Tokyo Boogie-woogie and D.T. Suzuki

MICHIGAN MONOGRAPH SERIES IN JAPANESE STUDIES

NUMBER 95

CENTER FOR JAPANESE STUDIES
UNIVERSITY OF MICHIGAN

Tokyo Boogie-woogie and
D.T. Suzuki

Shoji Yamada

Translated by Earl Hartman

University of Michigan Press
Ann Arbor

Originally published in Japan as *Tokyo bugiugi to Suzuki Daisetsu*,
by Yamada Shoji
© 2015 by Jimbun Shoin

For questions or permissions, please contact um.press.perms@umich.edu

Published in the United States of America by the
University of Michigan Press
Manufactured in the United States of America
Printed on acid-free paper
First published June 2022

A CIP catalog record for this book is available from the British Library.

Library of Congress Cataloging-in-Publication Data

Names: Yamada, Shoji, 1963– author. | Hartman, Earl, translator.
Title: Tokyo Boogie-woogie and D.T. Suzuki / Shoji Yamada ; translated by
    Earl Hartman.
Other titles: Tōkyō bugiugi to Suzuki Daisetsu. English
Description: Ann Arbor : University of Michigan Press, 2022. | Series:
    Michigan monograph series in Japanese studies ; 95 | Includes
    bibliographical references and index. | Translated from Japanese.
Identifiers: LCCN 2022004655 (print) | LCCN 2022004656 (ebook) |
    ISBN 9780472075300 (hardcover) | ISBN 9780472055302
    (paperback) | ISBN 9780472220052 (ebook)
Subjects: LCSH: Suzuki, Daisetz Teitaro, 1870–1966—Family. | Suzuki,
    Masaru, 1905–2000. | Buddhist scholars—Japan—Biography. | Conflict of
    generations—Japan—20th century. | Beats (Persons)
Classification: LCC BQ988.U887 Y3613   2022 (print) | LCC BQ988.U887
    (ebook) | DDC 294.3/9270922 [B]—dc23/eng/20220222
LC record available at https://lccn.loc.gov/2022004655
LC ebook record available at https://lccn.loc.gov/2022004656

This publication was supported by funding from the Suntory Foundation.

Cover image: Courtesy of Kamei Eiko and Nippon Columbia Co., Ltd.

Contents

Digital materials related to this title can be found on
the Fulcrum platform via the following citable URL:
https://doi.org/10.3998/mpub.12268621

Preface and Acknowledgments

This book attempts to illuminate the relationship between D.T. Suzuki (who styled himself "Daisetz") and his adopted son, Masaru "Alan" Suzuki. Various catalysts spurred me to take up research on this topic. One was that I came to know Alan's daughter by his first wife: meeting her was what initially motivated me to start this book project. After that first encounter with her, I made contact with people connected with Alan and traveled around Japan visiting various individuals, including elderly people living solitary lives, businesspersons in the prime of their careers, and a retired university professor. I even visited a family whose home had been washed away in the 3/11 tsunami and who were living in cramped temporary housing.

Another important catalyst was the publication of Daisetz's complete English-language diaries (hereafter the "Daisetz Diaries") that are housed in the Matsugaoka Bunko Library, Kamakura, where Daisetz lived during his final years.[1] It is well known that he wrote entries in his diary in English on almost a daily basis. The word "diary" may bring to mind the image of a modern diary in which a person writes about what they thought on a particular day, but Daisetz's diary was not like that. If one wants to be critical, his diaries are rather dry and bland, just records of who visited and where he went on a particular day.

Until the publication of the complete diaries, only carefully selected sections translated into Japanese had been released.[2] Since an editor was involved in choosing which portions to include or disregard, these published

---

1. Kirita Kiyohide, ed., "D.T. Suzuki's English Diaries," published in *MBKN* 19–29 (2005–2015).

2. *SDZ* 40, 105–264; Kirita Kiyohide, ed., *Suzuki Daisetsu kenkyū kiso shiryō* (Kamakura: Matsugaoka Bunko, 2005).

diaries are insufficient for tracing Daisetz's day-to-day activities. However, the "Daisetz Diaries" that began to be newly released in 2005 could be relied upon as more or less complete, unedited records. Evidence for this is that the diaries contain passages that are not conducive to idealizing the image of Daisetz. With regard to Alan as well, I was able to discover new things in the "Daisetz Diaries" about the frequency of Alan's interactions with Daisetz and Daisetz's feelings as a father toward his child. Comparing the information in the diaries with the letters and essays contained in *Suzuki Daisetsu zenshū zōho shinban* (The Complete Works of D.T. Suzuki, Expanded New Edition) brought many things into focus.

At the same time, I also became convinced that there was information in unpublished documents that would enable me to decipher Daisetz's family relationships more precisely. In particular, it appears that the letters and diaries of Daisetz's wife, Beatrice, are housed in the Matsugaoka Bunko; however, most of them are not yet publicly available. The translator of Daisetz's letters, Yokoyama Wayne Shigeto, who has seen these documents, has stated that "the sensei is not always presented as a great person" and "this material could have the opposite effect of causing the D.T. Suzuki full of human faults to make a strong impression on our minds."[3]

I have not used any of the unpublished documents housed in the Matsugaoka Bunko in the preparation of this book, nor have I asked for permission to view those materials. The reason is that I did not want my freedom of expression to be held hostage by the institute, which is known for not having an open attitude toward scholars. Surviving family members showed me copied materials that had evidently come from the Bunko, but I drew a careful distinction between these materials and published documents, and did not include or discuss the former in this book. Instead I sought to uncover new knowledge about Alan and his relationship with Daisetz by exploring other avenues and sources.

However, digging up Alan's past, who has been slapped with the label of "undutiful," is not something that surviving family members or other people connected with D.T. Suzuki will welcome. For example, if the persons concerned are still alive, obviously some materials should be kept undisclosed to protect their privacy. Nevertheless, I thought that trying to trace the outline of the father-and-son relationship between Daisetz and Alan using what I

---

3. Yokoyama Uein Shigeto, "Kaisetsu: Biatorisu fujin no tegami ni han'ei sareru ningen Suzuki Daisetsu no shōzō," in Matsugaoka Bunko, ed., *Suzuki Daisetsu botsugo 40 nen* (Tokyo: Kawade Shobō Shinsha, 2006), 77.

have learned up to this point would be a meaningful contribution. I am sure that new materials will be discovered or made available in the not so distant future, and researchers who are better equipped than I am will no doubt write a more complete story about Alan than I have been able to do.

I would like to express my gratitude to those who aided me in writing this book, especially Ms. Ike Maya and the members of the Suzuki family who graciously consented to be interviewed. I would also like to acknowledge Mr. Matsuoka Takahiro of the publisher Jimbun Shoin, who took on the task of editing the original Japanese edition. In addition to them, I thank Professor Markus Nornes, Mr. Christopher Dreyer, and Professor Iino Tomoyuki for this English edition. This book is one facet of what I consider my life's work: research into the generation, dissemination, transformation, extinguishment, and regeneration of cultural information. At the same time, it is the second volume in my Zen culture series, following *Shots in the Dark: Japan, Zen, and the West* (2009).[4] Like a number of my previous works, this monograph is also one that cannot be neatly categorized on a bookstore shelf. I will be happy if the reader considers it to be the result of my modest unearthing of a subject that falls in the gaps between disciplines and is ignored by respectable scholars working in academia.

Finally, I want to thank my wife Kazue, for whose unfailing support of my work I am eternally grateful.

• • •

This book was originally published as *Tōkyō bugi-ugi to Suzuki Daisetsu* in 2015 by Jimbun Shoin. I have adapted and expanded the translation by incorporating corrections to the Japanese edition, adding new footnotes, and modifying some of the Japanese expressions to make the text more understandable to an English-speaking audience. Dr. Patricia Fister, professor emeritus at the International Research Center for Japanese Studies (Nichibunken), edited the draft of the English edition. This book is not a word-for-word translation of the original Japanese volume. All mistakes and inadequacies are mine. For publishing this English translation, I received support from the director's discretionary fund of Nichiubnken and from Suntory Foundation.

4. Shoji Yamada, *Shots in the Dark: Japan, Zen, and the West*, trans. Earl Hartman (Chicago: University of Chicago Press, 2009). Originally published as *Zen to iu na no Nihon-maru* (Tokyo: Kōbundō, 2005).

A Note on the Text

Abbreviations

MBKN: Zaidanhōjin Matsugaoka Bunko kenkyū nenpō (*The Annual Report of Researches of the Matsugaoka Bunko*), Kamakura: Zaidanhōjin Matsugaoka Bunko [1987–2015]; *Kōeki Zaidanhōjin Matsugaoka Bunko kenkyū nenpō* (*The Annual Report of Researches of the Public Interest Matsugaoka Bunko Foundation*) Kamakura: Kōeki Zaidanhōjin Matsugaoka Bunko [2016–]

SDZ: Suzuki Daisetsu zenshū zōho shinban, 40 volumes (The Complete Works of D.T. Suzuki, Expanded New Edition; Tokyo: Iwanami Shoten, 1999–2003)

Macrons

This book uses macrons in accordance with the modified Hepburn system. Long vowels are indicated using ō, ū, ā. Macrons are used for all long vowels except in anglicized words such as "koan" and "Tokyo." Macrons are likewise omitted for Japanese institutions and personal names if they are omitted from the official English notation or citation (for example, Otani University, Teitaro).

Dates

Pre-1873 dates are rendered according to the traditional calendar (for example, D.T. Suzuki's birthday, October 18, Meiji 3, is denoted as October 18, 1870, not as November 11, 1870).

Names

Japanese names are rendered according to the traditional order (last name comes first), except Daistz Teitaro and Masaru Alan Suzuki. In this book, "Tokyo bugi ugi" is rendered as "Tokyo Boogie-woogie."

Introduction

This book focuses on the great twentieth-century scholar of Buddhism D.T. Suzuki, but is not a book about his philosophy or Zen. I barely refer to his most representative works, such as *Essays in Zen Buddhism, Zen Buddhism and Its Influence on Japanese Culture*, and *Japanese Spirituality*, and I have no illusions that I understand Daisetz's philosophy. Even more so, I do not have the slightest qualifications to discuss Zen itself. For readers who wish to learn about such topics, I recommend reading books on the subject or visiting a Zen temple. Perhaps some readers will be dissatisfied that this book does not contain any discussion of his philosophy; however, I assure that you will come to know a side of Daisetz that is not discussed in depth elsewhere and have the opportunity to expand your understanding of D.T. Suzuki, the man.

In the hours just before dawn on July 12, 1966, the ninety-five-year-old Daisetz Suzuki (given name: Teitarō; 1870–1966) was on his deathbed. Daisetz had been stricken with sudden abdominal pains the previous day and had been taken by sleeper taxi from his residence-cum-library, the Matsugaoka Bunko, located on top of a hill behind the Tōkeiji temple in Kita-Kamakura, Kanagawa prefecture, to St. Luke's International Hospital in Tsukiji, Tokyo. The eminent scholar, student of Buddhism, and recipient of the Order of Culture,[1] known as "The Teacher of Humanity" who had spread Zen throughout the world, was preparing to breathe his last.

Hayashida Kumino (maiden name: Suzuki; 1918–2011), the eldest daughter of Daisetz's nephew, described the scene in detail in her book *Ōoji Suzuki Daisetsu kara no tegami* (Letters from My Granduncle D.T. Suzuki; hereafter

---

1. The Order of Culture (Bunka kunshō) is a prestigious honor awarded to Japanese scholars and artists in recognition of their outstanding contributions to Japanese culture.

Granduncle).[2] Daisetz, who had been admitted as an emergency patient, was surrounded by an oxygen tent to help him breathe. The attending physician was Hinohara Shigeaki (1911–2017), who would later become famous in Japan as the doctor who was still working at the age of one hundred. Daisetz would occasionally open his eyes and appeared to be trying to look at something.

Among the people who had heard of the emergency and rushed to the hospital was a middle-aged man with good-looking Western features. He was Daisetz's adopted son, Masaru Suzuki (ca. 1916–1971), also known as Alan. Father and son were meeting after a long separation. Alan bent over and brought his face close to Daisetz from outside the oxygen tent. Daisetz's secretary, Okamura Mihoko (1935–), called to Daisetz: "Sensei, it's Alan." Her voice appeared to reach him, and Daisetz, saying "Ohh, ohh . . . ," crawled close to the tent, opened his eyes wide, and moved his hands.[3]

What were Daisetz's feelings as he moaned, "Ohh, ohh"? There is no record of what Alan said at that time. Nobody even knows how long he stayed at the hospital. Dr. Hinohara did not remember the presence of a man named Alan.[4] However, Alan was not just some anonymous person. He wrote the lyrics to "Tokyo Boogie-woogie" (1947),[5] the pop song that epitomized postwar Japan, and he had once been married to the singer Ike Mariko (1917–2000), known as "The Queen of Swing." For a person who presented to the world a song that represented a generation, however, there is surprisingly little information about Alan available. No one speaks much about the fact that Daisetz had an adopted son named Alan. For the people who surrounded Daisetz, Alan had become something they did not want to touch; some even considered Alan to be an "undutiful son." There was a reason for this: in his forties, normally the time when a person has developed

---

2. Hayashida Kumino, *Ōji Suzuki Daisetsu kara no tegami* (Kyoto: Hōzōkan, 1995), 130–43.

3. Hayashida, *Ōji Suzuki Daisetsu kara no tegami*, 141.

4. Telephone interview with the secretary of Dr. Hinohara on March 12, 2010.

5. "Tokyo Boogie-woogie" has been one of the most popular songs in Japan since World War II. The song was composed under the influence of American culture and gave defeated Japanese hope for a new era. Its popularity has continued for over seventy years. According to the J-WID database of the Japanese Society for Rights of Authors, Composers and Publishers, "Tokyo Boogie-woogie" had been covered by fifty-nine artists as of August 2019. The song also ranked twelfth in royalty revenue among Japanese popular songs between 2008 and 2017 (https://www.jasrac.or.jp/release/pdf/190417_1.pdf). Regarding its popularity, sociocultural background, and position in the history of Japanese popular songs, see chapter 4 of Hiromu Nagahara, *Tokyo Boogie-Woogie: Japan's Pop Era and Its Discontents* (Cambridge, MA: Harvard University Press, 2017).

a sense of discretion, Alan was the main character in an incident that became grist for the mills of a mass-circulation magazine.

Few people have been able to write about Alan without having to rely on secondary sources. *Granduncle*, however, was written by someone who had devoted herself to Daisetz over an extended period and had been, at one point, Alan's fiancée. Precisely for that reason, it is rich with first-person testimonies that cannot be found in other publications. As such, it has been an invaluable resource for this book. Kumino had known Alan, who was the same age as she, from his childhood. While being careful to be discreet, she stated, "I am forced to speculate that there was some problem in the family environment that caused Alan to grow up to be a person who lost his way in life."[6] Even allowing for the possibility that fathers in that period were more or less the same, Kumino wrote that "Daisetz was not the kind of father who would take time away from his study to play with his son or, when spending time with him, would forget the passing of time."[7]

Most researchers are silent about Alan and seem to show no desire to consider Daisetz via his relationship with his son. The translator of Daisetz's letters, Yokoyama Wayne Shigeto (1948–) addresses this issue in some depth, albeit briefly.

> Once Alan reached adulthood, his many gifts came wonderfully to the fore, and he grew into an elegant and free-spirited person. It is a fact that while Alan esteemed his father Suzuki-sensei and held him in high regard, Suzuki-sensei adopted a standoffish and indifferent attitude toward Alan. It was an unfortunate thing. What I mean by that is that the sensei could have learned a lesson of "humility" from his son.[8]

This paragraph appears in a publication commemorating the fortieth anniversary of Daisetz's death, and can be read as Yokoyama's positive assessment of Alan's life and criticism of Daisetz's parenting. Yokoyama was in charge of transcribing Daisetz's handwritten English-language diaries for the purpose of printing and publication, and therefore in comparison to other persons, has had a markedly greater number of opportunities to view the primary resources housed in the Matsugaoka Bunko. It is significant that a man in Yokoyama's position asserts that while Alan esteemed Daisetz, his father was standoffish.

---

6. Hayashida, *Ōoji Suzuki Daisetsu kara no tegami*, 63.
7. Hayashida, *Ōoji Suzuki Daisetsu kara no tegami*, 63.
8. Yokoyama, "Kaisetsu," 77.

The novelist Iwakura Masaji (1903–2000), a disciple of Daisetz, is one of those who wrote about Alan in some depth, or, should I say, one of those who was able to do so. Iwakura was asked by Daisetz to look after Alan when he reached puberty and was too wild for Daisetz to control. Iwakura had the following to say in *Suzuki Daisetsu no hito to gakumon* (D.T. Suzuki: The Man and His Work; 1961), edited by Daisetz's leading disciple, Furuta Shōkin (1911–2001).

> Subsequently, Sensei [Daisetz] did not want to talk very much about Alan, whom he had disowned. It wasn't a matter of who was in the wrong; I think it is better to call this a tragedy with its roots in generational differences and life circumstances. I feel sorry for both of them.
>
> The relationship between Sensei and Alan, however, is a conspicuous example of how even a person such as Sensei, who was a perfect model of the human character, can be unequal to the task of educating a young person. I could really feel his pain.[9]

This text was written in November 1960, while Daisetz was still alive. It appears to say that Alan was not the only one in the wrong and that Daisetz was also to be blamed.

Kumino, Yokoyama, and Iwakura all imply that Daisetz was not able to raise his son in the way that he wanted. However, we cannot divine from these snippets the manner in which Daisetz was shut off from his son or what sort of worries he experienced. What is even more invisible is the agony of Alan, the "undutiful son."

There really has been very little written about Alan. I am sure that if he had been dedicated to carrying on Daisetz's scholarship, much more would have been left to posterity. Daisetz's writings amount to unfathomable numbers of words. His published complete works (*Suzuki Daisetsu zenshū zōho shinban*; hereafter abbreviated as *SDZ*)[10] alone comprise forty volumes, and it appears that there are quite a number of documents that were not included in this compilation. Even today, a massive trove of Daisetz's manuscripts, diaries, and books is carefully stored at the Matsugaoka Bunko. Moreover, I am sure there are as yet unknown writings in libraries and private hands all over the world. A lifetime would not be enough to read and digest all of this material.

---

9. Iwakura Masaji, "Ōtani Daigaku jidai no Suzuki Daisetsu," in Furuta Shōkin, ed., *Suzuki Daisetsu no hito to gakumon* (Tokyo: Shunjūsha, 1961), 90.

10. Suzuki Daisetsu, *Suzuki Daisetsu zenshū zōho shinban* (The Complete Works of D.T. Suzuki, Expanded New Edition), 40 vols. (Tokyo: Iwanami Shoten, 1999–2003).

What I am interested in hearing is not the voice of the garrulous father, but that of the son who was not able to leave many words for posterity. Some important message is hidden within this seemingly failed father-son relationship: how should a parent relate to a child who did not grow up into the person one was hoping for? Daisetz was also troubled by this universal question. It seems to me that researchers have failed to see their agony.

In his excellent critical biography, *Suzuki Daisetsu no genfūkei* (The Origins of D.T. Suzuki; 1993), the high-ranking Rinzai Zen priest Nishimura Eshin (1933–) obliquely criticizes biographies of Daisetz written by his disciples, saying, "The biographies of famous people are generally recorded by direct disciples who are eyewitnesses, and therefore the stories are embellished, leading to needless mythologizing. It is precisely by demythologizing such biographies that the objective truth is brought truly into relief."[11] While taking the position of not engaging in the mythologization of D.T. Suzuki, Nishimura, who was not Daisetz's disciple, hardly mentioned Alan in his book. Even though his work reconstructed a significant part of Daisetz's life in great detail, Nishimura did not have anything to say about Alan. Why was that?

In order to present someone as a good person, it is necessary to hide some things. For the D.T. Suzuki legend, perhaps that was Alan. If this is true, however, an important aspect of Daisetz's life becomes invisible. I believe that not averting our gaze from Alan will allow us to see a different side of Daisetz. It will bring the feelings that Daisetz had for his son as well as the troubles he had with him, concealed within Daisetz's words, to the surface.

Zen Buddhism, the Rinzai school in particular, seems to be weak in the areas of the inner workings of human emotions and family relationships. Practitioners of Zen attempt to break away from logical thinking through the device of koans, which are presented as cryptic riddles. For example, there is the koan "What was your original face before your parents were born?" It appears to be asking, "Who was the original you who existed before your parents were born?" Insofar as it is urging the practitioner to search for his or her original self that exists beyond the parent-child relationship, it appears that Zen does not prioritize such relationships. The novel *Mon* (Gate; 1910) by Natsume Sōseki (1867–1916), one of Japan's most famous novelists, depicts a protagonist who is wrestling with this koan. Perhaps Sōseki was given this koan by the Zen priest Shaku Sōen (1859–1919), who was the teacher of both Daisetz and Sōseki. Presumably Daisetz experienced the state of mind induced by this koan.

---

11. Nishimura Eshin, *Suzuki Daisetsu no genfūkei* (Tokyo: Daizō Shuppan, 1993), 4.

Eminent scholar of Buddhism Sueki Fumihiko (1949–) relates the following thoughts regarding Zen and parent-child relationships:

> Having spent many years reading the *Blue Cliff Record*, what I can say in general is that while it is deeply involved in the issue of language, I cannot escape the feeling that the issue of emotion gets lost and that problems on that level are not explained. Today, when considering various social problems, for example those dealing with children, the subtleties of human feelings take on a significant meaning, and I cannot shake the feeling that Zen is lacking in this area.[12]

It can be said that not only Zen, but Buddhism in general, does not emphasize the parent-child relationship. Saying this might make some people uncomfortable, because the popular image of present-day Japanese Buddhism revolves around things like funerals, cemeteries, and memorial services for ancestors during the *obon* season. Buddhism, however, originally was quite different. Entering Buddhist orders meant severing family relationships, including those with one's parents. Religious precepts did not allow priests or nuns to have sexual relations, so those in religious orders could not become the biological parents of children. In sum, Buddhist teachings do not include anything that can serve as a guidepost for how parents and children should relate to one another. Even if Daisetz, who was a Zen Buddhist, was having trouble relating to his son, this does not diminish his worth. Instead, realizing his pain and learning from it should be seen as an homage to Daisetz and Alan.

Buried deep within their relationship was the suffering of a child with a parent who was too highly acclaimed, and the distress of a parent whose child did not grow up as he wished. It is a worthwhile endeavor to find out the true identity of Masaru "Alan" Suzuki, who wrote the lyrics to "Tokyo Boogie-woogie," and learning more about D.T. Suzuki. Like Don Quixote, who, driven by passion, went on a reckless journey, I would like to take readers on a tour of discovery to search for the true identity of Masaru Suzuki and to learn more about D.T. Suzuki.

---

12. Sueki Fumihiko, *Nihon Bukkyō no kanōsei: Gendai shisō to shite no bōken* (Tokyo: Shinchō Bunko, 2011), 189. Originally published by Shinchōsha in 2006.

ONE

Hidden Origins

The Adopted Child

July 7, 1916—this is the date that appears in the Suzuki family register as the birth date of Masaru Suzuki (commonly known as "Alan"). In this book, this date will be treated as Alan's birthday, though it is just the official date recorded in the register, and even Alan himself did not know if it was his actual date of birth. Daisetz and his wife, Beatrice Erskine Lane (1878–1939), might have known Alan's actual birthday; however, no record certifies the date.

Determining Alan's actual date of birth is further complicated by conflicting information in modern publications. From an academic point of view, the most reliable source is the chronology found in *Suzuki Daisetsu kenkyū kiso shiryō* (D.T. Suzuki, Primary Research Sources; 2005), edited by Kirita Kiyohide (1941–2016).[1] This chronology gives July 7, 1917, as Alan's birth and adopted day in their family registry. The date matches the chronology in *SDZ*.[2] According to a certified copy of the family registry obtained by surviving members of the Suzuki family, however, July 7, 1916, is the correct date. What this means is that the "definitive" chronology contains an error. The certified copy of the family registry lists Masaru Suzuki not as an adopted child, but as the natural child of Daisetz and Beatrice.[3] His place

---

1. Kirita, *Suzuki Daisetsu kenkyū kiso shiryō*.

2. *SDZ* 40, 134.

3. In traditional Japan, if a family did not have any sons, it was customary to adopt the groom of one's biological daughter and designate him as the successor to the family name and fortune. Alan can be classified as a *moraigo* (foster child). It was possible to raise a *moraigo* without officially adopting him or her (Takeda Akira, "Yōshi no gainen to mokuteki: Yōshi kenkyū no sōkatsu o megutte," in Ōtake Hideo, Takeda Akira, and Hasegawa Zenkei, eds.,

of birth is recorded as the residential quarters at Gakushuin University in Tokyo, where the couple lived at the time, and the person who submitted the notification was Daisetz himself. At the time, Daisetz was forty-five and Beatrice was thirty-eight years old. Nowadays, thirty-eight is an age at which a woman can give birth without any difficulties, but in that era Beatrice would likely have been past child-bearing age.

Could Alan have been Daisetz's biological child? The following two facts refute this supposition. First, Daisetz himself clearly wrote in a private letter to his relatives that Alan was adopted. In a letter dated March 10, 1921, and addressed to Hatsuko (1885–1945), the wife of Daisetz's nephew Suzuki Ryōkichi (1877–1920), Daisetz wrote, "Please do not let the maid know that the boy was adopted."[4]

According to the book *Granduncle*, by Hayashida Kumino (Hatsuko's daughter), the home of Hatsuko's parents (the Matsuzaki family) was adjacent to Daisetz's family home in Kanazawa, and Daisetz's oldest brother, Gentarō, married a woman from the Matsuzaki family. If Daisetz had not gone to the United States, Hatsuko's mother Shikako and Daisetz probably would have gotten married. Upon Daisetz's return from his first extended stay in the United States, Ryōkichi and Hatsuko rented a house next to their residence in Aoyama for Daisetz to live in, and she took care of him there.[5] This shows the close relationship between Hatsuko, the recipient of this letter, and Daisetz.

In the letter Daisetz wrote that he wanted to hire the maid whom Hatsuko had recommended; he discussed the salary to be paid and asked Hatsuko not to tell the new maid that Alan was adopted. At this time Alan was four years old, an age when children are considered to be most endearing, and Daisetz was worried about how to prevent the maid from looking askance at Alan as an adopted child.

Daisetz's English-language diary provides the second piece of proof that

---

Gisei sareta oyako: Yōshi [Tokyo: Sanseidō, 1988], 303–6). Civil law in old Japan prohibited parents who had a biological son from adopting a boy; however, such parents were permitted to take in *moraigo*. It should be noted that the social and legal status of *moraigo* was lower than their pseudosiblings. An adopted son was deemed to be in a blood relationship with his adopted parents and could therefore inherit the family headship (Nobe Yōko, *Yōshi engumi no shakaigaku: "Nippon-jin" ni totte "ketsuen" to wa nanika* [Tokyo: Shin'yōsha, 2018], 61). Since Alan's biological parents were unknown, Daisetz and Beatrice were unable to register him as an adopted son. I presume that recording Alan as a natural child in the family registry reflects their compassion and wish to avoid having Alan be insulted as a *moraigo*.

4. *SDZ* 36, 409.

5. Hayashida, *Ōoji Suzuki Daisetsu kara no tegami*, 12–16.

Alan was not his biological child. In his entry for May 28, 1939 (when Alan was twenty-two), Daisetz recorded that he had told Alan about his birth. One week later, Daisetz wrote that he found it strange that Alan was not interested in knowing who his birth parents were or the details about how he came to live with Daisetz and Beatrice. Since Daisetz's diary presumably was not intended to be seen by anyone other than himself, we should regard Alan as adopted and not as Daisetz and Beatrice's biological child, regardless of the family registry. In other words, although Daisetz registered Alan as his "real" son, this is not true to life.

Nevertheless, Daisetz wanted to raise Alan as his real son. He was deeply in love with his wife, Beatrice, and when she died, Daisetz wrote a letter to his friend Yamamoto Ryōkichi (1871–1942) saying, "I have lost half of myself."[6] It was rare for a Japanese man from this period in history to write so straightforwardly of his love for his wife. It is natural for a couple to long for the fruit of their love, and when they realized that this was unobtainable, their desire for at least an adopted child seems quite natural.

Nothing is known for sure about where Alan came from. Kumino heard that Alan was the offspring of an English man and a Japanese woman, but in *Granduncle*, she wrote, "I do not know any details."[7] Surviving Suzuki family members speculate that Alan was the illegitimate child of a Scottish tailor who worked at the Mitsukoshi Department Store and a Japanese woman. In the brief biography appended to the book *Bukkyō no taii* (Outline of Buddhism; 1947) published in celebration of Daisetz's seventy-seventh birthday, Daisetz's student Iwakura Masaji wrote that Alan was "the outcome of a relationship between a Scottish man and a Japanese woman."[8]

Around the time of Alan's birth, a cloth cutter from London was employed at a dry goods store at the Nihonbashi branch of the Mitsukoshi Department Store in Tokyo. It cannot be confirmed whether he was Scottish or not. There is a picture of this man in a magazine published by Mitsukoshi, and he appears to resemble Alan, but it is impossible to know for certain. This cloth cutter worked at Mitsukoshi until January 1916, and one can infer from various records that he returned to England in February of the following year.[9] Since Alan's date of birth recorded in the family registry is July 7, 1916, the timing surrounding this date is problematic. If this person

6. *SDZ* 36, 667.

7. Hayashida, *Ōoji Suzuki Daisetsu kara no tegami*, 19.

8. Suzuki Daisetsu Kyōju Kiju Shukugakai, ed., *Bukkyō no taii* (Kyoto: Hōzōkan, 1947), 156.

9. *Mitsukoshi* 6: 1 (January 1916): 22–25; *Mitsukoshi* 7: 2 (February 1917): 6.

was Alan's biological father, I would like to think that he returned home after seeing that his child had been adopted into the family of a scholar.

Judging from his features, one can have no doubt that at least one of Alan's biological parents was a Westerner. Beatrice's maternal grandparents were of the Scottish nobility. Being a mixed-race child whose mother was Japanese and whose father was Scottish, Alan was, serendipitously, a perfect fit for assuming the role of Daisetz and Beatrice's real child. Regarding Alan's age at the time of his adoption, Kumino wrote that "he had just been born,"[10] but in actuality, it is more likely that he was at an age where he no longer needed to nurse, a little more than one year old. Iwakura also wrote in the previously mentioned brief biography of Daisetz that Alan was adopted after he was one year old.[11] In short, it is possible that Alan was older than stated in the family registry. If this is true, then it makes sense that Alan later was deemed a precocious child, mature beyond his age.

Beatrice was known as an animal lover. In the book *Suzuki Daisetsu: Hito to shisō* (D.T. Suzuki: The Man and His Thoughts; 1971) the scholar of literature and close friend of the Suzukis Jugaku Bunshō (1900–1992) reminisced about Beatrice's love of animals and Alan's adoption as follows:

> Beatrice was an animal lover down to the marrow of her bones; if she encountered an abandoned dog or cat on the street, she would always take it home and look after it. If she saw a draft horse or a draft ox being mistreated by the cart driver, she would lecture the driver on how he should treat animals more kindly. I witnessed such scenes many times when I accompanied her. I think that she probably would even have taken in the abused horses and oxen if there had been space in her house for them. Thus it was natural for the Suzuki family to take in Alan, who had been orphaned in the Great Kantō Earthquake.[12]

The statement that Alan had been orphaned in the Great Kantō Earthquake is apparently a misunderstanding or a *lapsus memoriae* on Jugaku's

10. Hayashida, *Ooji Suzuki Daisetsu kara no tegami*, 19.

11. Suzuki Daisetsu Kyōju, *Bukkyō no taii*, 156.

12. Jugaku Bunshō, "Kateijin to shite no Daisetsu koji," in Hisamatsu Shin'ichi et al., eds., *Suzuki Daisetsu: Hito to shisō* (Tokyo: Iwanami Shoten, 1971), 209–10. Originally published in *Suzuki Daisetsu zenshū geppō* (July 1969).

part. After all, the Suzukis adopted Alan in 1916, and the Great Kantō Earthquake did not occur until 1923. Leaving such an error aside, the way Jugaku described Beatrice adopting a human child as being an extension of her love for animals is quite intriguing. Jugaku must have been very familiar with Alan's behavior. By comparing Alan with horses and oxen, Perhaps Jugaku was trying to say that Beatrice's philanthropy came back to haunt her in the end. By presenting Alan as an orphan whom the Suzukis had saved, he may have been trying to protect their reputations. As an intellectual who associated with Daisetz, Jugaku's attitude toward Alan is easy to understand.

Daisetz's Parents

Here I would like to give an account of Daisetz's life up until the time he adopted Alan. The following three texts are the most representative of Daisetz's memoirs.

"Watashi no rirekisho" (My Resume; *Nihon Keizai Shimbun*, September 28–October 18, 1961)[13]

"Yafūryū-an jiden" (Memoir of the Yafūryū-an; in *Suzuki Daisetsu no hito to gakumon*, Furuta Shōkin, ed., dictated in 1961)[14]

"Memories of My Younger Days" (*The Middle Way*, 1964)[15]

"My Resume" was compiled from Daisetz's oral dictation to his disciple Furuta Shōkin, and published after being revised by Daisetz.[16] "Memoir of the Yafūryū-an" was based on an oral presentation by Daisetz that was broadcast by NHK Radio 2 on February 1, 1961. The name "Yafūryū-an" was the name Daisetz gave to his hermitage and was taken from the phrase "fūryū narazaru tokoro mata fūryū" (Even where there is no refinement, there is still refinement) appearing in the *Biyan Lu* (The Blue Cliff Record;

13. *SDZ* 26, 499–539.

14. *SDZ* 29, 147–63. Originally published in Furuta, *Suzuki Daisetsu no hito to gakumon*, 165–81.

15. *SDZ* 34, 399–410. Originally published in Daisetz T. Suzuki, "Early Memories," *The Middle Way* 39: 3 (November 1964): 101–8.

16. *Suzuki Daisetsu zenshū* 32 (Tokyo: Iwanami Shoten, 1971), 582.

Case 67), a Sung dynasty Chan (Zen) text.[17] Both of these memoirs were published at around the same time, and appear to be based on oral dictations of Daisetz's memories from the same period in his life.

His disciples have published many critical biographies of Daisetz. For details regarding his younger days before he became famous, however, they cannot be regarded as primary sources because they rely upon Daisetz's memoirs. In this book, therefore, I would like to trace the outline of Daisetz's early life utilizing these personal memoirs, the chronology found in *D. T. Suzuki, Primary Research Sources*,[18] and the brief history that Iwakura Masaji wrote in *Outline of Buddhism*.[19]

Suzuki Daisetz Teitarō was born in Honda-machi in the city of Kanazawa on October 18, 1870. The family were vassals of the Honda family, who served as the head of the chief retainers of the Maeda clan.[20] His father's name was Ryōjun (later changed to Jū, ca. 1822–1876) and his mother's was Masu (ca. 1831–1890); Ryōjun was a samurai, a doctor, and a Confucian scholar. Teitarō (Daisetz) was the last of five children (one girl and four boys). Daisetz's older sister's name was Ryū (dates unknown); his older brothers were named Gentarō (ca. 1857–ca. 1925), Kōtarō (ca. 1862–1939), and Ritarō (ca. 1866–1877). If one lines up the first characters of the boy's names the result reads *gen kō ri tei* (Ch. *yuan heng li zhen*). The characters of this phrase are taken from the *I Ching* (one of the five classics of Confucianism) and represent the four heavenly virtues. The "Tei" of Teitarō, for example, means "the accomplishment of all things." Very fitting names indeed for a Confucian scholar to give his sons.

According to Iwakura Masaji, Daisetz's oldest brother, Gentarō, was something of a rogue, which one often sees among sons of the warrior class. His next oldest brother, Kōtarō, was adopted into another family whereby he took the name Hayakawa. Iwakura wrote that "he was not particularly intelligent, but his persistence knew no bounds, and once having set his heart

---

17. *The Blue Cliff Record*, vol. 2, trans. Thomas Cleary and J. C. Cleary (Boulder, CO: Shambhala, 1977), 426.

18. Kirita, *Suzuki Daisetsu kenkyū kiso shiryō*.

19. Suzuki Daisetsu Kyōju, *Bukkyō no taii*, 137–63.

20. The Maeda clan ruled Kaga (present-day Ishikawa and Toyama prefectures), one of the largest feudal domains in the Edo period. About two years before Daisetz was born, the Japanese feudal system collapsed via the Meiji Restoration, which was the power transition from the Tokugawa shogun to Emperor Meiji in 1868. After the Restoration, the new government rapidly imported Western civilization and promoted the modernization of Japanese society, economy, culture, education, and industry. Daisetz grew up during this period of transformation.

on becoming a lawyer, he took the exams over a period of ten years, finally passing at the age of seventy-two."[21] Daisetz's father Ryōjun died at the age of fifty-four when Teitarō was six years old. As a result, Daisetz had practically no memory of his father. Daisetz wrote that after his father's death, he began to wonder, "Why do people die? Also, what exactly is death?"[22] His third brother, Ritarō, died the following year at the age of eleven, and his mother, Masu, was left to raise four children alone.

In elementary school, Teitarō was a delicate child, but he would run about like a puppy in more than a foot of snow, barefoot and hatless with his kimono cinched up to his waist.[23] He was good at whistling and rock-throwing, and his grades in school were head and shoulders above his peers. At the age of eleven, Teitarō entered the first level of the middle-school curriculum offered by the Ishikawa Prefectural Technical School and met Yamamoto Ryōkichi, who would later become a well-known ethicist. At sixteen, he entered the Number Four Higher Middle School. One of his classmates was Nishida Kitarō (1870–1945), who later became a famous philosopher; he and Daisetz became friends and influenced one another.

Next I would like to address the religious environment in the Suzuki home. The Suzuki family belonged to the Rinzai sect, but Daisetz's mother was a member of the Hijibōmon sect of the Jōdo Shinshū branch of Buddhism. The Hijibōmon practiced magical rites, and it had been banned by Rennyo (1415–1499), the rejuvenator of Jōdo Shinshū. Teitarō had no memory of the fact, but his mother apparently registered him as a member of this sect.

When Teitarō was young he visited Zuikōji, the Rinzai temple to which his family belonged. There he asked the head priest to explain Zen. The priest told him there was a lot written about Zen in a book called *The Blue Cliff Record*, but when Teitarō asked to see it, the priest replied that he did not have a copy. Until late in life, Teitarō often wondered whether that priest knew anything about Zen or not. Around the age of fifteen, Teitarō also spoke with a Christian missionary several times, but Christianity did not interest him.

When he was in the higher middle school, Teitarō decided he wanted to try *sanzen*, so, carrying a book titled *Oradegama* (1747) by the Edo-period Zen priest Hakuin Ekaku (1686–1769), without introduction he went to visit

---

21. Suzuki Daisetsu Kyōju, *Bukkyō no taii*, 139.
22. Suzuki Daisetsu Kyōju, *Bukkyō no taii*, 140.
23. Suzuki Daisetsu Kyōju, *Bukkyō no taii*, 140.

the Kokutaiji temple in the city of Takaoka in Toyama prefecture. There an *unsui* (a novice monk who has undertaken Zen training) instructed him in how to sit zazen. However, when Teitarō asked the head priest to explain the meaning of some of the terminology in *Oradegama*, he was scolded severely and chased out of the temple. In this manner, Teitarō's first Zen experience ended after four or five days.

Unable to afford the tuition, Teitarō had to leave the Number Four Higher Middle School after attending for less than a year. He subsequently became an assistant at the elementary school in Iida-machi in the county of Suzu, Ishikawa prefecture (present-day Suzu city), where he taught English to the upper-level students. His eldest brother, Gentarō, was an instructor at another elementary school in Suzu county, so Teitarō probably enlisted Gentarō's help in securing the position. At that time, Teitarō took a preconscription army physical examination but failed due to his nearsightedness.

In 1890, when Teitarō was nineteen, his beloved mother passed away at the age of fifty-nine. His mother's death was a much more significant emotional blow than his father's had been. According to Iwakura, Daisetz came to feel that "my mother's death made me realize that the world was not just something to be looked at prosaically and scientifically as stages of life and death. A new world, which I had been unaware of, opened up."[24] The following year, Teitarō quit his job as an elementary school instructor and left his birthplace behind.

Zen Training

After leaving Kanazawa, Teitarō's first destination was Kobe, where his older brother Kōtarō lived. After staying there for four months, Teitarō went to Tokyo, where he initially stayed in the Kyūchōkan in Hongō-magome. The Kyūchōkan was a dormitory for people from the Kaga domain (the pre-Meiji name for what became Ishikawa and Toyama prefecture). There Teitarō became fast friends with Ataka Yakichi (1873–1949), who was also from Kanazawa. They talked about their ambitions, and Ataka said that when he became successful as a businessman, he would provide Teitarō with financial support for his studies. Ataka later founded Ataka & Company and, true to his word, supported Daisetz as his patron. At the Kyūchōkan, Teitarō also met Hayakawa Senkichirō (1863–1922), who would later become director of Mitsui Bank, a member of the House of Peers, and the president of the South Manchuria Railway Company.

---

24. Suzuki Daisetsu Kyōju, *Bukkyō no taii*, 144.

After arriving in Tokyo, Teitarō began attending the Tōkyō Senmon Gakkō (Tokyo Professional School; today's Waseda University). At the time, the novelist Tsubouchi Shōyō (1859–1935), who had an enormous impact on modern Japanese literature and theater, was teaching English literature. Tsubouchi reportedly evaluated Teitarō's essays as follows: "Your answers are too simple, and your translations stray too far from the original. Reading your essays, I can't tell whether you understand grammar or not. There's no way for me to grade them."[25]

In July 1891, while he was attending the Tōkyō Senmon Gakkō, through the introduction of Hayakawa Senkichirō, Teitarō asked to be accepted as a pupil at the Engakuji temple in Kamakura and began receiving instruction in Zen from the chief priest, Imakita Kōzen (1816–1892). Teitarō was twenty years old at the time. Then, as a layman, Teitarō undertook more rigorous Zen training. The initial koan that Kōzen gave to Teitarō was "What is the sound of one hand clapping?" At that time, Nishida Kitarō, Yamamoto Ryōkichi, Ataka Yakichi, and Natsume Sōseki were all training at Engakuji. About six months after Teitarō began going to Engakuji, however, his teacher, Imakita Kōzen, passed away. Shaku Sōen took over Kōzen's mantle, and so Teitarō naturally came to receive Zen instruction from him. Meeting and training under Sōen would change Teitarō's life.

Three months prior to Kōzen's death, Teitarō quit the Tōkyō Senmon Gakkō after only four months. In September 1892, he matriculated at the Faculty of Philosophy, College of Letters of Tokyo Imperial University as a special student (*senkasei*). Until he dropped out of college after three years, Teitarō avidly pursued Zen practice, frequently walking from Tokyo to Engakuji in Kita-Kamakura (about fifty kilometers). No matter how hard he tried, however, he could not solve the riddle of "the sound of one hand clapping." Perhaps giving up on Teitarō because of his inability to solve it, Sōen gave him a different koan, often referred to as the *mu* (nothingness) koan. Around 1894, Teitarō received the Buddhist name "Daisetsu" from Sōen. This name was taken from the following phrase found both in the Chinese classic *Tao Te Ching* and the Zen text *The Blue Cliff Record*: "A person of great (*dai*) talent does not show off and therefore appears to be inept (*setsu*)." Daisetz's name literally means "great clumsiness."[26]

Iwakura related that among his Zen compatriots, Daisetz was seen as "a person one could be at home with. He neither smoked nor drank, and

---

25. Suzuki Daisetsu Kyōju, *Bukkyō no taii*, 145.

26. From his early career as a translator, Daisetz preferred to spell his name "Daisetz" rather than use the standard romanization "Daisetsu."

never behaved in a lewd manner. He never had any interesting anecdotes or sob stories to tell. But he loved gobbling down the sweet bean cakes that he bought at Mitsuhashidō, a shop near Engakuji. Daisetz was a refined person who rarely said much, and appeared to exist on an otherworldly level, above the mundane world."[27]

In 1893, an event occurred that would prove to be for Daisetz, or perhaps I should say, for Japanese Buddhism as a whole, of earthshaking importance. The first World's Parliament of the Religions was held in Chicago, and the various sects of Japanese Buddhism sent delegations. Sōen participated as the representative of the Rinzai sect and gave a presentation introducing Mahayana Buddhism. This conference is considered to be the worldwide debut of Japanese Zen Buddhism as "Zen." In addition, it was Daisetz who was given the responsibility of translating the draft of Sōen's lecture into English. There is a story that Natsume Sōseki, who was also training Zen with Sōen, corrected Daisetz's translation, but it is impossible to ascertain whether this is true or not.

Bottom of the Heap

One of the attendees at the World's Parliament of Religions was a gentleman named Paul Carus (1852–1915), an editor at a small publishing house called Open Court Publishing Company, located in La Salle, a city near Chicago. Inspired by Sōen, Carus wrote a book titled *The Gospel of Buddha* (1894).[28] Sōen ordered Daisetz to translate this book, and it was published in Japan the following year. Carus asked Sōen to recommend someone who could assist him so he could publish more books on Eastern thought, and it was Daisetz whom Sōen introduced.

According to a letter that Daisetz sent to Carus on May 14, 1896, Daisetz intended to go to the United States after he was ordained as a Zen priest.[29] Daisetz thought that being a priest would come in handy for keeping his costs low and that having clerical status would be helpful to him during his stay in the United States. However, something prevented Daisetz from becoming a Zen priest.[30] As the time for him to leave the tutelage of

27. Suzuki Daisetsu Kyōju, *Bukkyō no taii*, 146.
28. Paul Carus, *The Gospel of Buddha according to Old Records* (Chicago: Open Court Publishing, 1894).
29. *SDZ* 36, 75.
30. *SDZ* 36, 66.

Sōen relentlessly approached, after completing the "Rōhatsu Sesshin,"[31] as Daisetz was leaving the monastery he suddenly understood the "Mu" koan. According to Iwakura, Daisetz had an enlightenment experience: "I completely forgot the distinction between myself and the great pine tree in the moonlight."[32]

Subsequently, in 1897, the twenty-six-year-old Daisetz began his eleven-year life of obscurity in the United States. Daisetz had difficulty coming up with the fare for his voyage. In addition to Sōen, he asked his friend Yamamoto Ryōkichi for help.[33] Daisetz was planning on studying in the United States, with Carus paying his tuition. In a letter to Yamamoto, Daisetz wrote: "Since I intend to depend on Mr. Carus for all of my tuition while I am in the U.S., I believe that it will not be necessary for me to rely on your kindness."[34] Daisetz, however, was unable to attend school during his time in La Salle. In a letter addressed to Shaku Sōen, Daisetz revealed his feelings about the distressful first year he spent in the United States.

Even though almost a year has passed since I left Japan, I have had no significant experiences here . . . when I have free time I study academic subjects that interest me and save the material for another day. I have no idea whether my life will see rainy or cloudy days; so, waiting patiently I try to carve out a niche for myself.[35]

Approximately three years after his arrival in the United States, Daisetz was finally employed by the Open Court Publishing Company. A post for a proofreader opened, and Daisetz was given the job. At that time Daisetz wrote to Sōen saying, "Without asking him, I don't know how much Mr. Carus intends to offer, but I believe that he will pay me something."[36] That wisp of hope, however, was soon dashed. In a letter to Sōen two months later Daisetz wrote, "My position as Japanese proofreader is a decent position, but it is just like being a slave, and I am not paid at all. . . . . I have kept my head down here for more than three years now, but I have nothing to show for

---

31. A week of intensive seated meditation with no sleep or rest, commemorating Buddha's enlightenment that took place after meditating from December 1 to 8, according to the lunar calendar.

32. Suzuki Daisetsu Kyōju, *Bukkyō no taii*, 147.

33. *SDZ* 36, 63, 65.

34. *SDZ* 36, 66.

35. *SDZ* 36, 126–27.

36. *SDZ* 36, 190.

it. . . . Even so, I hope that when I return to Japan, this experience will help me."[37] Later, in 1904 after four years had passed, Daisetz wrote in a letter, "Carus is a stingy man."[38] Daisetz's position in the United States was basically that of an unpaid helper. At the time, prejudice against people of color was the norm, and there was a strong exclusionary attitude toward Japanese immigrants. Bluntly speaking, for Carus, Daisetz was more or less a Japanese slave who did intellectual work.

Daisetz's primary job at Open Court Publishing Company was Japanese to English translation and proofreading. Beginning with the English translation of the *Tao Te Ching* by Laozi that Carus had planned, Daisetz's personal projects included an attempt to translate the *Dasheng Qixin Lun* (Awakening of Faith in the Mahayana; ca. 550) into English and the publication of *Outlines of Mahayana Buddhism* (1907).[39]

One significant incident that occurred during Daisetz's eleven years in the United States was his meeting with Beatrice, who would later become his wife. When Sōen revisited the United States in 1905 on a lecture tour, Daisetz accompanied him as his interpreter. Beatrice attended Sōen's lecture in New York in April of the following year. Interested in Buddhism, she visited Sōen privately and Daisetz served as the interpreter. Over the next five years, until Beatrice went to Japan to marry Daisetz, the two of them nurtured their love through letters.

Daisetz's Image of Women

Before Daisetz began his platonic love affair with Beatrice, what was his image of women? A clue for understanding this appears in a letter that he penned to Yamamoto Ryōkichi on October 3, 1897, shortly after going to the United States.[40] Daisetz, who had been observing American manners and customs, wrote that in order for young people not to fall into immorality, it is necessary to take a lenient attitude toward association between the sexes and that educational standards for women should be

---

37. *SDZ* 36, 193. Carus's father-in-law and the founder of the Open Court Publishing Company, Edward C. Hegeler (1835–1910), apparently paid for Daisetz's expenses while he was in La Salle. I am grateful to the anonymous reviewer who informed me of this.

38. *SDZ* 36, 262.

39. Daisetz Teitaro Suzuki, *Outlines of Mahâyâna Buddhism* (London: Luzac and Company, 1907).

40. *SDZ* 36, 100–102.

raised. Japanese society did not allow men and women to freely associate with one another, with the result that men frequented prostitutes and geisha, and women were influenced by immoral members of their own sex. He believed that red-light districts should be abolished so that young boys could not witness illicit relations between men and women, that women should be allowed to attend college, and that schools should be coeducational so men and women could associate freely. For the times, this was quite a liberal philosophy.

When it came to relating to an actual woman, however, Daisetz could not hide his discomfort. In a letter to Sōen dated June 11, 1898, Daisetz wrote that he was nonplussed about having to accompany women or converse with them. While the American custom is to humor women, he wrote that "discussing scholarly subjects with them was one thing, but worthless and idle chatter about the doings of society is a duty for which I am particularly ill-suited."[41] Daisetz went on to say that he would stay in his rooms as much as possible to avoid contact with women. In a letter to Yamamoto Ryōkichi dated January 6, 1901, he stated, "The way in which (unmarried) women whisper about men is just like what geisha do."[42] For a man of around thirty years of age, his innocence is something to behold. With such an attitude toward women, it was only natural for Daisetz to be attracted to Beatrice, who was earnest in her pursuit of the Buddhist way.

I would like to touch upon the correspondence between Daisetz and Beatrice up until the time they were married. The first letter that Daisetz wrote to Beatrice included in *The Complete Works of D. T. Suzuki, Expanded New Edition* is dated March 29, 1907, one year after their fateful meeting in New York. It is a brief letter, saying simply: "I did not have time to write last night. Monday you may look for two. T. It rained all day yesterday and it seems to be going windy to-day. Did you succeed in finding a suitable room? Where shall I send my next letter?"[43] From the language, one can divine that at this time they were corresponding with some frequency. Every one of Daisetz's letters from this period is short. He wrote about trivial things such as the weather, the situation in Japan, and things like that. It appears that the primary purpose was just to send letters, but perhaps that is what love letters are, after all.

As for love letters from Beatrice, a few of them were published in Jap-

---

41. *SDZ* 36, 145.
42. *SDZ* 36, 202.
43. *SDZ* 36, 303.

anese translation in *Suzuki Daisetsu botsugo 40 nen* (Forty Years after the Death of D.T. Suzuki; 2006):

> I will be lonely not being able to see you for a while, but believing in your love for me and the fact that we are together brings me much happiness. . . . I am sure the longed-for day will come when we see each other again. My dearest, dearest love Tei-sama, please keep me in your heart always. Please love me. Even if we are apart, I think of you always.[44]

It appears that corresponding with Beatrice was great spiritual support for Daisetz. After returning to Japan, he wrote to her saying, "I have not heard from you since last Friday, and wonder what you are doing & how you are getting along."[45] While it is unclear where he found the money, Daisetz also sent Beatrice a pendant as proof of his love. The pendant was inscribed in Sanskrit "TAT TVAM ASI" (lit. Thou art that). While the truth of the matter is unclear, the belief that Daisetz ordered the pendant from Tiffany on Fifth Avenue in New York has entered the realm of legend.[46] From the Zen point of view, which disdains attachments and worldly desires, this may seem like a contradiction, but I think we should pay more attention to the real-life Daisetz.

Daisetz's Marriage

In March 1909, Daisetz ended his eleven-year stay in the United States and returned to Japan. According to Hayashida Kumino, it appears that Daisetz did not have a firm outlook for the future. He thought of becoming a photographic technician, and he had brought back with him a camera and an enlarger for photographs. Daisetz maintained a keen interest in photog-

---

44. The suffix "sama" is a honorific title, often used for the person to whom the letter is addressed. Because the original letter is not available, the English text here is a translation based on the Japanese version by Yokoyama in Matsugaoka, *Suzuki Daisetsu botsugo 40 nen*, 78.

45. *SDZ* 36, 325.

46. Ueda Shizuteru, "Suzuki Biatorisu fujin," in Ueda Shizuteru and Okamura Mihoko, eds., *Suzuki Daisetsu to wa dareka* (Tokyo: Iwanami Gendai Bunko, 2002), 227–28. Originally published in *Zen bunka* 175 (2000).

raphy until the end of his life.[47] Alan would later share his father's interest in photography, if nothing else.

In August 1909, Daisetz was hired as an instructor in the English Department of Gakushuin University. For a period of two and a half years beginning that October, he was also appointed as an instructor at the College of Letters, Tokyo Imperial University, where he taught English. At the time Daisetz was not regarded as a scholar of Buddhism, but rather an English teacher returned from abroad.

From 1910 to 1915, Daisetz did not confine himself to doing research solely on Buddhism; he also translated the principal works of the Swedish mystic Emanuel Swedenborg (1688–1772) into Japanese and left his mark as the one who introduced Swedenborg to the Japanese public. He even published a biography titled *Suedenborugu* (Swedenborg) in 1913.[48] There are arguments for and against the thought of Swedenborg, who claimed to have seen the spiritual world. In particular, since Zen disavows the existence of "an afterlife," I think that there are probably some Zen scholars who would prefer to avoid the subject of "the Zen scholar D.T. Suzuki" being interested in Swedenborg.[49]

The Buddhist scholar Masutani Fumio (1902–1987) related that "Daisetz told me that at the time he still needed money, so he undertook the translation job for payment."[50] I find it hard to believe that Daisetz accepted a job that was at odds with his principles just because he needed the money. Daisetz did not speak much about Swedenborg after that, but it appears that Swedenborg was of some interest to him. In fact, in his later years Daisetz made the following comment on the subject of spiritualism: "There are many things in our world that we still don't understand."[51]

Beatrice ultimately followed Daisetz to Japan. By curious coincidence, the day that she arrived—February 14, 1911—was St. Valentine's Day. The two of them had their wedding ceremony on December 12 the same year at the American Consulate in Yokohama. The groom was forty-one and the bride was thirty-three. Even today, a mixed marriage between a Japanese

47. Hayashida, *Ōoji Suzuki Daisetsu kara no tegami*, 15.

48. Suzuki Daisetsu, *Suedenborugu* (Tokyo: Hinoeuma Shuppansha, 1913).

49. Recently a number of scholars have noted the abiding effect Swedenborg's work had on Daisetz: e.g., Andō Reiji, *Daisetz* (Tokyo: Kōdansha, 2018), chapter 3.

50. Masutani Fumio, "Suzuki Daisetsu ron," in Matsugaoka, *Suzuki Daisetsu botsugo 40 nen*, 129. Originally published in *Zaike bukkyō* 1490 (1966).

51. Okamura Mihoko, "'Shi'nin' Daisetsu," in Hisamatsu et al., *Suzuki Daisetsu*, 372. Originally published in *Suzuki Daisetsu zenshū geppō* (August 1970).

man and a Caucasian woman is rather rare. I am sure that in the early twentieth century people must have found it very unusual.[52] Apparently some members of Daisetz's circle were opposed to the match. Even Daisetz's close friend Yamamoto Ryōkichi was not entirely in support of it. In a letter that he sent to Daisetz before the wedding, he warned him that "taking a foreign wife will be expensive." In particular, he wrote that she would want more expensive food than a Japanese wife and would require high-quality personal effects, and that it was doubtful that she would be able to become accustomed to the Japanese way of life.[53] In view of Daisetz and Beatrice's subsequent married life, however, his fears proved to be groundless.

The precise date is not clear, but at some point around the time Daisetz and Beatrice were married, Sekiguchi Kono (1882–1948; known as Okono) began to work for Daisetz as a maid. For more than thirty years until her death from acute pneumonia in July 1948, Okono would care for Daisetz and Beatrice and, later, Alan.

On July 7, 1916, Daisetz and Beatrice, who were unable to have children, adopted a baby boy of unknown origins whom Okono had managed to locate for them. They submitted a notice of birth naming him Masaru and designating him as their natural-born son. According to the chronology found in *D. T. Suzuki, Primary Research Sources*, on July 20, about two weeks after the notice of birth was submitted, Beatrice left for the United States on a temporary home visit.[54] In a letter sent to Beatrice on August 9, Daisetz wrote: "The baby seems to be getting on all right."[55] This is the first record of Daisetz writing anything about his son.

When Daisetz and Beatrice got married, they lived in Takadaoimatsu-chō, Koishikawa-ku (present-day Mejirodai, Bunkyō-ku); however, some-

52. Some Japanese women (including prostitutes) married foreigners before the Meiji Restoration, but it was in 1873 that international marriage was first authorized by a declaration from the Dajōkan (Grand Council of State). Kamoto Itsuko clarified that the number of mixed marriages in Japan from 1873 to 1898 was 265. She classified mixed marriages into four types: (A) a Japanese bride enters into a foreign male's family register; (B) a foreign groom enters into a Japanese bride's family register; (C) a foreign bride enters into a Japanese groom's family register; and (D) a Japanese groom enters into a foreign bride's family register. The total number of type C mixed marriages was fifty-eight from 1873 to 1898 (Kamoto, *Kokusai kekkon no tanjō: "Bunmei koku Nippon" eno michi* [Tokyo: Shin'yōsha, 2001], 94–97). Although I could not find data for the year 1911, I believe that the marriage of Daisetz and Beatrice represents a rare case.

53. Yamamoto Ryōkichi, *Daisetsu ate Yamamoto Ryōkichi shokan: Suzuki Daisetsu mikōkai shokan [bessatsu]* (Kyoto: Zen Bunka Kenkyūjo, 1989), 58.

54. Kirita, *Suzuki Daisetsu kenkyū kiso shiryō*, 37.

55. *SDZ* 36, 399.

time before adopting Alan, it appears that they had moved to an official residence of Gakushuin University. From this time, they would also occasionally lodge at the Shōden-an, within the precincts of the Engakuji temple in Kita-Kamakura, perhaps when visiting Shaku Sōen.

In December 1916, Beatrice's mother, Emma Erskine Hahn (1846–1927), came to Japan. Emma was a very talented and versatile person; she had a PhD in medicine, debated social issues, managed a farm, and lectured on Russian literature. She was opposed to using animals in medical experiments and was active in the animal welfare movement. Her husband and Beatrice's father, Thomas Lane, had died early in their marriage, so Emma had taken a second husband, a German scholar by the name of Hahn.[56] Emma spent the remainder of her life in Japan and died in Kyoto. She lived close by Daisetz and Beatrice, but it is unclear whether she actually lived with them.

Daisetz continued to serve as an English instructor at Gakushuin University and also acted as dormitory leader. However, people whispered behind his back that Daisetz, with an American wife, had become "too foreign,"[57] and in 1921 Daisetz resigned from Gakushuin. Almost simultaneously, Daisetz became professor at Otani University in Kyoto. Beatrice also became a part-time instructor there, teaching preparatory courses, and so the whole family moved to Kyoto. Two years previously Daisetz's Zen teacher Sōen had died, and so there was no longer any reason for Daisetz to remain in the Tokyo and Kamakura area. Daisetz, however, continued to make use of the Shōden-an at Engakuji, so perhaps it is more appropriate to say that the family split their time between Kyoto and Kamakura.

Beatrice and Okono

During this period, it was Beatrice and the maid Okono who were the supporting pillars of Daisetz's life. What were these two women like? Beatrice was born of the union between her father, an American diplomat, and her mother, a daughter of the Scottish aristocracy. Beatrice's father died very soon after she was born, so like Daisetz, she grew up having no memory of her father. Beatrice graduated from Radcliffe College (now a college of Harvard University), which was known at the time as "the Harvard for women" and had an MFA from Columbia University.[58] After coming to

56. Suzuki Daisetsu Kyōju, *Bukkyō no taii*, 150.
57. *SDZ* 26, 530.
58. Hayashida, *Ōoji Suzuki Daisetsu kara no tegami*, 45.

Japan, Beatrice became devoted to researching esoteric Buddhism of the Shingon sect and would frequently visit Mt. Kōya, where the head temple of the sect is located. She published a lecture titled "Buddhism and Practical Life" (1933),[59] and after her death Daisetz published her work *Shōren bukkyō shōkan* (Some Observations of Blue Lotus Buddhism; 1940).[60]

Compared to Daisetz, Beatrice was quite a strong personality. Perhaps due to her mother's influence, she was very devoted to animal welfare and would take in animals that others were no longer able to care for or that had been abandoned. In 1929, Beatrice opened what is thought to be the first animal shelter in Japan—Jihien (Charity Garden)—near the Shōden-an. Hayashida Kumino remembered the Jihien as follows:

> The room for the cats had a wooden floor and was quite spacious. The walls of the room were lined with shelves, and from them mosquito netting was hung like curtains. Each cat had its own sleeping area in the interior behind the curtains. Okono-san brought her younger brother and his wife from her home province of Niigata to care for the dogs and cats. When Okono-san's brother rang a bell, all of the cats would jump out at the signal and begin to eat.[61]

Beatrice loved animals unconditionally. There were many times when Daisetz had to throw in the towel in the face of her irrepressible love of animals. An example of this is seen in his letter to Beatrice dated April 8, 1921.

> When you come back, you <u>must</u> dispense of the two dogs—I mean two of the three dogs—somehow. You don't realise how much money, how much human labour is to be devoted to them. I reckoned up that it takes at least <u>20</u> yen to feed them—dogs and cats, without taking notice of the damage they do to the yard. . . . You <u>must</u> promise to send the two dogs away as soon as you come back. I have at present too many things to occupy myself with and I don't wish to be bothered with the animals. I am <u>quite</u> decided now on that point. . . . P.S. This time I am quite serious about the dogs and I must earnestly hope that you will mind my advice.[62]

---

59. Beatrice Suzuki, "Buddhism and Practical Life," in *Bukkyō to jissai seikatsu*, trans. Yokogawa Kenshō (Nagoya: Shindō Kaikan, 1933).

60. Suzuki Biatorisu, *Shōren bukkyō shōkan* (Kyoto: Suzuki Teitarō, 1940).

61. Hayashida, *Ōoji Suzuki Daisetsu kara no tegami*, 31–32.

62. *SDZ* 36, 410–12.

Even though there were occasions like this, Daisetz exhibited an understanding of Beatrice's love of animals. In the Buddhist newspaper *Chūgai nippō*, Daisetz wrote: "For a Buddhist in Japan to attempt to set up an animal shelter is not just a matter of liking or disliking animals; rather, I believe that setting up such a facility is one method to teach the general public about the Way of Compassion."[63] Daisetz himself was an animal lover as well who was especially fond of cats.

Certain people in Daisetz's circle, however, did not think highly of Beatrice. For example, Jugaku Bunshō wrote as follows:

According to Daisetz's students at Gakushuin University, such as the late Yanagi Muneyoshi, compared to the scale of Professor Daisetz's influence, his wife did not have a very good reputation. They would say, "Daisetz-san is fine, but his wife, well . . ." and then become vague and evasive.[64]

Beatrice reportedly had a very hot temper. Asahina Sōgen (1891–1979), the head priest at Engakuji, relates the following reminiscence that supports this.

The following story concerns Mrs. Suzuki's impulsiveness. Around 1910, when electric lighting was first introduced to Engakuji, Mrs. Suzuki flew into a rage since she was of the opinion that the whole temple compound should be preserved in its traditional form without bringing in electrical lighting. She offended people in the temples by walking around and yelling in a loud voice in her halting Japanese so that all could hear her. Sensei, however, made no attempt to defend or explain her actions.[65]

Jugaku Bunshō also touched upon Beatrice's extraordinary love of animals, her mediocre cooking skills (she was a vegetarian), and her relationship to Theosophy, which has something of a disreputable air about it.

However, it seems that forcing cats and dogs to be vegetarians goes against nature somewhat. The barking and meowing of the cats and

63. *SDZ* 31, 449. Originally published in *Chūgai nippō* (August 15–18, 1929).
64. Jugaku, "Kateijin to shite no Daisetsu koji," 208.
65. Asahina Sōgen, "Katei ni okeru Daisetsu sensei," in Hisamatsu et al., *Suzuki Daisetsu*, 118. Originally published in *Suzuki Daisetsu zenshū geppō* (April 1969).

dogs that one could hear at the Suzuki residence had an unnatural air of unsatisfied hunger. We—this included Dr. Hatani Ryōtai—were used to vegetarian cuisine, but even so, we recoiled from the flavors of the Western-style vegetarian cuisine that was served at the Suzuki home and would wink at one another while praising it as "very good."[66]

As befitted her deep attraction to esoteric religion, Ms. Beatrice had an uncommonly strong interest in Theosophy as well. She set up a Japanese branch of Krishnamurti's "The Order of the Star in the East" in the Suzuki home, holding regular meetings and inviting those who were interested. Having a change of heart, Krishnamurti decided to disband the organization in 1929, but up until just before that time, meetings of this somewhat spooky and disreputable organization were held at the Suzuki home, and a fellow believer, a Dutch woman named Mattheisen, lodged temporarily with the Suzukis.[67]

It appears that Jugaku saw Beatrice as a member of this "somewhat spooky and disreputable organization." He also praised Daisetz's compassion in taking such a person [Beatrice] in. Jugaku's writings give the impression that Daisetz had nothing to do with Theosophy. However, according to the chronology in *D. T. Suzuki, Primary Research Sources*, in the decade of the 1920s Daisetz himself frequently participated in Theosophy meetings.[68] Since the meetings were held at his house, there would have been nothing strange about him attending. Jugaku must have known about Daisetz's relationship with Theosophy, but by writing that Daisetz had no connection with this "somewhat spooky and disreputable organization," suggests he was trying to protect Daisetz's reputation as a scholar.

Leaving aside the fact that Beatrice's poor reputation can be used as material for mythologizing Daisetz, the two of them were genuinely in love. There is a story that a student at Otani University asked Beatrice, "Why do you love Japan?" and Beatrice, blushing furiously, replied, "Because it's Tei's country."[69]

The other woman who was close to Daisetz was the maid Okono.[70] It is

66. Jugaku, "Kateijin to shite no Daisetsu koji," 210.
67. Jugaku, "Kateijin to shite no Daisetsu koji," 210.
68. Kirita, *Suzuki Daisetsu kenkyū kiso shiryō*, 43–68.
69. Ueda, "Suzuki Biatorisu fujin," 233.
70. Information about Okono can be found in the following publications: Hayashida,

impossible to know what Okono, who was from Niigata prefecture, did before she came to the Suzuki house. The Buddhist scholar Kusunoki Kyō (1915–2000), who lived near the Matsugaoka Bunko, reported that Okono entered Daisetz's employment before he got married, whereas Hayashida Kumino said that it was two years after he married Beatrice. Okono was a small, thin woman who could neither read nor write, and according to Kumino, she was a bad cook as well. Kusunoki, however, described her as "extremely intelligent and quick-witted and very observant and alert to her surroundings, with a deep love of animals; and she had great respect for Daisetz as an eminent scholar."[71] She was also the doorkeeper of the Suzuki home, and chased away first-time visitors with a loud shout, yelling, "Don't bother the sensei."[72] In her own way, Okono aided Daisetz's studies from the shadows.

Okono and Beatrice often butted heads, though they could not speak each other's language very well. According to Kumino, Okono would frequently incur Beatrice's wrath by commenting on the affairs of the Suzuki household, leading an exasperated Beatrice to say, "I am the wife of this house, not you."[73] According to Kumino, "Okono and Beatrice were like two peas in a pod: dedicated if seen in a positive light, opinionated and mercurial if one looks at it negatively."[74] Even though they often fought, Okono, with her love of animals, was a great help to Beatrice as far as the animal shelter was concerned. Daisetz was very fond of the quirky Okono and took good care of her. Kumino remembers that on many occasions Daisetz would say, "It may very well be that the way Okono lives her life is the Zen way of living."[75]

Alan in the "Daisetz Diaries"

Alan makes his first appearance in Daisetz's English-language diaries (hereafter the "Daisetz Diaries")[76] in 1920. In the entry for January 18, Daisetz

---

Ōoji Suzuki Daisetsu kara no tegami, 85–90; Kusunoki Kyō, "Okono-san no tsuioku," in Hisamatsu et al., *Suzuki Daisetsu,* 389–92 (originally published in *Suzuki Daisetsu zenshū geppō* [June 1970]); Furuta Shōkin, "Daisetsu sensei to yūen no hitobito (1)," in *SDZ* 18 *geppō* (March 2001): 8–11.

71. Kusunoki, "Okono-san no tsuioku," 390.
72. Furuta, "Daisetsu sensei to yūen no hitobito," 9–10.
73. Hayashida, *Ōoji Suzuki Daisetsu kara no tegami,* 88.
74. Hayashida, *Ōoji Suzuki Daisetsu kara no tegami,* 87.
75. Hayashida, *Ōoji Suzuki Daisetsu kara no tegami,* 86.
76. Kirita, "D.T. Suzuki's English Diaries."

wrote: "B. goes to Shoden with Allan." The "B" is for Beatrice, and Shoden refers to the Shōden-an at the Engakuji temple. According to the family register, Alan would have been three years old. At this time, Daisetz spelled Alan's name as "Allan," but starting about three years later he would change it to "Alan."

Here I would like to clarify the nature of the "Daisetz Diaries" according to the account left by the Buddhist scholar Kirita Kiyohide, who published the diaries.[77] Starting around 1920, Daisetz diligently kept a diary in English. Kirita posits that he was following Beatrice, who had the custom of keeping a diary. The original copies of the "Daisetz Diaries" are the property of the Matsugaoka Bunko and were kept strictly private; it was not until around 1980 that their existence became publicly known. Even today, the number of scholars who are allowed to see the originals is quite limited. Their contents are not secret, and sequential publications by Kirita and Yokoyama Wayne Shigeto appeared in the journal *Matsugaoka Bunko kenkyū nenpō* (Annual Research Report of Matsugaoka Bunko; hereafter *MBKN*) from 2005 to 2015. In the monthly report in the fortieth volume of *The Complete Works of D. T. Suzuki, Expanded New Edition*, Kirita described the nature of the "Daisetz Diaries" as follows:

> So far as I have examined, Daisetz did not forget a single entry in the diaries. It appears that over a period of several decades, Daisetz did not miss a single day, and writing in the diary appears to have been entirely habitual. The diaries offer a window into how Daisetz approached his day-to-day life. The diary entries were constructed so that each day included, without fail, the high and low temperatures, the weather, and what he did. . . . The entries regarding his activities comprised the important correspondence he would send and receive, the names of visitors and the places he visited, and the writing, proof-reading, and revisions he did, as well as what he read, and the entries were arranged so as to be divided, generally, into morning, afternoon, and evening. . . . The diaries contained what Daisetz did each day, but there is hardly any mention at all of things such as goings on in the wider world. Also, other than extraordinary events such as the death of a family member, Daisetz usually wrote nothing about what he may have thought or felt at any given time.[78]

77. Kirita Kiyohide, "Chūki Suzuki Daisetsu eibun nikki ni tsuite," *MBKN* 19 (2005): 157–58.
78. Kirita Kiyohide, "Zenshū no kanketsu ni atatte: Kongo no Daisetsu kenkyū no tameni," *SDZ* 40 *geppō* (2003): 9–10.

As was typical of diaries at that time, the "Daisetz Diaries" contain nothing more than a matter-of-fact record of daily events, and as noted above by Kirita, do not touch upon Daisetz's thoughts and feelings. To put it another way, we can say that for Daisetz to write about what he thought and felt meant that something was an "earthshaking event" for him. Such earthshaking events involving Alan cropped up frequently.

According to Kirita, the Matsugaoka Bunko contains almost complete diaries of the thirty-one years during 1920, 1923–1933, 1936–1948, and 1950–1955; only one month from 1949; and memoranda during the years 1956–1959, 1961, and 1962.[79] Unfortunately, there are no complete diaries from the middle of the 1950s, Daisetz's most active years, until his last years in the 1960s. Kirita finds this extremely questionable, saying, "It is quite clear that something strange is going on."[80] Scrutinizing why diaries from such an important period are missing from the Bunko is beyond the scope of this book, so I will not discuss it further.

Kirita and Yokoyama's reprint of the "Daisetz Diaries" in the *MBKN* seems trustworthy, since there is no arbitrary editing of the text and because there are entries about incidents that might tarnish Daisetz's image. In a paper written prior to the reprinting of the "Daisetz Diaries," Kirita made the following proposal to the Matsugaoka Bunko.

> In criticizing or praising Daisetz, the question is: on what data and on what grounds are the discussions based? The more data, the better, even if it is just a little bit. It is not a good idea to judge by "this data has no value" or "this data could cause problems, so we won't make it public." The reason is because it goes against the fact that the data exists, and judgments that "this data has no value" or "this data could cause problems" are not related to Daisetz himself, but nothing more than personal value judgments determined by the times, societal constraints, and personal likes and dislikes of the person making them. It goes without saying, but value judgments differ according to the person, era, and society, and they change over time. Therefore, evaluations of Daisetz will naturally differ and transform throughout the ages. What is essential is to uncover and present data as it is, without making any arbitrary selections.[81]

---

79. Kirita, "Chūki Suzuki Daisetsu eibun nikki ni tsuite," 157; Kirita Kiyohide, "Kōki," *MBKN* 29 (2015): 59. At the time of writing this book, the memoranda of the year 1961 are not published.

80. Kirita, "Chūki Suzuki Daisetsu eibun nikki ni tsuite," 157.

81. Kirita Kiyohide, "Matsugaoka Bunko to Suzuki Daisetsu kenkyū," *MBKN* 18 (2004): 89–90.

If all of the people and organizations that are in possession of historical data had such an attitude, there is no telling how much progress would be made in historical research. If one reads between the lines, one can view this as criticism of the fact that up until that time, data on Daisetz had not been presented "as it is" but had been "arbitrarily edited." On the other hand, it appears that the entries regarding the temperature and the weather, which Daisetz presumably included without fail, were omitted from the "Daisetz Diaries" that Kirita published. Since the originals have not been made public, it is impossible to verify whether or not the published "Daisetz Diaries" are complete. All of that being said, Kirita and Yokoyama no doubt published the "Daisetz Diaries" with the lofty goal of not sifting through the data and selecting what to keep and what to discard. Thanks to the "Daisetz Diaries" and the way in which they were published, we can clarify the relationship that Alan had with his father from the time he was a child up through his young adulthood.

Kirita is also the editor of *The Complete Works of D. T. Suzuki, Expanded New Edition*, on which this book heavily relies. Upon the completion of the volumes, however, Kirita issued the following warning, saying that *Works* was not perfect.

> In my opinion, the concept of "complete works" means that what that person has left to posterity, including notes and memoranda, are collected, organized, faithfully reproduced, and published with nothing left out, great or small. There is, of course, the issue of the extent of the effort, but at a minimum, great effort should be expended in that direction. In the publication of the present volumes of the "complete works," we faced limitations dictated by the times and societal norms regarding things like the protection of privacy, as well as time restrictions, and as one of the people involved in this project, I blame myself for those occasions when I did not put forth my maximum effort.[82]

Here I would like to present one example of the limitations to which Kurita was obliged to conform. It concerns an entry regarding a slaughterhouse that appeared in *Ichi shinjitsu no sekai* (The World of One Truth) published in 1941.[83] In the *Complete Works of D. T. Suzuki, Expanded New*

82. Kirita, "Zenshū no kanketsu ni atatte," 9.

83. Suzuki Daisetsu, *Ichi shinjitsu no sekai* (Tokyo: Kondō Shoten, 1941).

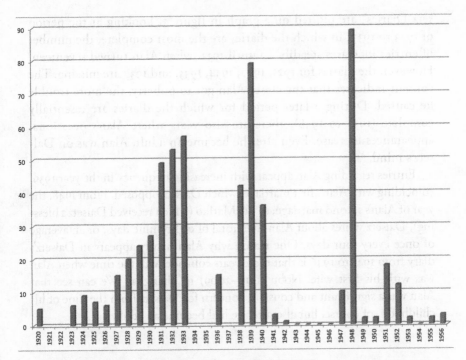

Fig. 1. The number of days with references to Alan in the "Daisetz Diaries"

Edition, the editors omitted this episode, citing as their reason "the use of a discriminatory expression that is clearly inappropriate in today's society."[84] In the original text of the omitted section, Daisetz digressed to give the impressions he felt when he saw the people working at a slaughterhouse in Chicago. In the old (first) edition of *The Complete Works of D. T. Suzuki*, published in 1969, this section was not omitted.[85] It is not clear whether the decision to delete this from the *Expanded New Edition* was made by Furuta Shōkin, the Buddhist scholar and senior disciple of Daisetz who was the managing editor for both editions, or by others such as Kirita. What we should keep in mind, however, is the fact that ultimately the data included in new edition of *The Complete Works of D. T. Suzuki* was subject to editorial decisions as to what to include and what to exclude.

Let's return the discussion to the diaries. The number of days on which references to Alan appear in the published version of the "Dai-

84. *SDZ* 16, 543.
85. Suzuki Daisetsu, *Suzuki Daisetsu zenshū* 16 (Tokyo: Iwanami Shoten, 1969), 43–44.

setz Diaries" are plotted on a graph in figure 1. Looking at the period of 1923 to 1937, in which the diaries are the most complete, the number of entries increases steadily up until 1933, when Alan turned seventeen. However, the diaries for 1921, 1922, 1934, 1935, and 1937 are missing. The content indicates that the closer Alan got to puberty, the more trouble he caused. During a later period for which the diaries are essentially complete (1938 to 1948), there are also years where Alan's occasional appearances increase. Even after he became an adult, Alan was on Daisetz's mind.

Entries regarding Alan appear with increasing frequency in the year 1939, coinciding with Alan's first marriage, which Daisetz opposed. From 1948, the year of Alan's second marriage, to Ike Mariko (which received Daisetz's blessing), Daisetz writes about Alan for a total of eighty-nine days, or an average of once every four days. One reason why Alan hardly appears in Daisetz's diary from 1941 to 1946 is that these years coincide with the time when Alan was with his first wife, Nobu (1916–2009) in Shanghai. We can see that Alan was a significant and constant concern for Daisetz from the time of his childhood, of course, but also after he had become an adult.

Daisetz's Dependent Family

Let's bring the discussion back to Daisetz's family. It was not only his wife, child, and the maid Okono whom Daisetz was supporting; throughout his life, Daisetz also provided for his oldest brother Gentarō's eldest son, Ryōkichi, and his children. Ryōkichi dropped out of the upper level at Aoyama Gakuin School and went to the United States, where he worked to support himself while attending Harvard and New York University. Daisetz, who was also in the United States at that time, met with Ryōkichi in Boston and New York and, taking pity on his nephew, who like him was struggling, emptied his wallet for him despite his own poverty.[86] After Ryōkichi returned to Japan, he married his cousin Hatsuko, who took care of Daisetz in the early days after his return from the United States. Ryōkichi and Hatsuko had five children: Rei (1909–1990), En (1912–1923), Ō (1914–1991), Kumino, and Ichio (1920–1985). Kumino married (becoming Hayashida Kumino) and went on to author *Granduncle* in her later life. Among the children, it was the second son, En, for whom Daisetz had the highest expec-

---

86. Hayashida, *Ōoji Suzuki Daisetsu kara no tegami*, 10–11.

tations. Unfortunately, En died without ever finishing elementary school. Daisetz was grief-stricken, saying, "[En] was not only very intelligent, but also a good person; however, because he was thoughtlessly made to study at school, he contracted meningitis or something of the sort, and without being sick for even a day, slipped away from his mother's embrace almost as though nothing had happened."[87]

In September 1920, the year before Daisetz moved from Tokyo to Kyoto, Ryōkichi died of illness at the age of forty-two. He left behind his wife Hatsuko (who was thirty-five years old) and five children, from eleven-year-old Rei to Ichio, with whom Hatsuko was pregnant at the time. Ryōkichi's father Gentarō and the entire Suzuki family were of the opinion that Hatsuko should remarry and that the younger children should be put up for adoption.[88] It was Daisetz who put a stop to this. In a letter to Hatsuko on May 30, 1921, Daisetz wrote: "Today, I feel that the children should not be scattered to the four winds, and even though that I want to take the youngest one in myself, at this time, given the circumstances with my family, unfortunately, this is impossible. Therefore, I would like to offer you some monetary support."[89] Later, in a letter dated July 1, Daisetz encouraged Hatsuko, writing, "I want you to honor Ryōkichi's memory and raise your children to be upstanding people. It is the vital role of a mother."[90] Unfortunately, Hatsuko's father-in-law, Gentarō, died in June 1925. Hatsuko was now at the end of her rope, and just as he promised in his letter, Daisetz supported and her children financially, eventually adopting the youngest, Ichio.

It was undoubtedly chivalrous behavior on Daisetz's part, but this could have had an adverse effect on Alan's education. Since he was able to keep sending money to distant relatives, Alan probably thought that his father was wealthy. As far as Alan was concerned, it would be perfectly natural for him to expect the same treatment that his father gave to his grandnephews and grandnieces.

87. *SDZ* 17, 195. Originally published in Suzuki Daisetsu, *Hyakushū sensetsu* (Kyoto: Chūgai Shuppan), 1925.
88. Hayashida, *Ōoji Suzuki Daisetsu kara no tegami*, 20–22.
89. *SDZ* 36, 415–16.
90. *SDZ* 36, 417.

TWO

The Juvenile Delinquent

A Prison without Bars

After taking up a position at Otani University at the age of fifty, for a while Daisetz moved from place to place, accompanied by his family and maid. Among the places he lived are Rikkyoku-an, a sub-temple on the grounds of Tōfukuji, and the Chishin dormitory at Otani University (present-day Chishin dormitory at Otani High School). In 1924, the Western-style house that Ataka Yakichi was building for Daisetz in Koyamaōno-chō, Kamigyō-ku in Kyoto was completed, and in March 1926, Daisetz, Beatrice, the nine-year-old Alan, and Okono moved in. The outer walls were pink, and branches of akebia vines formed an arc over the path from the gate to the entrance of the house. A large ginkgo tree also grew there.[1] As of this book's writing, the house still exists as a private residence.

In 1941, after Beatrice had died and Alan had left home, Daisetz asked Hatsuko, the wife of Daisetz's late nephew, and her daughter Kumino to come and live in the house as helpers, and they agreed. Kumino remembers the pink, Western-style house as follows:

After passing under the akebia arch and going into the entranceway, one saw the kitchen and the dining room on the left-hand side on the first floor. The lavatory and the bath were at the end of the hall. Further inside, there was an old Japanese-style structure that seemed to have been added as an afterthought. That was where the maid lived. Adjacent to that was the library, which stood on its own, independent of the rest of the house. . . . On the second floor were the bedrooms of Daisetz

1. Hayashida, *Ōoji Suzuki Daisetsu kara no tegami*, 71.

34

and the deceased Beatrice. A door connected the two rooms so that one could go between them without having to go into the hall. Okono's room was across the hall. And then there was Alan's room. . . . The most magnificent rooms in the house were the individual studies of Daisetz and Beatrice. The shelves on the walls were jam-packed with books.[2]

Kumino, who was in her twenties, said that she could not get used to life in the Suzuki home. Even though it was done out of concern for his young great-niece, the limitations that Daisetz put on when Kumino could go out and where she could go were quite strict. Kumino did not get along very well with the strong-willed Okono either. Kumino wrote that "the quiet life in the home of an old scholar made me feel like I was suffocating, and I wanted more freedom. Plainly put, I wanted to be able to do what I wanted, like practice my hobbies to my heart's content."[3] In secret, Kumino called Daisetz's residence "a prison without bars," after the name of a film.[4] A prison without bars—this is how an average young person, the same age as Alan, felt about life with Daisetz.

Daisetz's Fears

Looking at the entries of the "Daisetz Diaries" during the first half of 1923, one finds that the six-year-old Alan became sick and the maid suddenly quit, which saddened Alan. When a child is at the cute, adorable stage, every issue can be chalked up to "mischievousness." However, even after Alan had reached the age where a person should know the difference between right and wrong, his pranks and lies continued to escalate. He entered a Shinshū Ōtani sect elementary school in April 1924, and according to the "Daisetz Diaries," Daisetz was summoned to the school over Alan's "misconduct" in the next month. Meetings between Daisetz and the teachers at the school are also recorded in July 1925 and March 1926.

In a letter to Beatrice dated July 14, 1926, Daisetz expressed his concern about Alan's habit of lying. Alan had told someone named Numaguchi that he had a headache, but as far as Numaguchi could see, Alan was perfectly

---

2. Hayashida, *Ōoji Suzuki Daisetsu kara no tegami*, 72–73.

3. Hayashida, *Ōoji Suzuki Daisetsu kara no tegami*, 82.

4. Hayashida, *Ōoji Suzuki Daisetsu kara no tegami*, 82. Kumino was referring to a French film *Prisons sans Barreaux*, directed by Leonide Moguy (Films OSSO, 1938).

Fig. 2. Daisetz, Beatrice, and Alan, circa 1925. Photographer unknown. Source: Barbara R. Sims, *Traces That Remain: A Pictorial History of the Early Days of the Baha'i Faith among the Japanese* (Tokyo: Baha'i Publishing Trust Japan, 1989), 85.

fine. Daisetz said that feigning a headache was a stratagem of Alan's. Daisetz also wrote that whenever he did not want to do something, Alan would beg off claiming a headache and that it was necessary to get him to stop indulging in this habit.[5] Hayashida Kumino also clearly remembers Alan as a wild and unruly child.

> The only thing I recall from when Alan was a young boy is the time when Alan, who was in the fifth or sixth grade in elementary school, I think, came from Kyoto to our house in Tokyo for a visit and acted in a rude, insolent manner. He would climb up on the roof and run around, then jump down through the kitchen skylight and run along the top of the wall around the house. He really frightened my mother.
>
> It was so bad that the impression I had of him was that he was a

---

5. *SDZ* 36, 450.

wild boy who made my dear mother worry a lot, and I just wanted him to go home as quickly as possible.[6]

Asahina Sōgen also remembers Alan's wild ways. When the Suzukis were living at the Chishin dormitory at Otani University, Sōgen lived under the same roof with them for about two months. In addition to learning English from Beatrice, he supervised the studies of Alan, who had just started elementary school.

Then there was Alan. He was a wild and impetuous child, and one day when I accompanied him to school, after passing through the school gate, all of a sudden he went barefoot and with his shoes in his hand, ran deep into the interior of the school grounds without a backward glance. I was quite surprised. . . . In every way he was more active than Japanese children.[7]

One can see from the final sentence that Sōgen regarded Alan as a foreigner with his unusual behavior. In today's world, Alan would have been diagnosed as having some syndrome. At that time, however, he was just seen as an unruly child who could not sit still and was left alone without any medical intervention.

As Alan grew up, Daisetz grew more worried and uneasy. One can sense this here and there in the letters he wrote to Beatrice. In a letter dated August 23, 1927, Daisetz mentioned a telegram that Alan was supposed to have sent but did not, saying, "No doubt he is still irresponsible"[8] and that it would be best for Alan to live at the school dormitory. Daisetz had a premonition that at some point he would not be able to control Alan and was hoping that Alan could be reformed by leaving home and having the school train him to be disciplined. This does not mean that Daisetz abandoned Alan. On September 12, 1928, Daisetz sent a letter to Beatrice from the Shōden-an in which he expressed concern about Alan, who was about to start a new term at school.[9] In particular, in a letter to Beatrice dated January 8, 1929, Daisetz voiced his earnest hopes for his son.

---

6. Hayashida, *Ōoji Suzuki Daisetsu kara no tegami*, 58–59.
7. Asahina, "Katei ni okeru Daisetsu-sensei," 120.
8. *SDZ* 36, 469.
9. *SDZ* 36, 497.

With Alan you must be patient. He may not learn very much just now, or may not show any decided inclination to learn. But when he is old enough later he will remember the love and labour you have spent on him, and this will get him thinking anew about his life. Education is done generally in this way I think. Not to try to see one incredible result is [the] great secret of success in education. Some day he may wake up.[10]

The difficulty with Alan lies not just in the fact that he was wild, but that he was an adopted child who was being raised as the Suzukis' natural son. There is a strong possibility that he was born out of wedlock. If Alan learned of this in the future, what would he do? For Daisetz, this was a serious matter that could erupt at some point. In his book *Zen: Zuihitsu* (Zen Essays) published in 1927, Daisetz included an essay entitled "Shiseiji o chūshin ni shite" (Centering on the Illegitimate Child).[11] In it a female teacher went on a cruise, had a relationship with a man, and became pregnant. She gave birth to a boy whom she gave up for adoption. The boy believed that his adoptive parents were his birth parents. His biological mother, pretending to be his "aunt," maintained communication with him. Before he was to enter middle school, however, he became aware of his real family background. Upon visiting his "aunt," who was his real mother, he was crushed when the meeting did not match the fantasy he had created in his mind.[12] After introducing this story, Daisetz wrote the following:

> When I am confronted with a real-life example of this, the various problems that I occasionally see and ponder in the course of my everyday life become real, and I am strangely stirred to action, struck by the seriousness of the problem and the feeling that I must do something as soon as possible.[13]

Without the existence of Alan, it would be impossible to understand the reason why Daisetz wrote something like this. Alan was eight years old when this essay was first published. Already at this time, Daisetz was seriously

---

10. *SDZ* 36, 500.

11. This first appeared in the September 1924 issue of *Chūgai nippō*.

12. Suzuki Daisetsu, "Shiseiji o chūshin ni shite," repr. in Suzuki Daisetsu, *Zen: Zuihitsu* (Tokyo: Daiyūkaku, 1927). Originally published in *Chūgai nippō* (September 1924), *SDZ* 19, 385–93.

13. *SDZ* 19, 386.

concerned about what would happen if and when Alan found out about his true origins. He was impatient: "I must do something as soon as possible."

"Even if they are not illegitimate, there can be no doubt that there are many children who are growing up in such circumstances. The question is: how can we save such children?"[14] Daisetz concluded that "today, the only way to save illegitimate children is through religion."[15]

> In any case, once a person has been born as a human being, regardless of how that person came into being, that person is a spiritual entity. That is what we need to concentrate on. The illegitimate label is a label that is put on a person by society and by people. From the view of God, however, each person is an individual spirit. Viewed from the highest possible human awareness, each person has a dignity and a worth that cannot be judged by society.[16]

Daisetz is saying that illegitimate children also have dignity. He believed that Alan was also "an individual spirit" who had worth. If this is so, those who shun Alan do not understand Daisetz's feelings.

Much later in his life, Daisetz discussed artificial insemination in one of his articles (1962), asking, if a couple cannot conceive, what will happen if a child finds out that he or she has been born as a result of the artificial insemination of his mother from sperm that is not from her husband?

> No matter how hard one tries to keep such a thing secret, the child who was created artificially will find out about it from somewhere. If not when he is a child, after he grows up a bit and wonders where he came from, surely he will find out the truth. Unless that person is a philosopher or a man of religion by nature, it is certain that such an "artificially made person" will suffer a great psychological and, thus, moral upheaval in his mind, resulting in a spiritual abnormality. There is no way of knowing what effect this will have on society. It is not just an issue of the unhappiness of the person; it is a matter of the responsibility of the parents. It is a crime against society.[17]

---

14. *SDZ* 19, 391.
15. *SDZ* 19, 391.
16. *SDZ* 19, 392–93.
17. *SDZ* 34, 292–93. Originally published in *Yomiuri Shimbun* (November 5–26, 1962).

Even if the situations of a child who is the result of artificial insemination using sperm that is not of his father and that of an adopted child differ in certain respects, the confusion such children will experience upon finding out the truth of their origins is certainly similar. In fact, Alan was aware that he was adopted before Daisetz told him. This experience is reflected in the passage above. It was one cause of Alan's "spiritual abnormality," and Daisetz must have felt that he also bore some of the responsibility.

Daisetz's Philosophy of Education

Let us digress for a moment and take a look at Daisetz's views on the education of children. Reading *Kōjō no tettsui* (The Iron Hammer of Improvement), which was published in 1915, the year before Alan was adopted, it appears that Daisetz's philosophy was to be strict with children, entirely different from mainstream thinking today. According to *The Iron Hammer of Improvement*, Japanese parents do whatever their child says. It is impossible to expect that a child raised in this manner will live an orderly and disciplined life, gain self-respect and independence, and be capable of self-control after he or she reaches adulthood. Particularly in affluent households, children are corrupted by being spoiled and being called "young master" or "little lord." There is no need to abuse children, but parents should teach them self-restraint, making sure that their children go to bed on time and not giving them what the adults are eating even if they want it. Daisetz wrote that if parents do their best to guide a child, paying attention to everything the child does and says, it should be possible to achieve this in a short period.[18]

The letters that Daisetz sent to Kumino's mother Hatsuko reveal his philosophy of education. In a letter dated May 27, 1921, Daisetz wrote: "It is the duty of parents to give their child the best possible education. For that purpose they should be more frugal than frugal, and within their area of activity, children should not handle objects roughly. I believe that if such things are in place from the start, as a matter of course children will come to understand naturally."[19]

A Zen master does not teach his disciples in any detail. In a study Daisetz published in 1916, he wrote that Zen education is centered on the individual.

---

18. *SDZ* 17, 169–71. Originally published in Suzuki Daisetsu, *Kōjō no tettsui* (Tokyo: Kōseikan Shoten, 1915).

19. *SDZ* 36, 414. Originally published in Suzuki Daisetsu, *Zen no tachiba kara* (Tokyo: Kōyūkan, 1916).

When a disciple does zazen, the teacher does not teach him anything. If the disciple's understanding is incorrect, the teacher does not make a counter-argument; he simply says it is wrong. While it would be possible to break down a problem and explain the answer in detail, according to Daisetz, it would kill Zen.[20] I think that Daisetz's approach to education was to watch the child and wait patiently until the child found his way on his own.

Daisetz approved of what is called the "Spartan" way of education. In *Bunka to shūkyō* (Culture and Religion) published in 1943, agreeing with the educational philosophy of the Jōdo Shinshū priest Ashikaga Jōen (1878–1960), Daisetz wrote: "In Mr. Ashikaga's experience, since a somewhat incompetent child will not behave like a fine horse that obeys even when it is only shown the whip but is not actually struck with it, there are times when measures such as striking a child are necessary. This is an important matter."[21] Daisetz went on to say that for dull-witted people, stimulating them by using out-of-the-ordinary means such as hitting can give them the opportunity to display hidden talents.

In a Zen training hall, a senior monk will strike the back of a trainee whose mind is wandering using a stick called a *keisaku*. It is not considered to be a violent punishment; instead, the *keisaku* is recognized as the "stick of compassion." There was a prominent Chinese priest, Deshan Xuanjian (780–865), who was famous for hitting his disciples with the "Staff of Thirty Blows." I do not think that Daisetz, who had penetrated to the essence of Zen, would have felt any ambivalence about striking the person he had to guide. One can easily imagine Daisetz seeing Alan, with his insolent behavior, as a "somewhat incompetent child" and striking him accordingly. However, one can also say that this was common parental behavior in Japan before World War II. Zen disciples are also taught that one should throw away everything one has learned since one was born and be like a newborn baby. Is it possible that perhaps Daisetz saw the Zen state of mind in Alan, the uninhibited child?

In his eulogy for Shaku Sōen, Daisetz touched upon a conversation between Beatrice and three-year-old Alan at the private funeral held for Sōen. Daisetz heaped scorn upon himself, saying that the young Alan was closer to enlightenment than he was, shattered as he was by the loss of his lifelong teacher, Sōen.

---

20. *SDZ* 16, 483–85.
21. *SDZ* 19, 164. Originally published in Suzuki Daisetsu, *Bunka to shūkyō* (Nagoya: Shidō Kaikan, 1943).

CHILD: "Are we going to see Kwancho-San now?"
MOTHER: "You won't see him anymore. He's gone away to Buddha."
CHILD: "Has he gone away to meditate with Buddha?"
MOTHER: "Yes, my dear child."

Hearing this he said "Umm," and appeared to be completely satisfied. This child is at a higher level than I am.[22]

Moreover, in a lecture given in 1939, Daisetz described the childhood years of Bankei Yōtaku (1622–1693), an Edo-period Buddhist priest whom he had studied extensively, as follows:

By the way, the Zen priest Bankei was apparently quite a strong-willed child in his youth. He was what would be called a ringleader today; when anything happened, he would be the leader of the gang, and he was apparently an extremely unruly and bratty child who, if there were a fight, would be the first one in on it. . . . There is a tendency to put such a child in an inferior elementary school rather than a good school, and if the teacher's guidance is not appropriate, such a child will drift more and more off track. In this case, if an especially good teacher does not look after his education, the child will do poorly rather than improve. Just because a person does not listen to instruction does not mean that he or she is wrong; we are led to believe that this means that the person who could not get him to listen is at fault. I think this is something to which we must pay attention. . . . If a headstrong child can be guided appropriately, it is certain that such a child will show great development. If this guidance breaks down, the child will turn out badly.[23]

It is natural to assume that Daisetz equated the brattiness of Bankei and Alan in mind. What Daisetz is saying is that if such a headstrong child cannot be guided, it is the fault of the adults, parents, and teachers. Daisetz must have gained something from Alan's wildness in his youth. Yokoyama Wayne Shigeto wrote, "In a lecture delivered five years before his death, Suzuki-sensei, who had reached a dead end with the problem [of Alan], said

---

22. *SDZ* 31, 133–34. Originally published in Suzuki Daisetsu, "Ryōga rōshi o itamu," *Zendō* 112 (January 5, 1920).

23. *SDZ* 20, 77–79. Originally published in *Asoka* (July 1960).

something along the lines that the state of Zen enlightenment is the same as the state of the natural exuberant activity of a child who jumps around all over the place. It must be one of the lessons he learned from the Alan problem."[24] If this is so, then we can say that the existence of Alan thrust Daisetz into the contradiction that exists between the state of Zen mind and sociality, between satori and the responsibilities of a parent.

A Parent's Hope

In April 1929, Alan entered the Kyoto Municipal Number Three Middle School (Sanchū; present-day Yamashiro High School), and Daisetz arranged to have Alan lodged in the school's dormitory. However, Daisetz thought that rather than Kyoto, with its many temptations, it would be better for Alan to live as a student away from the mundane world. In a letter dated March 25, 1929, just before Alan was to enter the Number Three Middle School, Daisetz wrote the following to Beatrice, who was at the Shōden-an in Kita-Kamakura: "If he does not get into Sanchyu [*sic*] dormitory, the best place will probably be Koya [*sic*] [Middle School] for him to go. It may not be advisable for him to be in Kyoto any longer."[25]

Daisetz had never liked the culture of Kyoto. In one of his most important works, *Nihonteki reisei* (Japanese Spirituality; 1944), he summed up Japan until the Heian period (794–1185/ca. 1192) with the word *jōseiteki*, alluding to people living their lives by force of habit—a culture characterized by inert passivity.[26] Suzuki described the *Genji monogatari* (The Tale of Genji; ca. 1008) as "filled with the love complications, sensual pleasures, and literary and rhetorical pastimes of aristocratic life"[27] and even goes so far as to say of the *Makura no sōshi* (The Pillow Book; ca. eleventh century), "There is little to learn from its thought, passion, spirit, or religious or spiritual

---

24. Yokoyama Uein Shigeto, "Eibun shokan no mado kara mita Suzuki Daisetsu: 'The immediate present is a despot'," *SDZ* 35 *geppō* (August 2002): 4.

25. *SDZ* 36, 505.

26. *SDZ* 8, 34. In an earlier translation of Suzuki's article, "jōseiteki seikatsu" was rendered as "emotional life." However, it seems more appropriate to translate *jōseiteki* as "inertial passivity." See Daisetz Suzuki, *Japanese Spirituality*, trans. Norman Waddell (Tokyo: Japan Society for the Promotion of Science, 1972), 28.

27. Daisetz Suzuki, *Japanese Spirituality*, 37.

aspirations."[28] According to Daisetz, it was the Kamakura period (ca. 1185–1333) in which the Japanese really awoke to religious or spiritual life, and the culture of the Heian period was preparation for that.[29] Daisetz further claimed that the reason Shinran (1173–1262) was able to mature was that he left Kyoto when he was exiled: "[F]or although Buddhism did exist there [in Kyoto], it did not possess the experience of Japanese spirituality."[30] As far as Daisetz was concerned, the culture of Kyoto had been decadent since the Heian period, and it generated a harmful influence on Alan.

Daisetz, who raised Alan as his natural child with the hope that he would grow into a respectable adult, arranged for him to live in the dormitory at the Number Three Middle School, where he would no longer be under his supervision. Daisetz's feelings were just like those of any other parent who sends his child out into the world. His letters and diaries from April of that year are full of entries about Alan. For example, Daisetz wrote the following in a letter to Beatrice dated April 2, 1929.

> Alan is out since early this morning. He [says] thanks for being permitted to see moving pictures but not for his books[,] and anything in connection with school life is fool[ish]. He can never be a scholar.[31]

Since Daisetz and Beatrice wanted Alan to become a scholar, they wished that he would be more interested in books than in the cinema. In a letter to Beatrice dated the next day, April 3, Daisetz wrote the following:

> Now that part of my business over[,] the next thing I have to do with him will be going to the San-chu on the seventh (7th) and put him up at the dormitory. Thus his entering into the middle school costs me a great deal. I hope he deserves it. His text-books [sic] are tied up in a *furoshiki*[32] and not one glance is given there. . . . he is very much concerned with his outward appearance and the impression he makes on others—superficially. I wonder if he is going to amount to anything. If he does not show any inclination to be studious in [sic] two years from now, I am afraid all our hopes about him are departed.[33]

---

28. Daisetz Suzuki, *Japanese Spirituality*, 37.

29. Daisetz Suzuki, *Japanese Spirituality*, 46.

30. Daisetz Suzuki, *Japanese Spirituality*, 80.

31. *SDZ* 36, 506.

32. A *furoshiki* is a square wrapping cloth that can be used to pack up and transport a variety of items, including books.

33. *SDZ* 36, 507.

Despite his parents' concerns, Alan was unable to rid himself of the habit of lying about almost everything. A letter from Daisetz to Alan dated April 10 contains the following passage.[34]

Dear Alan, —I am at Shōden now and will be back in Kyoto before 14th, Sunday. Okono says she never received your letter which you said you sent to her. I am afraid you did not tell the truth. I doubt whether you wrote to Mr. Numaguchi. I hope you are writing to Mamma at Beppu [city], or you already did so. If you do not, she will be terribly disappointed. I want to see you this coming Sunday morning, as I have some important matter[s] to talk [about] with you. Hope you are doing well and trying to be a good student. /Yours, /Father[35]

Among the letters of Daisetz that have been made public, this is the oldest one written to Alan. Daisetz scolded his son while at the same time expressing his hopes for him. The meeting on Sunday morning that Daisetz had been planning did not materialize, as Daisetz had to stay in Kamakura longer than expected. Daisetz sent Alan another letter two days later in which he wrote that he had wanted to discuss a number of important things in addition to Alan's behavior in the dormitory.[36] On the one hand, we have Alan, who neglected his studies and ran around and played all the time, and who lied without feeling shameful. On the other hand, we have Daisetz, who, faced with such a son, believed he would straighten out one day and therefore continued to admonish him strongly yet compassionately. It was probably the same basic tenor of their relationship when Alan was a child. In a lecture given at the Myōchūji temple in Osaka on May 12, Daisetz spoke the following words:

Therefore, the desire on the part of Amida Nyorai of the Shin sect to save people cannot be helped, since it is the Original Vow of the Bodhisattva, who is obliged to save people, who will chase after a person to save them even if the person refuses to be saved and runs away. . . . The vow to save is the Original Vow of Amida; therefore, there is nothing that can be done about it. From a child's point of view, the child wants to be free, so he will run around trying to get away; but from the point of view of Amida Nyorai, this is not real freedom, and

34. Like Beatrice, Daisetz spoke to Alan in English, so the original letter is in English.
35. *SDZ* 36, 508–9.
36. *SDZ* 36, 510.

so Amida, overcome with pity for the child, will chase after him to the ends of the earth to save him.[37]

On the surface, it appears that Daisetz was discussing Jōdo Shinshū, but in reality, he was expressing his feelings for Alan. Through his confrontation with Alan, Daisetz was able to get closer to the Original Vow of Amida Nyorai.

Alan Goes Wild

Daisetz scolded Alan for his lying, but at the same time, Daisetz hid the fact that Alan was adopted. It was only much later that Daisetz revealed the secret of Alan's origins, but according to discussions I had with Daisetz's family members, Alan may already have heard a rumor that he was not Daisetz's biological son by the time he was in middle school. In other words, the father who told him not to lie was lying to him. It is quite possible that this contradiction may have warped Alan's spirit even further. Not only that, but at that time mixed-race people were rare in Japan, and it is easy to imagine that Alan's classmates teased him for being a "mongrel" (*ainoko*).[38]

Despite Daisetz's expectations, putting Alan in the middle school dormitory did not calm him down. Almost as soon as he started school, he began causing all sorts of trouble. In letters written to Beatrice around this time, Daisetz remarked that perhaps it would be better to put Alan to work at a Zen temple, or perhaps they should send him to Mt. Koya [*sic*] after all.[39] Daisetz seems to have believed that a stricter dormitory life would benefit Alan.[40]

Sports (including the competitive rugby club) were very popular at the Kyoto Municipal Number Three Middle School, and the school tradition was characterized by earnestness and strong-mindedness. There was a room

---

37. *SDZ* 27, 128–29.

38. Mixed marriages were uncommon in traditional Japan, with the majority of half-Japanese children being the offspring of Japanese prostitutes in the late nineteenth century (see Kamoto, *Kokusai kekkon no tanjō*, 72). It is highly possible that as a Western-looking boy, Alan was regarded as the result of an immoral relationship. After World War II, a number of half-Japanese children were born between Japanese females engaged in prostitution or other service jobs and soldiers of the Occupation forces. Under the circumstances, Alan may have suffered from being under discriminatory gaze throughout his life. For the widespread discrimination against and ambivalence toward half-Japanese, see Shimoji Rōrensu Yoshitaka, *"Konketsu" to "Nihonjin": Hāfu, daburu, mikkusu no shakaishi* (Tokyo: Seidosha, 2018).

39. *SDZ* 36, 514.

40. *SDZ* 36, 518–25.

for supervising the students in one corner of the dormitory, and a commissioned officer from the army was posted to the school to keep a sharp eye on them. Students who were late were disciplined in this room, and those who did not get a permission slip could not attend class. Even so, the student body was made up entirely of adolescent boys, so the school also had a soft-hearted side commensurate with this. According to the recollection of a student of Alan's generation who graduated from the school, the schoolboys often dropped by the Nikkatsu film studio that was nearby. Their playground was shared with young actresses from this studio, and they would engage the girls in games of "hide-and-go-seek and tag" (using his words). The streetcar that the students took to school was a place for secret trysts with the students at the girls' school that was located along the train's route. Since it was a time when rules governing relations between the sexes were strict, there were cases where suspensions and expulsions resulted from romances being discovered.[41] This "soft" side of the Number Three Middle School made Alan happy, but for Daisetz, it must have been a bitter pill to swallow.

At this juncture, Daisetz's disciple Iwakura Masaji entered into Alan's life. In response to a request from Daisetz, Iwakura lent his aid to the attempt to reform Alan. According to the "Daisetz Diaries," on June 1 of the year when Alan entered middle school, Iwakura went in lieu of Daisetz to talk with the director of the dormitory about Alan. Later, in the entry for February 24, 1930, Daisetz stated that he spoken with Iwakura about Alan.

From this point on, Iwakura started taking Alan to his hometown of Inami-machi (present-day Nanto city) in Toyama prefecture. In addition to hoping that Alan would grow up to be a good citizen, Daisetz had begun to harbor the feeling that he wanted to rid himself of the curse of a juvenile delinquent who was not even his biological son. In a letter to Yamamoto Ryōkichi, Daisetz wrote: "Last year we managed to place our child in the Number Three Middle School; however, not only is he failing, but he also seems to be a cinema addict, and it is a great embarrassment. We would like to send him to a boarding school someplace far away—do you know of a good place? It is a damned nuisance."[42] Also, in a letter to Suzuki Hatsuko, Daisetz wrote: "We have sent Masaru to Toyama during his vacation. There would be nothing but harm and no good at all for him to be in Kyoto."[43]

---

41. Ōhashi Tadanari, "San-chū kōshinkyoku," in Hirao Kiyoshi, ed., *Kyō san-chū Yamashiro-kō sōritsu 60 shūnen kinengō* (Kyoto: Sōryō Dōsōkai, 1971), 176–80.

42. *SDZ* 36, 536.

43. *SDZ* 36, 537.

Let us try to decipher Alan's state of mind at this time from the "Daisetz Diaries" and the letters Daisetz wrote to Beatrice. In the summer of Alan's second year of middle school, Daisetz hired a student from Kyoto Imperial University to be Alan's tutor. Alan had been planning to enjoy himself over the summer vacation with Suzuki Ō (Hayashida Kumino's older brother), who had become his friend, and therefore he was upset at Daisetz's scheme. One evening, Daisetz scolded Alan severely for his attitude. The next morning, Alan apologized and said he would study hard over the summer vacation.[44] His grades, however, continued to fall.

In May 1931, in Alan's third year of middle school, Okono discovered that Alan had not been to class for three days at most since April. At that point, Daisetz started thinking seriously about transferring Alan to the Mt. Kōya Middle School. When Daisetz scolded Alan for his misbehavior, Alan would apologize and promise to be good, but he would immediately revert to his former behavior. In the "Daisetz Diaries" entry for June 14, 1931, we find the following describing Alan's conduct.

At 12.30 last night Alan found not in his bed, house searched but no trace, had his door locked. In the morning when the door was unlocked he was found in the room. Hiding himself all the time in the closet[,] where we failed to look into. A talk with him in the forenoon.[45]

There is no way to see hiding in the closet as anything but a childish deception. I am sure that Alan snuck out of the house at night and went off to amuse himself somewhere. That summer, Daisetz decided to put Alan in Iwakura's care. Iwakura wrote about this in his biography of Daisetz. The passage is a bit long, but it is a crucial testimony for understanding Alan's adolescence.

One year in the summer, the sensei spoke with me regarding Alan.

"Could I ask you to please take Alan back to your hometown over the summer? I want you to train him by having him help the farmers. Work him hard. I want him to know how important labor is." Sensei was seriousness itself. "If he continues like this, that boy will be a complete washout in life. When I think he's studying in the evenings, before I know it, he has hung a rope from the second-story window and is off gallivanting around somewhere. Like a stuntman

---

44. *SDZ* 36, 546.
45. *MBKN* 20, 46.

in American westerns. I can deal with it, but his mother is worried about him and it's hard on her."

Being young, I listened to this with conflicting feelings. I believe that Alan was in his fourth or fifth year of elementary school at the time. Despite his youth, the handsome and precocious boy could already handle himself on a motorcycle and a horse and loved doing stunts like throwing a lasso the way cowboys did, and he was good at it. This perceptive and precocious boy apparently could not deal with school learning, with its formality and hypocrisy. I could not simply lay all the blame on him.

The sensei, however, who had seriously and earnestly thought about life from a young age and then immersed himself in Zen training, probably found it impossible to tolerate being shown at close range, morning to evening, the New Wave that was current at the time. In fact, once one has taken it upon himself to be responsible for the education of another person, there may come a time when duty requires that one throw one's whole life down the drain along with that of the other person. For the sensei, whose entire life was devoted to the study of Buddhism and who lived for the avocation of spreading Buddhism throughout the world, this was impossible.

I acceded to the sensei's request. I put Alan under a lenient "house arrest" in the poor house where I had been born, and tried to instill a sense of discipline in him by taking him out to the fields under the blazing sun to weed and cut grass. Alan resisted, saying that he would escape by borrowing a horse from a horse-riding club in a nearby town and ride it to Kamakura. He claimed that he would ride from my hometown, in the southwest corner of Toyama prefecture, all the way to Kamakura. Believing in his seriousness, and because I loved him, I pleaded with him tearfully and was able to dissuade him.[46]

Iwakura wrote that Alan was "in his fourth or fifth year of elementary school, I think" when he spent a summer in Toyama. Comparing this to the "Daisetz Diaries," however, we find that it was in 1931 when Alan was in the third year of middle school. In any case, this reminiscence helps us understand Alan's wayward behavior. Iwakura, however, did not place all of the blame on Alan. It was because Iwakura sympathized with Alan, who had a special parent named Daisetz Suzuki, that he decided to undertake the difficult task of overseeing Alan's education.

---

46. Iwakura, "Ōtani Daigaku jidai no Suzuki Daisetsu," 90–91.

Womanizing Rears Its Head

Alan was an active child. As he entered puberty and became aware of his sexuality, he became more "active" than the average boy at his age in that aspect as well. As I noted earlier, it is unclear how old Alan actually was. There is a strong possibility that Alan was already more than one year old by the time of his birth date as recorded in the Suzuki family register. Considered together with his inborn temperament, if he was older than the age indicated by his academic year, then Alan's "precociousness" makes sense. In a letter to Beatrice dated April 1, 1931, Daisetz wrote: "Alan gets some letters from girls or a girl. Two letters are here, evidently from one. I wonder what kind of girl she is. He is premature in these respects. Isn't he?"[47] Here, looming large as life is the image of the father worried about what appear to be love letters addressed to his son.

So far as one can tell from the "Daisetz Diaries," the first entry regarding what could be called an "incident" of this kind is dated June 28, 1931. By that day, Alan had been missing for three days. Daisetz sought the help of Okono and Iwakura and even went to the police. Alan returned to school six days after his disappearance, but he left early and was seen in the evening accompanied by a girl. Since the entry in the diary is fragmentary, we do not know the details of this "incident." What we do know is that a boy who was fourteen years old at the time according to his family register was missing from his school dormitory for six days, and it seemed that a female was involved in his "escape." Daisetz discussed Alan's future with him, and the conclusion to which he came was that Alan should spend the summer with Iwakura in the Toyama countryside. Six days after the night Alan came back from his escapade accompanied by a woman, Daisetz packed him off to Toyama. Hayashida Kumino remembered Alan's womanizing in the following passage, tinged with bitterness.

> After that, Alan came to our house many times after he started middle school, and at that time he was busy playing around with my older brothers, Rei and Ō. The three of them would go out to Asakusa, which was where the action was at that time. . . . It seems that Alan had a passion and a knack for amusement that far exceeded my two brothers, who were older than him.

However, it is clear that Daisetz and Beatrice did not want a child

---

47. *SDZ* 36, 560–61.

who enjoyed playing around. Not only that, one could be amused and wave it off if the kind of play had been childish games, but once Alan reached puberty and was in his teens, I have heard that he got into the habit of womanizing, to use an unpleasant word. Alan was what one would call today a "half" [mixed race]; he was tall and had the kind of face that people notice, and I heard that he was popular with worldly and sophisticated women who were well versed in relations between men and women.

In any case, what I heard was that he would slip out of the second story of his house in Kyoto at night, and climb up the drainpipe to his room in the morning. He did this repeatedly.[48]

At this time, Daisetz and Beatrice wanted Alan and Kumino to get married in the future. This, of course, was conditional on Alan becoming a responsible adult. Every time Alan had a problem with a woman, he used the fact that he had a fiancée named Kumino as an excuse to break up with her. As far as Kumino was concerned, aside from whether she liked or disliked Alan, the more fundamental issue was that she just was not interested in him, considering him to be "a person who lived in a world different from mine."[49]

Daisetz's Views on Sexual Desire

Let us digress for a moment and take a look at Daisetz's views on sexuality and sexual desire. In 1900, when he was living in the United States, Daisetz wrote a paper entitled "Seiyoku ron" (Views on Sexual Desire).[50] Even though this was before he established a relationship with Beatrice, it gives us a good picture of Daisetz's chasteness, so I would like to introduce it here.

First, Daisetz wrote that his purpose in writing "Views on Sexual Desire" was to address the breakdown in morality in Japan and to defend the practice of a person remaining celibate and unmarried for individual spiritual cultivation. Sexual desire contributes to the continuation of the species by weakening a person's vitality. In the life of an individual, the exercise of sexual desire is nothing other than a physical sacrifice for the sake of the

---

48. Hayashida, *Ōji Suzuki Daisetsu kara no tegami*, 59.

49. Hayashida, *Ōji Suzuki Daisetsu kara no tegami*, 60.

50. *SDZ* 30, 239–52. Originally published in *Nihonjin* 126, 127, 129 (November 5, 20 and December 20, 1900).

species as a whole. Fecundity and intelligence are in inverse proportion to one another. It is a fact that people possessed of wisdom are not blessed with children. If one gets carried away with sexual desire in one's youth, physical growth is impeded and psychological problems result. From the view of ethical religion as well, the indiscriminate indulgence of one's sexual appetite is a crime against nature and the character of the individual. Even between married couples, indulging in sexual pleasure is a kind of fornication. If a child learns that he or she was born as a result of the physical desires of his or her parents, that child will develop superficial ideas about sex. If that happens and the child follows his or her sexual desires unchecked, the parents will not be able to guide the child properly. Prostitution must be stamped out by all means. People with physical defects should not marry. Birth control is a sin. What is preferable is that a person keeps his or her heart pure and indulge in actions that are in tune with the universe and the meaning of human existence.

The above is an outline of Daisetz's "Views on Sexual Desire." In short, sexual desire is sinful and sex should only be engaged in by married men and women for the purpose of procreation. It appears that Daisetz's views on the sexual love between men and women did not fundamentally change even after he met Beatrice. With a parent like that, any child, let alone Alan, would have felt suffocated. It is possible that because of the continuous repression he experienced at home, Alan's "natural qualities" began to blossom in a direction diametrically opposed to what Daisetz was hoping for.

"Confinement" on Mt. Kōya

In the summer of 1931, the year that Daisetz put Alan in the care of Iwakura Masaji, he conferred by letter with Beatrice, who was staying at Mt. Kōya, about how to educate their son. In a letter dated August 12, Daisetz wrote: "When I see Alan when going up to Tokyo[,] I will have a talk with him and see if it is really better for him to go to Koya [sic] this year. . . . However[,] it may be better for him to go out into the practical world right away. Let him do whatever things he likes, and find out by himself what is best for him to do in the world. The only thing that will cure him is a hard life."[51]

The conclusion to which the Suzukis came was to immediately remove

51. SDZ 36, 570.

Alan from Kyoto with its many temptations and transfer him to the Mt. Kōya Middle School. Beatrice stayed at Mt. Kōya on occasion to research esoteric Shingon Buddhism. Part of the reason behind their decision was probably the familiarity both of them had with the atmosphere of such sacred places. Hayashida Kumino wrote that the reason for Alan's transfer was because he "had been expelled from the Kyoto Municipal Middle School,"[52] but Daisetz's letters and diary indicate that it was a voluntary transfer rather than a forcible expulsion. So after having completed half of the five years of middle school, Alan withdrew from the Kyoto Municipal Middle School.

In September 1931, Alan transferred to the Mt. Kōya Middle School (present-day Mt. Kōya High School) and went to live in the school dormitory. The policy of banning women from Mt. Kōya had ended in 1904, but there had been no change in the fact that Mt. Kōya was a sacred space removed from the mundane world. Moreover, even inside that space, the school was in a valley surrounded by mountains almost entirely bereft of human activity. It was a huge change from Kyoto, where one could easily walk to the busy downtown district. Daisetz and Beatrice thought that it would be the ideal environment for Alan. In addition to the fact that it was a religious school, the educational program was very strict, complying with the spirit of the 1930s, when military training was emphasized. The following is a typical day's schedule.

Wake Up	5:30 (6:00 in the four months of December, January, February, and March).
Cleaning	Room cleaning and personal toilet finished by 6:00.
Service	Students from all dormitories gather at the Kōdō Lecture Hall and recite the Principle of Wisdom sutra (*Rishu-kyō*).
	[snip]
After Classes	Undergo training in Patriotic Youth Group
Bathing	Baths open on alternate days; start bathing by 6:00.
Dusk Service	4:30 to 5:00, reading and studying sutras.
Dinner	5:00 (in groups).
Inspection	Line up in the hall for roll call. Receive occasional instructions from the dormitory supervisor (6:00).

---

52. Hayashida, *Ooji Suzuki Daisetsu kara no tegami*, 59.

Self-Study   Study in your own room from 6:00 to 8:50. Absolutely
no talking with students in other rooms. Rounds
by the dormitory supervisor to exercise strict supervision.

Sleep   Lights out and in bed at 9:00.[53]

At this time, an active duty officer from the army was posted to the
school, and he had a powerful voice in all aspects of education. Military
training was conducted in the schoolyard, and the school ordered the students to spend three days in the army so they would gain military experience.[54] It is impossible to imagine that the lackadaisical Alan could have
been comfortable with this.

Repeated Offenses

Alan was unable to settle down even in the atmosphere of the religious
solemnity of Mt. Kōya. Although Daisetz had sent his son far away, he had
not completely severed his relationship with him. When the school was on
holiday, Alan would go back home to Kyoto or the Shōden-an in Kita-
Kamakura, and sometimes went to Tokyo to spend time with Suzuki Ō
and his friends. Daisetz's purpose in doing so is unclear, but in the winter
of 1931 he sent Alan to Taiwan. The entry in the "Daisetz Diaries" for April
4 recorded that Daisetz and Alan took a two-hour walk in the mountains.
From these entries, we can divine that as a father, Daisetz continued to
involve himself in Alan's education and that he felt obliged to do so.

In retrospect, was Daisetz's decision to place Alan in a boarding school
the correct one? In an article he wrote about five years later, Daisetz compared Japanese boarding schools to those in Britain and the United States.

All of the schools we have in Japan were built after the Meiji Restoration; they did not develop naturally. The schools are blessed with the
full complement of rules and regulations, which is a bit dubious in
itself, but, in any case, there is no spirit and the schools lack humanity.
No matter which school one goes to, one cannot see anything that has

---

53. Harada Ryōsuke and Saeki Ryūjō, eds., *Gakuen kaiko roku* (Kōya: Kōyasan Kōtōgakkō,
1956), 43–44.

54. Harada and Saeki, *Gakuen kaiko roku*, 57.

the development of character as its central concern. One is forced to conclude that there will be nothing but a sorry result no matter how many years a student attends such a school. In particular, middle school and high school dormitories are the sorriest of the lot. Not only is it doubtful whether such places could produce a scholar, but it is also my opinion that there is not the slightest possibility whatsoever that such places could produce great men.[55]

In sum, Daisetz was not satisfied with the education at boarding schools. He probably had no respect for an "education" that could not even properly guide a single student, his son Alan. It is also possible that this view of Daisetz's was influenced by his experience as a dormitory supervisor at Gakushuin University in Tokyo.

On July 24 of the same year, in a letter to Beatrice, who was at Mt. Kōya at the time, Daisetz wrote of his intention to send Alan and Suzuki Ō for Zen training at Kojirin, a sub-temple of Engakuji in Kamakura.

> He has to get up early, do sweeping, cleaning, and so on—according to the regulations they have there. It is a kind of layman's Zendo. He has to practice Zazen, though he may not go to Sanzen as the rest do. The young man who is directer [director] there is quite an earnest man, and stays there all the time. I will ask him to look after Alan.[56]

The editor of *The Complete Works of D. T. Suzuki, Expanded New Edition* noted that the paragraph that immediately follows this section was deleted. This letter itself did not appear in the old edition of the *Works*. From the flow of the text, one can infer that it is possible that Daisetz wrote something about Alan that could not be made public. This kind of concealment of facts distorts the image of Daisetz. It may very well be that one of the aims of this sort of "editing" is to manipulate the image of Daisetz in a specific direction.

In the summer of 1932, Alan was enjoying himself in Tokyo with Suzuki Ō and his friends as usual. He became ill toward the end of the vacation and recuperated at home until October. In the entry for September 16 in the "Daisetz Diaries," Daisetz wrote that a doctor in a sanatorium examined Alan. Also, in a letter to Suzuki Hatsuko dated October 18, while expressing

55. *SDZ* 19, 42. Originally published in Suzuki, "Kyōiku to rekishiteki keizokusei," *Shindō* 12: 4 (1937): 2–6.
56. *SDZ* 36, 582.

sympathy for her eldest son Rei, who was ill, Daisetz touched upon Alan: "[the illness] is closely connected to air and sunlight,"[57] suggesting the possibility that Alan had some sort of pulmonary disease.

According to the November 9 entry in the "Daisetz Diaries" from the same year, Alan had been suspended from the Mt. Kōya Middle School. The reason is not apparent. The family was busy with trying to deal with the situation; Okono went to Mt. Kōya immediately, and Daisetz wrote a letter to the school. By a strange coincidence, Alan's friend Suzuki Ō was expelled from school around the same time, probably for bad conduct. A letter that Daisetz wrote to Ō at that time has been preserved. Daisetz supported Hatsuko's children (Rei, Ō, Kumino, and Ichio) financially as though they were his own. This letter conveys the style in which Daisetz would remonstrate with problematic children, so I am including some excerpts from it.

A man's spirit lies in his ability to turn misfortune into good. The students of today must not follow the path of indecisiveness, and instead with great vigor and unyielding resoluteness go out into the world wherever life takes them. One must not forget the spirit one has today, since, as it is said, vows made in stormy times are forgotten in times of calm, and when all is said and done, a man must treasure spirit above all and have fortitude. What happens to you today may be an excellent impetus. You should rouse yourself to do your best.[58]

The entry in the "Daisetz Diaries" of December 27 reads, "Talked to Alan about his future course of study,"[59] and the entry for March 26 of the following year stated, "After supper serious talk with Alan."[60] Did Daisetz tell Alan to "rouse yourself to do your best"? If so, Alan did not take this advice to heart either.

In a letter from Daisetz to Beatrice dated April 10, 1933, Alan's true voice makes an appearance in a quote. After spending the spring vacation in Kamakura, on the morning of the day Alan returned to Kyoto with Daisetz, the father once again lectured the son on his attitude at school. In response, Alan said: "When the parents are so worried over me, do you think I am going to behave so bad as to be expected?"[61] Of course, Daisetz did not

57. SDZ 36, 587.
58. SDZ 36, 589.
59. MBKN 20, 99.
60. MBKN 20, 111.
61. SDZ 36, 596.

believe him. Sure enough, on the way back to Kyoto, Daisetz witnessed two schoolgirls coming to meet Alan when the train arrived at Shizuoka Station, even though the train only stopped at the station for a minute.[62]

According to the "Daisetz Diaries," in the autumn of that year, Alan ultimately caused a violent incident at school. Daisetz rushed to the school, met with the principal, and probably wrote a petition asking for a lenient punishment. He met with the official in charge at the court and paid damages to the victim.[63] Thanks to Daisetz, Alan was not expelled, and he managed to graduate from Mt. Kōya Middle School in March 1934. Therefore it is clear that while Daisetz adopted a strict attitude with Alan, he could not completely abandon his son. It is difficult to say whether this kind of assistance was beneficial to Alan or not.

62. *SDZ* 36, 596.
63. *MBKN* 20, 134–37.

THREE

Glimpses of Brilliance

Japan-America Students Conference

After graduating from Mt. Kōya Middle School, Alan decided to attend Doshisha University, which was fairly close to the Suzuki home in Kyoto. His choice of Doshisha was probably encouraged by Daisetz, and he decided to major in English literature. Alan lived in the dormitory just as he had in middle school, but it appears that he frequently visited the Suzuki residence. Daisetz did not refer to Alan in his diaries and letters from this period as often as he did when Alan was in middle school, but as previously mentioned, the diaries from 1934 to 1935 are missing, so we cannot be sure.

Alan had one remarkable achievement in college that was the pride of the Suzuki family—his selection as a member of the Japan-America Students Conference (JASC) delegation two years in a row. The JASC was a conference in which students from Japan and the United States could meet and mingle, the objective being to improve the attitude of the United States toward Japan and to improve the relationship between the two countries. This conference has an illustrious history: the first was held in 1934, and, except for the break occasioned by World War II, it has continued to the present day. Many of the students who were selected for the delegation went on to assume key positions in political and business establishments as well as the academic world in both Japan and the United States. For the participants, the conference could be the first step on a course that would take them to the upper echelons of the elite. Among the older boys and girls who participated in the conference at the same time as Alan are Miyazawa Kiichi (1919–2007), former prime minister of Japan, and Yamamuro Yūshin (1917–2016), vice president of Mitsubishi Bank. Other prominent figures who are of the same generation as Alan include Tomabechi Toshihiro (1916–), who served as the vice president of Mitsubishi Corporation, and Kobori Sōhaku (Nanrei; 1918–1992), who was once the chief priest of Ryōkō-in, a sub-temple of Daitokuji in Kyoto. Later JASC alumni include people like Henry Kissinger (1923–), former US secretary of state; Glen S. Fukushima (1949–), former director for the Japanese Affairs Section of the Office of the United States Trade Representative; Inoguchi Kuniko (1952–), a political scientist and member of the House of Councillors of the Diet; and the neuroscientist Mogi Ken'ichirō (1962–).

The JASC began as an independent student conference. The students themselves would do the planning, recruit sponsors, and then hold the conference. On the Japanese side, the conference was supported by an organization called the Association of Japanese English Students. The conference was held every year, alternating between Japan and the United States, and had between fifty and two hundred attendees from each country. The conference itself lasted for one to two weeks, but if we include the round trip travel by ship, the students from the guest country would be eating and sleeping together for several weeks. Needless to say, this led to a lot of friendships and romances.

The first conference, in 1934, took place at Aoyama Gakuin University in Tokyo. One of the Japanese representatives at that conference was Matsumoto Tōru (1913–1979), who later served as an English instructor of NHK radio for twenty-two years and had a significant influence on English-language education in Japan. The second was held at Reed College in Portland, Oregon, and the third conference (the first one that Alan attended) was held in August 1936 at Waseda University in Tokyo.

How did Alan, a notorious wastrel who did not study much prior to entering Doshisha University, and who was always causing trouble, get selected to be a member of such a distinguished conference, filled with talented students? It is true that Alan, having been raised by a pair of scholars, was a literary-minded young man equipped with more than the usual amount of sophistication and culture. He was also completely bilingual in Japanese and English. A Japanese female college student who participated in the second conference in Portland reported that "the American female students spoke very quickly and used a lot of slang."[1] Matsumoto Tōru, who attended the same conference, reminisced as follows:

---

1. Sekiguchi Waichi, ed., *Kaisen zen'ya no disukasshon: Nichibei gakusei kōryū 50 nen no kiroku* (Tokyo: Nichibei Gakusei Kaigi 50 Shūnen Kinenjigyō Jikkō Iinkai, 1984), 34.

Calling it a debate is rather a stretch; rather than having a debate between the Japanese and the Americans, what happened was that the Japanese watched with mystified expressions on their faces as the Americans debated among themselves. Then, when the Americans asked the Japanese some important question, no one would answer right away; the Japanese were reduced to conferring among themselves and then selecting someone to answer for them.[2]

Even for a talented person, this was probably the English level of the participating Japanese students at that time. In a situation where it was necessary to understand and immediately respond to a question, Alan's language ability must certainly have been put to good use, and there is no doubt that he was a great asset to both the Japanese and the American students. In addition, the fact that Alan, with his Western features, was in the Japanese delegation must have been a walking advertisement for Japan's internationalism: just as there are Americans who are ethnically Japanese, there can be Japanese who are ethnically Anglo-Saxon.

Alan Discusses Zen

For the third JASC meeting in 1936, forty-three students were chosen as delegates for the US contingent, and more than four times that number (185) were selected for the Japanese delegation. The participants separated into four groups and held roundtable discussions on economics, culture, religion, and politics. Alan was in the religion group. It is interesting to note that Kubo Machiko, the elder sister of Kubo Nobu (Alan's first wife) was a participant in the economics discussion group.

The program of the religion group in which Alan participated shows there was a broad discussion. First, each member gave his or her opinion on religion and life, after which the relationship of the various religions (Buddhism, Shinto, and Christianity) to philosophy, science, and art was examined. Then they compared the respective religions and examined their relationships to economics, politics, culture, and education. Finally, the discussion moved on to the themes of nationalism, social work, race relations, interreligious cooperation, and Christianity in Japan and the United States.

The group met over a period of five days. There is no detailed record of

---

2. Sekiguchi, *Kaisen zen'ya no disukasshon*, 34.

the discussions, but the report published after the conference contains summaries of the presentations of the participants. Included is a summary of the presentation by Masaru Suzuki of Doshisha University. Before going further, I should mention that there are practically no records of the person known as Alan. In particular, existing writings of any length by Alan himself can be counted on the fingers of one hand. Thus this summary of a presentation by Alan in his youth is a very important record.

The theme of Alan's presentation was, of all things, "Zen Buddhism and Its Effects on the Culture of Japan." This title bears a striking resemblance to one of Daisetz's representative works, *Zen Buddhism and Its Influence on Japanese Culture*, published in 1938.[3] Although Alan's presentation was given approximately two years before the publication of Daisetz's book, the choice of this title was probably influenced by Daisetz's writings. It is inconceivable that Alan came up with this theme and the contents all on his own. It is most likely that Alan studied manuscripts of Daisetz's lectures and the draft of his book when preparing for his presentation.[4] In fact, Alan's presentation did not stray much from Daisetz's theory of Japanese culture, and one could easily dismiss Alan as a purveyor of Daisetz's goods at second hand. Before doing so, however, I would like to take a look at what the son tried to learn from his father.

During the eight hundred years history from the time Zen Buddhism was introduced into Japan, it has helped to mould and develop the life and mind of the Japanese people. In fact, every page of the cultural history of the nation records something contributed by Zen towards the intellectual, the aesthetic, and the spiritual life of the

---

3. Daisetsu Suzuki, *Zen Buddhism and Its Influence on Japanese Culture* (Kyoto: Eastern Buddhist Society, 1938).

4. In October 1935, Daisetz gave a lecture at the Kokusai Bunka Shinkōkai in Tokyo titled "Buddhist Philosophy and Its Effects on the Life and Thought of the Japanese People." He published it in 1936, which became the basis for his later book *Zen Buddhism and Its Influence on Japanese Culture*. I am grateful to the anonymous reviewer who kindly provided this information. After examining both texts, I found that Alan's account includes sentences that are nearly identical to his father's words. For example: "The best way to know what effect Zen philosophy and Buddhist thought had on Japanese cultural life, is to wipe out all the Buddhist temples together with their treasures, libraries, gardens, anecdotes, tales, and romances of various sorts, and see what we have left in the history of Japan. First of all, there would be no painting, no sculpture, no architecture, or even music and drama. Following this, all the minor branches of art would also disappear—landscape gardening, tea ceremony, flower-arrangements, and even the art of fencing."

people. So hence, I dare say, that without a vague understanding of the spirit of Zen, it is utterly impossible to understand the psychology and the culture of the Japanese people. This brings me however to a place where the explanation of "what is Zen?" is required, but such an attempt is indeed a vain task for a student like my self [sic]. Yet if the teaching and explanation of Christianity could be reduced to "utter faith in God," the teaching and philosophy of Zen may be reduced to the following words. "Enlightenment and the realization of truth through intuition."[5]

Zen is present in every nook and cranny of Japanese life, and without understanding that, it is impossible to understand Japanese culture—this is what Daisetz was trying to say in his *Zen Buddhism and Its Influence on Japanese Culture*. However, Alan modestly recognizes that as a mere student he is incapable of explaining Zen. Was this because Alan felt defeated by the fact that his father's learning was so far above his ability to understand it, or was this a defensive move on Alan's part, saying in effect, "I don't fully understand what Zen is, so don't ask me about it"? Alan defined Zen as "Enlightenment and the realization of truth through intuition." I searched for an identical expression in Daisetz's writings before 1936, but my narrow search turned up nothing. However, there is no doubt that this definition is embodied within the framework of the Zen that Daisetz expounded.

I would like to introduce some bits and pieces of what Alan included in his presentation. He said that the intuitive philosophy of Zen Buddhism could be seen a great deal in haiku poetry and ink painting, and that painting, sculpture, architecture, music, drama, landscape gardening, the tea ceremony, flower arrangements, and even the art of swordplay have been deeply influenced by Zen. Daisetz did not talk much about music and drama, but overall, the gist of Alan's presentation fits neatly into Daisetz's framework. In particular, in *Zen Buddhism and Its Influence on Japanese Culture*, the tea ceremony and swordsmanship are strongly emphasized.

Zen philosophy and Japanese Buddhism at large have left their permanent impressions in the arts, customs, culture, and ways of think-

---

5. Masaru Suzuki, "Zen Buddhism and Its Effects on the Culture of Japan," in Nozue Kenzō, ed., *The Third America-Japan Student-Conference 1936* (Tokyo: Nichibei Eigo Gakusei Kyōkai, 1937), 74.

ing, and ways of looking at life and the world, and these marks will be the perennial fountain of inspiration to the Japanese now and hereafter.

So those who really wish to understand the people and know their culture, should first of all try to find what lies hidden in the heart of Buddhism, and the spirit of Zen, and then like the faint rays of a rising sun on a misty morning, gradually will Japan and its people come closer to your hearts.[6]

At the end of his presentation, the fact that Alan took a step back and referred to the Japanese as "the people" and Japanese culture as "their culture" is cause for some concern. This can be read as indicating that Alan does not see himself as being completely on the Japanese side. If this is so, then it becomes a useful clue in considering whether Alan identified himself as being Japanese or Western. In English, however, there are times when one refers to oneself impartially in the third person. In the final sentence where he writes, "its people come closer to your hearts," Alan was putting himself on the Japanese side. From this passage, therefore, one cannot make a definitive judgment about Alan's position. However, the moment when he made this presentation in front of the elite of Japan and the United States was the point in Alan's life when he came the closest to Daisetz's philosophy.[7]

A Novelist's Misunderstanding

Out of all of the prewar JASC meetings, the sixth meeting, held in Los Angeles (1939), is the most well known. This is because the politician and former prime minister Miyazawa Kiichi (then a student at Tokyo Imperial University) participated, and the novelist Shiroyama Saburō (1927–2007) wrote a nonfiction novel about it titled *Yūjō chikara ari* (Friendship Is Pow-

---

6. Masaru Suzuki, "Zen Buddhism and Its Effects," 75.

7. During this conference Alan became acquainted with an American student of politics Richard Gard (1914–2007), who later became a Buddhist scholar. Alan and Gard kept up their friendship even after the conference, and Daisetz recorded in his diary that the three men got together during Gard's stay in Japan from 1939 to 1940. Daisetz later participated in Gard's dissertation defense in 1950. I would like to thank Dr. Laura Harrington for bringing this to my attention.

erful; 1988).[8] In *Friendship Is Powerful*, a person named Sassa Naruhide, who bears a striking resemblance to Alan, appears. In the following excerpt, Shiroyama related how the Japanese delegation crossed the Pacific and arrived in San Francisco, at which point the following accident occurred as they went out sightseeing.

> During the sightseeing tour of San Francisco, an unfortunate incident occurred.
>
> Sassa Naruhide from Keio University, walking unsteadily due to the influence of an anti-seasickness drug, was struck by a car and thrown to the pavement.
>
> Sassa's father was a scholar who taught Zen at Otani University and Columbia University. His mother was a British woman.
>
> Sassa looked like his mother, and this resulted in his often being mistaken for a member of the American delegation.
>
> Among the members of the student delegation, of course, Sassa's English ability was head and shoulders above everyone else's.[9]

Daisetz did not teach at Columbia University until much later, but no other scholar fits Shiroyama's description. Not only that, Sassa's mother was British, and his English was excellent. As mentioned previously, Alan's mother Beatrice was descended from the Scottish aristocracy. Was Sassa supposed to be Alan? According to *Gakusei nichibei kaidan* (Japan-America Students Conference; 1939), the record of the sixth JASC, a student from Keio University named Sassa Naruhide was actually a participant.[10] The report records the events that took place while the delegation was in the United States and contains the impressions of the students, but there is no mention of any accident involving Sassa. The most obvious discrepancy is that Alan participated in the fourth JASC conference in 1937, not the sixth one in 1939 that Miyazawa and Sassa attended. Moreover, the subsequent life of the Sassa Naruhide that Shiroyama Saburō created was decisively different from that of Alan. Shiroyama continued as follows:

---

8. Shiroyama Saburō, *Yūjō chikara ari* (Tokyo: Kōdansha Bunko, 1993). Originally published in 1988.

9. Shiroyama, *Yūjō chikara ari*, 26.

10. Takayanagi Kenzō, ed., *Gakusei nichibei kaidan* (Tokyo: Nihon Hyōronsha, 1939), 290.

However, Sassa was born under an unlucky star.

The Pacific War began soon after, and Sassa had a difficult time as a person of mixed race during those years. But those days didn't last long, for Sassa died during the war.[11]

Of course, Alan was not killed in the war. That being so, why did Shiroyama conflate Masaru Suzuki and Sassa Naruhide? Alternatively, did Shiroyama deliberately model the persona of Sassa Naruhide on Masaru Suzuki? There is no reason that would have required Shiroyama to fictionalize this point. In my own investigations I was unable to find any information about Sassa Naruhide. In the end, it may well have been a misunderstanding on the part of Shiroyama Saburō, who confused Masaru and Sassa Naruhide. Since it was intended as a novel, the book did not have to follow the truth completely.

However, it was not only Shiroyama who was wrong about when Alan went to the United States. Even Hayashida Kumino, who knew Alan personally, made the same mistake. Remembering Alan, who had been so uninhibited as a child, she wrote as follows:

> After that, Alan traveled to the United States in 1939 for the Japan-America Students Conference with the delegation that included Miyazawa Kiichi, who later became prime minister. Even if his behavior was somewhat questionable, there could be no doubt that he was a gifted individual, even if his talents were different from those of Daisetz and Beatrice.[12]

Why Kumino made such a mistake is a mystery. Leaving inquiry into the reason aside, I would like to clarify what happened at the JASC in 1937 (the one that Alan attended) using information in the conference report.[13]

---

11. Shiroyama, *Yūjō chikara ari*, 26.

12. Hayashida, *Ōoji Suzuki Daisetsu kara no tegami*, 64–65.

13. Miyamura Takamichi, ed., *Ruporutāju: The Fourth America-Japan Student Conference 1937* (Tokyo: Miyamura Takamichi, 1938); Executive Committee of the Fourth America-Japan Student Conference, ed., *Report of the Fourth America-Japan Student Conference August, 1937* (n.p.: Executive Committee of the Fourth America-Japan Student Conference, 1938).

Alan's Second Japan-America Students Conference

On July 15, 1937, the cargo and passenger ship *Asama-maru*, carrying forty-eight Japanese students (thirty-five men and thirteen women) accompanied by two supervising teachers, set sail from the Port of Yokohama. Multicolored streamers fluttered in the breeze and the sound of gongs and steam whistles announced the ship's departure. Accompanied by the strains of the Scottish folk song "Auld Lang Syne"[14] and the encouragement of family members who came to see them off, the spirits of the students were bolstered for the task ahead.

The *Asama-maru* was a luxury liner that regularly sailed the route connecting Yokohama, Honolulu, and San Francisco. With marble pillars in the dining room, it boasted Western-style interior decoration and service. Known as "The Queen of the Pacific" because of its grand appearance, the ship's length was 178 meters, and it had a displacement of seventeen thousand tons. Another ship that plied the North American sea lanes around the same time—the *Hikawa-maru*—is now a museum; it is open to the public at Yamashita Park in Yokohama, and thus it is possible to see the decks, passenger cabins, and dining room of a Japanese luxury liner of that period. One can view the extravagant interior and get an idea of the meals and service aimed at Westerners. The *Asama-maru* was a bit larger than the *Hikawa-maru*, but even so, it must have rolled quite a bit in the rough seas of the Pacific. Entertainment was limited, but for the delegation that was heading to the conference, it offered a space where they could study and prepare.

The *Asama-maru* as such served as a kind of floating school. At 7:00 a.m. the students would gather on the deck for morning assembly, and then after breakfast begin individual study at about nine. In the afternoon, they would break up into groups for workshops, and the evening hours were set aside for continuing the workshops or individual study. Since it was necessary for the students to submit a report to the supervising teachers by the time the ship docked in San Francisco, they studied diligently. In the aftermath of the Marco Polo Bridge Incident, which occurred in Beijing just one week before their departure, and with international attention being concentrated on Japan's actions in East Asia, the students were ready to confront the Americans as representatives of their country.

All that being said, these young people were all around the age of twenty. After about a week into life on the ship, a contingent of late risers surfaced,

14. In Japan, "Auld Lang Syne" is regarded as a farewell song; it is sometimes sung at graduations and used to signal closing time in stores.

and there was a movement to shift the morning assembly to 7:30, but this was opposed by the "orthodox" group. So as not to embarrass themselves in the United States, even social dance practice was held on the deck. One might think that the students had no experience in partner dances where men and women came into close physical contact, but this was not the case. Contrary to expectations, a majority of the women were conversant with social dancing, since they were all from good families and had received a Western-style education. In contrast, only four or five of the male students were acquainted with social dancing. As expected, the leader of the four men who were proficient dancers was "Suzuki." At a time when men and women generally were kept strictly segregated, the days on the ship must have been fun for the students. They were able to enjoy a monthlong trip together where they could exchange opinions and even dance hand in hand, even if it was only practice.

After the two-week voyage via Honolulu, the ship carrying the students passed under the Golden Gate Bridge, which had only been open for two months, and docked in San Francisco on July 28. The delegation stayed at a downtown hotel and enjoyed walking around the city, marveling at the unique and beautiful townscape as well as the cool climate. Dancing across the front pages of newspapers being hawked by young boys on the city streets were large black letters reporting on the Sino-Japanese War.

After spending a few days in San Francisco, the students moved to Stanford University, where the conference was to be held, and participated in the opening ceremony. The conference started on August 2 and lasted for one week. The US delegation consisted of seventy-nine students. The participants separated into nine roundtables: "Student Life in Japan and America," "Japan's and America's Economic Stake in the Pacific," "Armaments and National Security in the Pacific," "Government and the Individual in Japan and America," "Marriage and Family Life in Japan and America," "The Worker and His Job in Japan and America," "Moral and Spiritual Values in Present Day Life," "World Society and the National State," and "The Role of Arts in Japan and America." The conference was completely closed, and only those who were registered participants were allowed to attend.

Alan Discusses Japaneseness

Alan's name appears as a participant in three of the roundtables: "Government and the Individual in Japan and America," "Marriage and Family Life in Japan and America," and "The Role of Arts in Japan and America." In the

"Government and the Individual in Japan and America" roundtable, the discussion covered "Comparison of Constitutional Structure," "Government and Economic Activity," "The Political Status of the Subject and Citizen," and "Political Forces behind the Scenes." In the "Marriage and Family Life in Japan and America" roundtable, the subjects were "Approaching the Marriage Relationship," "Family Organization," and "Role of the Family in Society." Alan did not participate in the "Moral and Spiritual Values in Present Day Life" roundtable, the topic of which was religion, and it was Miyamura Takamichi of Taisho University who presented on Zen and Buddhism.

Among the roundtables he participated in, it appears that Alan played a central role in "The Role of Arts in Japan and America." A summary by Alan written in Japanese appears in the report that was published after the conference.[15]

> For me personally, it was somewhat unsatisfying to have to have spent the entire week of the conference confined to discussing the subject of "The Role of the Arts," which corresponded to the ninth topic of the Culture Group, explaining "What is Meant by Japaneseness?" and so-called Japanese things such as ancient Japanese art, architecture, flower arrangement, the tea ceremony, and martial arts; but nothing could give me greater satisfaction and happiness if, through the explanation of these things, my poor efforts in this group helped to deepen the understanding of, and interest in, Japan on the part of the American students.[16]

At this conference, too, Alan was put in the position of presenting his father's ideas at second hand, selling them on consignment, as it were. Alan was reduced to the role of a "mini Daisetz," using his father's theories to deepen the Americans' understanding of Japan. It appears that he was uncomfortable with being put in this position. The phrase "have to have spent the entire week of the conference explaining . . . so-called Japanese things" reveals how he felt.

Alan continued by saying that he believed American students would be surprised by the fact that Japan continued to transmit its unique spiritual culture while importing Western civilization and making it uniquely Japa-

---

15. Masaru Suzuki, "Sutanfōdo kaigi 9: The Role of the Arts," in Miyamura, *Ruporutāju*, 72–73.

16. Masaru Suzuki, "Sutanfōdo kaigi 9," 72.

nese. Moreover, Alan emphasized that he deliberately did not translate the subject of the discussion into Japanese and left it as "The Role of the Arts." Alan was of the opinion that there was no Japanese word that perfectly fit the English word "arts." "Arts" embodies a plethora of meanings, such as fine arts, contemporary arts, performing arts, martial arts, and even architecture; he felt that no one Japanese word could express all of these ideas. Alan's concerns are also those of modern humanities scholars in Japan today.

According to Alan, this group had other "peculiarities" in addition to the fact that it was impossible to translate the theme into Japanese.

> This was not the only peculiarity of the group. The other was that the chair, who worked diligently all throughout the week of the conference to move the discussion along in a vast and somewhat somber art classroom and who brought a sort of color and energy to the proceedings, was a pretty and lighthearted young woman who in body and spirit gave the impression of being one of the girls in a Hollywood revue.[17]

I would like to ask Alan just exactly what it was that was distracting him . . . He added that the pretty woman in question had astonishingly deep knowledge of the history of Japanese literature.

Returning to the roundtable on the role of arts, Alan presented the group with a somewhat fundamental question. He said that there is a huge chasm between ikebana, gardens, the tea ceremony, and the ancient arts of Japan and the current social situation and unemployment relief policies in Japan. In the United States, on the other hand, the government dealt decisively with the situation and, with unemployment relief and promotion of the arts working hand in hand, forged a socially meaningful movement. Here Alan discerned the innovativeness of capitalism.

The roundtable discussion saw many questions from the Americans on Japanese culture, which the Japanese side answered. It is likely that Alan, having a superficial understanding of Daisetz's theory of Japanese culture and speaking excellent English, spent all of his time answering questions. It appears that he did not like having to do that, but there was one question from an American student that left a deep impression on him. The question concerned how, in an industrialized future, traditional Japanese spiritual civilization and traditional Japanese things would be integrated with the

17. Masaru Suzuki, "Sutanfōdo kaigi 9," 73.

state of Japanese society. Alan replied that "the art traditions will continue to exist as antiquities, and what are seen as Japanese things will continue to exist in different forms."[18] In this exchange one can see how cultured a person Alan was.

Alan concluded his report by declaring, "Even though being old-fashioned, in various respects it can be said that out of all of the groups, this group was particularly outstanding."[19] It is here where we can see the adult Alan's perspective on Daisetz's work. The spiritual culture and traditions of Japan with which his father was concerned were "antiquities" for Alan. They would continue to exist in that form, but modern society would be seeking something different—this was Alan's view, I believe.

After completing the weeklong conference, the Japanese delegation toured Santa Barbara, Hollywood, Los Angeles, Portland, and Seattle and returned to Yokohama on September 10. Thus, Alan's two-month experience in the United States came to an end.

Daisetz's Indifference

The reason that Alan was selected as a member of the JASC delegation was probably because he was fluent in English, in addition to the fact that he was a literary-minded young man. Another reason could have been the fact that his father was a well-known scholar. In any case, he was selected as a delegate to a conference of the crème de la crème of student society, and it should have been a source of pride for both him and his parents.

However, there is no record that Daisetz took any interest in the fact that Alan was selected for the JASC. In his published letters, books, and other writings, Daisetz never mentioned the JASC. In 1936, while the JASC was taking place at Waseda University, Daisetz was in the middle of a trip to the United States and Europe, so perhaps he did not have an opportunity to write about Alan's participation. However, when Alan went to the United States in 1937, Daisetz was spending his time in Kyoto and Kamakura as usual.

The son who had caused Daisetz so much trouble with his conduct was now representing Japanese students. Not only that, but Alan had learned a certain amount from Daisetz's writings and was holding forth on Zen and Japanese culture on behalf of Japan. It seems that a normal parent would

---

18. Masaru Suzuki, "Sutanfōdo kaigi 9," 73.

19. Masaru Suzuki, "Sutanfōdo kaigi 9," 73.

be deeply moved in some way or another by this and would have left some record of it in his diaries or letters.

I assume that Daisetz provided the money for Alan's trip to the United States. However, it seems that he had no particular interest in what Alan might do. Even if it was only on the surface, the son was seemingly trying to get close to his father; nevertheless, the father's feelings do not seem to have been directed toward his son. Alan was very sensitive to Daisetz's attitude, and perhaps because of that expressed his irritation by talking about what his father was studying, even characterizing him as an "antique."

Two Red Threads of Fate

The journalist Sekiguchi Waichi (1959–), who has studied the history of the JASC, has written that the conferences at that time had another purpose: "The preparations for the conferences provided 'a venue where men and women could cultivate friendships,' which were rare at that time."[20] Since the JASC was a conference that involved visiting the host country, the trip itself taking several weeks, both before and after the students were busy for more than a year with elaborate preparations and the final wrap-up. Under such circumstances, romances were bound to blossom. For example, Miyazawa Kiichi later married Ijichi Yōko, who was with the delegation on the trip to the United States. According to what Shiroyama Saburō wrote, seeing Miyazawa and Yōko snuggled up together in deep conversation on the deck during the return journey caused their friends to tease them, saying that the JASC was "not just for Japan-American friendship, it was for Japan-Japan friendship."[21]

Alan was married three times over the course of his life, but he met the first woman who was to change his life—Kubo Nobu—at the conference at Stanford. Nobu was a student at Tokyo Woman's Christian University, and she went to the United States with her elder sister Machiko, who attended Tsuda University. Like Alan, Machiko was selected as a delegate two years in a row, starting the previous year. The sisters' father, Kubo Hisaji (1891–1961), was a scholar in the fields of law and economics and wrote *Kin kaikin bōkokuron* (A Theory That the Lifting of an Embargo on the Export of Gold Will Destroy Our Country; 1929).[22]

---

20. Sekiguchi, *Kaisen zen'ya no disukasshion*, 43.
21. Shiroyama, *Yūjō chikara ari*, 84.
22. Kubo Hisaji, *Kin kaikin bōkokuron* (Tokyo: Kubo Hōsei Keizai Kenkyūjo, 1929).

Fig. 3. Alan in his youth. Photographer unknown. Source: Hayashida Kumino, *Ōoji Suzuki Daisetsu kara no tegami* (Kyoto: Hōzōkan, 1995), 55.

There is very little documentation recording Nobu's views presented at the conference with the exception of one brief statement in English in the report on "Student Life in Japan and America": "Owing to the complex social influences which dominate the cultural institutions today, the universities which are meant for academic or cultural education are more or less inevitably putting stress on the vocational aspect of education."[23] According to the record of the conference, Alan and Nobu participated in two round-tables together: "Marriage and Family Life in Japan and America" and "The Role of Arts in Japan and America." However, there is no evidence that they were particularly close during the conference and no documentation about any relationship they may have had.

23. Executive Committee of the Fourth America-Japan Student Conference, *Report of the Fourth America-Japan Student Conference*, n.p.

The record of the conference includes characterizations of all of the delegates by someone referred to as T. M. (possibly the editor of the report, Miyamura Takamichi) He described Alan as follows:

> SUZUKI: A prodigy among the delegates. Mr. Cocktail Suzuki exudes the feeling of Kyoto, which permeates his lithe frame. The foremost authority on American literature. At times also lectures on "Japaneseness." (If I were a woman . . .)[24]

In a group comprising only very accomplished people, it appears that Alan was viewed as possessing unusual talents, as might be expected. It is hard to know what T. M. meant by "Mr. Cocktail Suzuki." Was it an allusion to the fact that Alan was half Japanese and half British, or was it perhaps because he looked like a model in a picture when he held a cocktail glass? By ending his characterization with "If I were a woman," T. M. seems to be implying that he would want to snuggle up to that "lithe frame," suggesting Alan had a sex appeal that even men recognized.

As to the matter of cocktails, it is not clear when Alan began drinking. He was a notorious troublemaker, so it is not hard to imagine that he began drinking in his teens. It may very well be that by the time Alan reached the age when drinking alcohol was legal, he was already a heavy drinker. Daisetz had to pay his bar tab many times, and up until the time of his second marriage, he would sometimes become drunk and go on rampages.

In any case, Alan was a handsome man who exuded buckets of charm and was gallant toward women. T. M. described Ms. Kubo Nobu, who later became Alan's first wife, as "burning with the American spirit. Physically she was very agile, and I seem to remember that a Nisei[25] person asked me if she had been born in the United States."[26] According to Nobu's surviving family, she was the sort of person who spoke her mind plainly. Perhaps that is what made her seem American to T. M.

If one didn't know what lay in his future, one might assume that Alan and Nobu met, fell in love, and lived happily ever after; however, that is not what happened. Even while he was seeing Nobu, Alan did not cease his romantic adventures. From around the time he entered college, he frequented the Higashiyama Dance Hall, which was located about halfway up the Higashiyama hills in eastern Kyoto. The dance hall was a place where the

---

24. T. M., "Pen sukecchi daihyōshū," in Miyamura, *Ruporutāju*, 103.
25. A second-generation Japanese American.
26. T. M., "Pen sukecchi daihyōshū," 104.

male and female customers could dance jazz and tango to live music. One
could also pay to dance with dancers who were employed by the dance hall.
The Higashiyama was known as the number one dance hall in East Asia, and
among its clientele were many foreigners, apprentice geisha, movie stars, and
intellectuals. In the 1930s, the novelists Tanizaki Jun'ichirō (1886–1965) and
Sakaguchi Ango (1906–1955) frequented the dance hall. Ike Mariko, Alan's
second wife, recalls its atmosphere as follows:

> After being ushered into the hall on the thick, bright red carpet,
> one saw widely spaced marble columns soaring up to the roof and a
> revolving chandelier that sent out a beautiful rainbow of colors. . . .
> On one side was a huge glass window that appeared to reach all
> the way to the ceiling, through which one could see a wide veranda
> stretching off into the distance, at the end of which was a huge foun-
> tain that sent multiple streams of water up into the air against the
> backdrop of the eastern mountains. The drops of water lit up as they
> fell, scattering light that seemed to be glittering in time with the
> music.
> Most of the men wore black suits and stood on the spacious,
> polished floor with their chests thrust out proudly. There were some
> foreign guests, and the women wore long evening gowns of varied
> colors. . . . Around the large oval hall were what seemed to be more
> than a hundred chairs for the dancers, and behind each chair was a
> lighted number. Numbers one to five were lit up so that everyone
> would know who the most popular dancers were.[27]

One summer evening at the Higashiyama Dance Hall, Alan's gaze fell
upon a pretty singer who had recently had her debut—Ike Mariko. It is
impossible to confirm with any accuracy what year this was, since there is a
discrepancy in the accounts written by both of the people involved. Judging
from various circumstances, I believe that it was either 1937, the year of the
JASC at Stanford, or the summer of the following year.

I would like to digress a bit and give an overview of the life of Ike Mariko,
using information gleaned from my interviews with people who knew her
and from her autobiography *Ike Mariko shō* (Ike Mariko's Sky; 2000).[28]

---

27. Shimizu Hideo, ed., *Ike Mariko shō* (Tokyo: Ike Mariko Ongaku Jimusho, 2000),
chapter 4.

28. Shimizu, *Ike Mariko shō*, chapter 4.

Mariko was born in 1917 in Kyoto at Manjuji, a sub-temple of Tōfukuji. However, she was not the daughter of a priest. In the past, it was not unusual for ordinary people with families to live in prominent temples. Mariko's grandfather, who was a vassal of the Tosa domain (present-day Kōchi prefecture), lived at Manjuji. Her father, a student at Kyoto Imperial University, married into the family, taking the family name of his wife, and Mariko was born. Mariko's father died of tuberculosis while she was still very young, and so Mariko grew up without anyone she could call her father.

The family moved their residence to Sōgon-in, another sub-temple within the precincts of Tōfukuji. When Mariko was in her third year of elementary school, the family moved to a new house that they had built near a botanical garden in Kamigyō-ku (the present-day Kyoto Botanical Gardens in Sakyō-ku). Mariko liked singing, and almost every day she would sit on the banks of the Kamo River and sing, with the murmuring of the river as her backup band.

After graduating from elementary school, Mariko entered St. Agnes' School, which was run by missionaries. Mariko chose the school after becoming enthralled by the hymns that echoed in the solemn chapel. She came to enjoy movies and started frequenting the Tōji-in Studio[29] in the hope of meeting movie stars. One day she went together with a friend who had run away from home for an evening, and Mariko's grandfather, in a rage, yanked her from St. Agnes' School and enrolled her in the Kyoto Women's School, run by Nishi Honganji, the head temple of the Honganji sect of Jōdo Shinshū. Even though the atmosphere at the Kyoto Women's School was the exact opposite of the westernized ambience of St. Agnes' School, Mariko was popular with the teachers and got good marks in her favorite subjects, music and English.

Because Mariko liked to sing, she aimed for admission to the Tokyo Music School in Ueno (present-day Tokyo University of the Arts). On the advice of a friend, however, she auditioned at the Takarazuka Music and Revue School in Hyōgo prefecture, which was affiliated with the Takarazuka Revue, and was accepted after passing the difficult test that twelve out of thirteen candidates fail. Mariko's grandfather was fiercely opposed to her entering Takarazuka, saying that it would be scandalous for her to dance in front of people, showing her legs, but her mother reassured him. After completing the difficult training at Takarazuka, Mariko made her debut under

---

29. The file studio established in 1921 by Makino Shōzō (1878–1929), who is said to be the founding father of Japanese film industry.

the stage name "Mikazuki Miyako." Over time, however, she developed an inferiority complex toward her rivals in Takarazuka Revue, whom she felt were more talented than she was.

Mariko would return home to Kyoto between performances, and one evening her cousin invited her to the Higashiyama Dance Hall. Mariko fell completely under the spell of a glittering world that was different from the Takarazuka stage. As a result, she quit the Takarazuka Music and Revue School after three years and began taking lessons from the jazz musician Jimmy Harada (1911–1995). She became a favorite at the Higashiyama Dance Hall as a jazz singer whose trademark was singing while waving a conductor's baton.

Alan approached Mariko, using the clever excuse that she had slightly mispronounced some of the English lyrics of a song she had sung. Mariko had remembered seeing Alan among the guests, but she had thought he was a foreigner. Trusting in the fact that Alan's father was a university professor and with Jimmy Harada's encouragement, Mariko and an actress friend of hers started taking regular English lessons from Alan.

Mariko's home was very close to that of the Suzukis, and the lessons took place either at the Suzuki residence or at Mariko's house. It seems that Alan had gathered several students and was teaching an English class at this time. In a letter to Beatrice on April 22, 1938, Daisetz wrote that "Alan has his pupils to-night."[30] When the lessons took place at Mariko's house, her grandfather, upon seeing Alan, apparently warned his granddaughter to be careful not to let the foreigner seduce her. Alan reportedly told Mariko that there was nothing in the world he hated more than his father, and Mariko considered him to be very "manly" for talking about his illustrious father in this way.

We do not know how long Mariko's lessons lasted. At some point, due to Alan's school schedule, Mariko's actress friend's shooting schedule, and the fact that Mariko herself quit working at the Higashiyama Dance Hall, the lessons ceased. It appears that there was nothing more to their relationship at the time other than the fact that Mariko thought Alan was a handsome teacher about her age and that Alan thought she was an attractive student. Eight years later, however, the goddess of fate would bring the two together again.

---

30. *SDZ* 36, 648.

Beatrice's Health Takes a Turn for the Worse

Unlike Daisetz, whose diaries and letters have been made public, there is very little information to help us understand how Beatrice related to Alan. It might be more accurate to say such information exists, but that it is not publicly available. Beatrice was in the habit of keeping a detailed diary. The "Beatrice Diaries" are kept under lock and key at the Matsugaoka Bunko, and very few researchers have been allowed access to the originals. If we could read her diaries, we might be able to understand how worried she was about Alan, with his wild ways.

Below I would like to quote from two letters with references to Alan that have been translated into Japanese and published. These were written in February 1937, which was in between the two JASC conferences that Alan attended. These excerpts from Beatrice's letters give us a good picture of the state of the parent-child relationship between Daisetz and Alan at this time. Even though Alan had been accepted at Doshisha University and selected as a JASC delegate, Daisetz did not recognize Alan's abilities. Not only that, the ruckus over whether Alan did or did not steal pocket money from his father's wallet hurt both parent and child.

> My Dearest Tei-sama, even though it has only been a few hours since you left, I'm already unbearably lonely. I'm particularly worried about Alan. After breakfast, he asked, "How much money did Papa leave?" I said "no," and when I then asked, "How much money did you get from Papa?" he answered, "Five yen." When I asked, "Is there any money aside from Papa's?" he looked at me with a strange expression on his face. I was sure that he had seen through me and realized I knew something. Even though I told him I would give him ten yen and the check from Doshisha University, he refused to take it, saying, "I'm not going to take this semester's tests at the university" and "You and Papa think I'm a disgrace to the family, so that's it." Then he stormed out of the house. I just don't know what to think anymore. I'm so worried and confused. Could Okono come for a few days? Anyway, goodbye. I pray that you have a good trip.[31]

---

31. Suzuki Biatorisu Rēn, "Saiai naru Tei-sama," trans. Yokoyama Wayne Shigeto, in Matsugaoka, *Suzuki Daisetsu botsugo 40 nen*, 79–80. Since the original English letters have not been published, the English passages included here were translated from the Japanese rendition.

My Dearest Tei-sama, there is nothing in particular to report today. However, I had a chance to talk to Alan, and the atmosphere at home was somewhat improved. Alan insisted that "Papa is making the biggest mistake of his life. I didn't take any money from his wallet." Perhaps it was because he was so startled at our question that he was unable to answer. It seems that Alan feels that "Papa always jumps to conclusions, so whatever I say won't make any difference." He was so hurt and upset that he seriously considered killing himself. This whole incident has left me exhausted, and I'm mentally and emotionally at the end of my rope.[32]

Considering Alan's character, I expect there may have been some instances where Alan pilfered money from his parents. Even if Alan did not steal the money, such protestations of innocence from a child who was a habitual liar from his youth would be difficult for his parents to believe. The relationship between Alan and his parents had fallen into a situation of mutual suspicion from which there was no escape. The constant problems that Alan caused must have exacerbated Beatrice's worries and anxiety. There is no doubt that this exhaustion was eating away at her body and spirit.

Alan continued to see Nobu after returning from the JASC at Stanford University, and Daisetz was aware they were dating. It was not a question of whether or not Daisetz approved; he no doubt had more than enough of his son's unending amorous liaisons. The entry in the "Daisetz Diaries" for March 10, 1938, reads, "One of Alan's girl friends left her house, and one of her relatives called early in [the] morning." The phrase "one of Alan's girl friends" suggests that Daisetz believed that Alan was seeing multiple women at the same time. From the context of the diary, there is a strong possibility that this particular girlfriend was Kubo Nobu.

Five days later, Beatrice was admitted to St. Luke's International Hospital after complaining of physical pain and fatigue. Beatrice's one-and-a-half-year battle with sickness had begun. We do not know what Alan's life at the university was like after he came back from the JASC. According to the April 7 entry in the "Daisetz Diaries," Alan went missing for four days. During that time, he was apparently at Beatrice's bedside in St. Luke's Hospital. In a letter to Daisetz, Beatrice mentioned that Alan was seeing "Miss Kubo." In his diary the day after receiving her letter, Daisetz records that he scolded Alan severely.

---

32. Suzuki Biatorisu Rēn, "Saiai naru Tei-sama," 80.

A Man with Many Loves

In May, a new woman-related problem of Alan's came to light: he had impregnated a woman named Ōtani Kinuko. This affair led Beatrice to lose faith in Alan completely. The particulars of this incident have already been publicized in the "Daisetz Diaries," so I will summarize them here.

On May 9, 1938, a person representing Kinuko contacted Daisetz, who was in Kyoto. This was probably the first time that Daisetz learned of her pregnancy. Daisetz immediately had to start considering a legal response. That day, he went to see his older brother Kōtarō, who was involved in legal work in Kobe city. The next day, Alan and Okono returned from Tokyo and Kamakura respectively. They spent an entire day discussing the problem that Alan had caused.

The entry in the "Daisetz Diaries" for May 10 reads: "Pity as much time wasted, which might be devoted to writing as there are not many more years left." Daisetz was sixty-seven at the time. It sounds very cold toward his son, but as far as Daisetz was concerned, this "incident" was impinging on his study. He spent several more days taking care of the problem, sending Okono to Kinuko's house and consulting with friends. It appears that Daisetz reached a private settlement by paying 200 yen to Kinuko's representative. The entry in the "Daisetz Diaries" for May 16 reads: "Hope this settles the matter for all the time to come. Will Alan be reformed after this? Some doubt about it."

The issue here is how much the 200 yen in settlement money was worth. For that, we need to know what the rate was at the time for consolation money in cases of this type. Several books were published in the 1930s on the issue of tarnishing a woman's virtue. I would like to cite from one of them, *Teisō jūrin to sono saiban* (Dishonoring a Woman and the Adjudication Thereof).[33] First, for a woman, nothing is more important than her chastity, and in some cases, it must be preserved over and above even one's life. Rape by violence, of course, dishonors a woman, but a divorce immediately following a marriage disgraces her as well. In his book, Jitsuda Jidao discusses some examples of the latter case. According to these examples, a twenty-nine-year-old woman in her first marriage is entitled to 400 yen in consolation money; a home economics teacher at a girls school, a woman who has graduated from high school, a worker at a vegetable store, a nurse, and the daughter of a local family of high standing are each entitled to 500

---

33. Jitsuda Jidao, *Teisō jūrin to sono saiban* (Tokyo: Nishodō Shoten, 1930), 117–58.

yen; a woman who gives birth to a baby girl is entitled to 600 yen; and, in the case of a woman who graduated from a prominent girls school and a man employed by the navy, the woman is entitled to 700 yen. It appears that the consolation money differed according to the woman's age, education, profession, and family, and the man's earning power. We do not know the age or the family background of Ōtani Kinuko, so it is difficult to determine whether 200 yen was a large or small sum.

On the other hand, how difficult was it for Daisetz to come up with the 200 yen? In Japan at the time, a cup of coffee was five sen (one sen was one one-hundredth of a yen), a double room at a hotel was 15 yen, yearly tuition at Tokyo Imperial University was 120 yen, and the prize money for the highest awards for literature (the Akutagawa Prize and the Naoki Prize) was 500 yen.[34] In December 1938, Daisetz gave Alan 55 yen for his Doshisha University educational expenses. Thus, 200 yen was approximately four times the amount that Daisetz was providing for Alan's yearly college tuition.

Hidden Facts

Since the fact that Alan impregnated a woman is not recorded anywhere in the "Daisetz Diaries" that have been made public, how can we be assured that it is true? The key to verifying this information can be found in the letters by Daisetz to Iwakura that are included in Iwakura Masaji's book.

> Greetings. I received the copy of the *Hagakure*.[35] Thanks. I don't have the time to meet with you regarding the issue with Alan. Let's try to do something in July.
> He's amoral, and there's something wrong with him on this point. He does not seem to have any regrets for the wrong he has done, and the fact that he can be so blasé about [thing omitted by Iwakura] is strange. It is a fact that this attitude gave my late wife a very bad feeling. We need to talk in more detail the next time we meet. I want to save him somehow. I'm sure he's feeling lonely.[36]

The date of the letter is April 23, but we do not know the year. If one reads this letter hastily, it appears to be nothing more than another letter from

---

34. Bungei Shunjū, *Bungei Shunjū 70 nenshi honpen* (Tokyo: Bungei Shunjū, 1991), 94.
35. A book on Bushido written for samurai (ca. 1716).
36. Iwakura Masaji, *Shin'nin Suzuki Daisetsu* (Kyoto: Hōzōkan, 1986), 112.

Daisetz worrying about Alan. If one looks at it closely, however, the original has been snipped. Iwakura decided to edit something out. When I inquired at the Toyama City Public Library, where this letter is kept, I was told that since the letter concerned private matters, it could not be disclosed even for academic research. It seems to me that if a public library is going to conceal material pertaining to a person who left his mark on postwar history and who has been dead for almost fifty years, claiming "privacy," then we might as well give up in trying to research modern personalities. I considered lodging a protest with the library, but soon realized there was no need to do so. The same letter that Daisetz wrote to Iwakura appears in *The Complete Works of D.T. Suzuki, Expanded New Edition*, and it is recorded as having been written on April 23, 1941.

> Greetings. I received the copy of the *Hagakure*. Thanks. I don't have the time to meet with you regarding the issue with ——. Let's try to do something in July.
>
> He's amoral, and there's something wrong with him on this point. He does not seem to have any regrets for the wrong he has done, and the fact that he can be so blasé about abandoning a pregnant woman is strange. It is a fact that this attitude gave —— a very bad feeling. We need to talk in more detail the next time we meet. I want to save him somehow. I'm sure he's feeling lonely.[37]

The situation should be obvious. Iwakura concealed the "thing" that Alan did; on the other hand, the editor of the *Works*, probably Furuta Shōkin, did not conceal the "thing" but the "who" that is the "subject." If we put both letters together, the original can be restored. In short, Alan impregnated a woman and felt no remorse about it, and this turned Beatrice against him. In 1941, the year the letter was sent, Alan was married to Nobu, so the woman in question was not her. Since the problem involving a woman that had caused Daisetz so much trouble was the Ōtani Kinuko affair, we can say for certain that the "pregnant woman" Daisetz spoke about in this letter was Kinuko. Iwakura and Furuta both covered up what Alan had done to protect Daisetz's "privacy." The facts, however, slipped through their fingers like water. We can divine even this much from public documents alone. Be that as it may, we do not know whether Kinuko gave birth to the child or not.

---

37. *SDZ* 37, 22.

A Mother's Death

Even after the incident with Kinuko, Daisetz occasionally would still give money to Alan. According to the "Daisetz Diaries," Daisetz supplied Alan with money on the following occasions: one month after the settlement with Kinuko, twenty yen on June 20, 1938; some money on July 4 (amount unspecified); fifty yen on October 21 "to pay his debts during summer"; fifty-five yen for tuition on December 15; "Alan's fees and debts paid" on January 31, 1939 (amount unspecified); and thirty yen on March 7. Looking through the "Daisetz Diaries," there are a lot of specific references to the amount of money Daisetz spent on Alan during this period. Perhaps because of the incident with Kinuko, the feeling was growing inside Daisetz that Alan was an expensive child. Alan probably used some of the money he got from Daisetz to play around, but that is not the whole story. As an alumnus of the JASC, Alan was cooperating in the effort to raise funds for the operation of the conference. In a letter addressed to Beatrice on July 5, 1938, Daisetz wrote that Alan was busy gathering funds for his juniors to bring over some students from the United States.[38]

Even as he was burdened by Alan's women problems in addition to his studies, Daisetz went to Tokyo several times a month to look after Beatrice at St. Luke's International Hospital. On May 3, 1938, Beatrice was temporarily released from the hospital and returned to Kyoto, but at that point the incident with Kinuko unfolded, and Beatrice saw the whole sordid story up close. In essence, what Alan did was to deliver a body blow to his already seriously ill mother. Beatrice was readmitted to St. Luke's Hospital on June 14; of course it is impossible to say with certainty whether or not it was Alan's fault. She was temporarily released from the hospital again on October 17 and then was readmitted for the final time on November 19.

The details are not clear, but on February 11, 1939, Beatrice wrote Daisetz a letter using language that indicated she was frantic.

Now, Tei-san, our family problems are far and away more important than Eastern Buddhism. I have come to realize that if you pass away now, I will be put in a position where I am penniless and with no rights. Please do not put me in such a dangerous situation. You must consult with a capable lawyer. There is an excellent lawyer in Yokohama.

---

38. *SDZ* 36, 651.

Have you consulted with Ataka-san about anything other than the books? Also, why is it necessary to catalog the books and the furniture? Are you going to entrust everything to Ataka-san? Hurry! Hurry!

I am not only in physical pain, but I am suffering greatly spiritually as well.

When will you be coming to see me? I have discovered a number of important matters and want to speak with you. It is dangerous to put this off any longer. Compared to my future (assuming I am still alive) and your future (assuming that you outlive me), how important is Eastern Buddhist thought? *Please do not put this off any longer.* You have not touched at all upon whether or not you have seen your siblings. Now that I have learned more about this situation, I am seized with a feeling of great desperation.[39]

Hayashida Kumino included this letter in *Granduncle*, but did not speculate about the substance of Beatrice's plea. Since this letter is introduced in the midst of a discussion about Alan, Kumino may have been connecting Beatrice's agitation to the issues with her son. Reading the letter with no preconceptions, however, such an interpretation is a bit forced. Daisetz was going forward with preparations for the establishment of the Matsugaoka Bunko with Ataka Yakichi and was making a catalog of the items that were to be entrusted to the Bunko. It is perhaps more natural to read Beatrice's letter as expressing her worries that if the management of the family possessions was signed over to the Bunko and Daisetz should die before she did, she might be left penniless.

According to Kumino, on her sickbed Beatrice not only said that Alan and Kumino's "engagement" should be treated as though it had never happened, but that it would also be necessary to disown Alan. However, Kumino wrote, "I don't know whether or not the parent-child relationship was actually dissolved, that is, whether Alan was disinherited, to use a complicated expression."[40] No mention of a dissolution of the adoption can be found in the family register. In fact, since Alan was the natural child of Daisetz and Beatrice so far as the family register is concerned, no adoption existed that could be dissolved in the first place.

---

39. Hayashida, *Ōoji Suzuki Daisetsu kara no tegami*, 61–62. Since the original English text is not published, the letter was translated into English from the Japanese rendition by Nakata Nagako.

40. Hayashida, *Ōoji Suzuki Daisetsu kara no tegami*, 60.

According to the entries in the "Daisetz Diaries," Alan visited Beatrice many times while she was in the hospital. Yokoyama Wayne Shigeto has translated an undated letter that Alan wrote at that time.

Dearest Mother:

Please forgive me. No matter what I do, all I do is cause trouble. All I do is make you suffer. I am just no good. I ruined your life. I want to leave home and reevaluate my destiny, and I think about where I went wrong in life. Mother, I regret everything. Please forgive me.[41]

Alan has realized that his mother's death is imminent and is apologizing for his conduct. In view of how Alan subsequently lived his life, it is hard to say whether he sincerely regretted what he had done. However, I would like to think that he had some feeling about how much suffering he caused his mother.

Alan graduated from Doshisha University in March 1939; his graduation thesis was on the American playwright Eugene O'Neill (1888–1953).[42] Perhaps what Alan meant by "I want to leave home and reevaluate my destiny" was that he wanted to go to some foreign country after his graduation, perhaps with Nobu. This would come to pass three years later.

Beatrice's illness became more and more serious. By 1939, Daisetz was spending almost half of each month visiting St. Luke's Hospital. In the midst of this grave situation, Alan attempted to persuade his parents to approve of his marriage to Nobu. Since Nobu was the daughter of a noted scholar, had a college degree, and was a talented woman who could hold intellectual discussions in English, in normal circumstances, she was well suited to the role of "marrying into the family of a scholar." Daisetz and Beatrice, however, were both firmly opposed to the match. The incident with Kinuko was still fresh, and Daisetz and Beatrice had progressively lost trust in Alan, who thought nothing about dating two or three girls at the same time. Even more than that, they were probably thinking of Nobu, whom they believed could probably never be happy being married to Alan.

41. Yokoyama, "Kaisetsu," 76–77. Since the original English text is not published, the letter was translated into English based on a Japanese rendition of it.

42. The Department of English, Faculty of Letters at Doshisha University retains a copy of Alan's graduation thesis titled "O'Neill's Attitude towards Life as Revealed in His Later Plays," in addition to the copies of two short reports published in November 1937 and June 1939 in issues of *L.L.L.*, the alumni bulletins of the faculty. I am grateful to playwright Ms. Tsutsumi Harue and Professor Kawashima Takeshi of Doshisha University for informing me of this.

In the context of discussions about marriage, Daisetz finally revealed the secret of Alan's origins to Alan on May 28. In his heart, Alan probably thought, "That? I've known about it for years." In Daisetz's June 4 entry in the "Daisetz Diaries" he noted that Alan had an hourlong discussion with Beatrice concerning the "Kubo girl." He also wrote, "Strange thing is that he is not worried over his real parents and circumstances in which he came to us."

Starting on June 27, Daisetz began staying at the hospital to take care of Beatrice. However, it was in vain, and Beatrice passed away on July 16 at the age of sixty-one, when Daisetz and Alan were sixty-nine and twenty-three, respectively.

Daisetz's Mourning

Beatrice's funeral was held on the following day. It was a very quiet affair, attended only by close relatives. As often occurs in Japan, Beatrice's ashes were divided and interred in separate locations: the Tōkeiji temple in Kamakura, the Suzuki family crypt at Nodayama cemetery in Kanazawa, and the Shin'nō-in temple on Mt. Kōya, which Beatrice had frequently visited while she was alive. On October 22, a relatively large-scale one-hundred-day memorial service was held at the Tōji temple in Kyoto, a major temple of Shingon esoteric Buddhism with which Beatrice had a deep relationship.[43] The following day, Daisetz wrote a letter to his old friend Yamamoto Ryōkichi, overflowing with his sense of loss.

> Following the general custom, yesterday we held what I suppose you could call a funeral or a farewell service. Saying that I remember my wife and am thinking of her is really not quite right; it is more accurate to say that I have lost half of myself.[44]

A eulogy that Daisetz wrote on December 16, the five-month anniversary of Beatrice's death, appears in the preface to *Shōren bukkyō shōkan* (Observations on Blue Lotus Buddhism; 1940), written by Beatrice and posthu-

---

43. October 22, 1939 was the nearest Sunday of Beatrice's one-hundred-day memorial (October 24). It is common to change the date of memorial service for the convenience of the attendees.

44. *SDZ* 36, 667.

mously published.[45] In his eulogy, Daisetz wrote with great emotion about his and Beatrice's spiritual connection.[46] The objective of their life from the time they were married was "to disseminate Eastern thought, or what might be called Eastern sensibilities, among the peoples of Europe and the United States." They believed that nothing would bring them more happiness than if, through them, the peoples of the East and the West could come to understand each other better. Rather than requiring such external goals, however, Daisetz wrote, "If we could discuss our feelings, thoughts, and opinions with each other and then commit them to writing, that would have been enough." Bound together by Buddhism, this international couple existed in a world that only the two of them inhabited. Their happiness lay in discussions between the two of them that led to East-West cultural exchange. However, Daisetz wrote that in the first fifteen years of their marriage "because of material obstacles, . . . we could not avoid spending time on other things." The "other things" probably refers to Daisetz's jobs as an English instructor at Gakushuin and Otani University. He wrote that Beatrice was constantly harping on her dissatisfaction with this obligation.

Beatrice was in the midst of organizing her ten years of research on Shingon Buddhism when she fell ill. Daisetz was informed that Beatrice did not have long to live, but he could not bring himself to tell her directly. He wrote that "this was because of my own weakness, but it was also because I was so thoroughly familiar with what was in her deepest heart."

In the teachings of Mahayana Buddhism, what most deeply moved Beatrice's heart was the bodhisattva ideal. Beatrice was attracted to the great compassion of bodhisattvas who sought to save not only people, but even animals, plants, mountains, and rivers. Initially, because of her concern for protecting wildlife Daisetz didn't prune the trees in their garden. When the family moved from the Kantō region to Kyoto, Beatrice brought all of the trees she had planted in her garden with her. It is said that in her later years she particularly loved evening primrose. Daisetz's eulogy continues:

My late wife's character was serene both internally and externally and was without pretense. Whatever she felt inside she expressed externally. In our house, in particular, she acted just as her natural personality moved her to, so things went very well. Once she trusted a person she would believe that person implicitly; thus, she could not tell

45. Suzuki Biatorisu, *Shōren bukkyō shōkan.*
46. *SDZ* 35, 16–27. Originally published in Suzuki Biatorisu, *Shōren bukkyō shōkan.*

a white lie. She was somewhat reserved with people whom she knew only slightly, but at home, she was candid and forthright, and so there was no end to our discussions from morning until night. She had little or no interest in politics, but as far as current events were concerned, regardless of whether it was East or West, whenever she read domestic or foreign newspapers and journals, she never neglected to express her opinion. Now that she is gone, it is natural for a person to feel a lack in this area of life.[47]

Daisetz referred to a couple as being an inseparable unit, and he ended his eulogy by writing that now "only half was left, . . . I must resign myself to the fact that no part of my life will be complete, . . . but the time will come when we will be 'as one' again."

First Marriage

As Beatrice became weaker day by day, Alan did not rush his marriage to Nobu. In the end, Beatrice died without giving them her blessing. However, after the memorial service marking one hundred days following her death, Alan proceeded to marry Nobu on November 3. According to surviving Kubo family members, not a single person from the Suzuki family, including Daisetz, attended the ceremony, which the family of the bride naturally resented. The entry in the "Daisetz Diaries" for November 3, 1939, reads, "Home all day doing miscellaneous work." The letters and writings of Daisetz that have been made public contain hardly anything about Alan and Nobu's marriage. Outwardly, Daisetz seems to have ignored Alan's wedding completely. Some possible reasons for this are that the wedding came immediately on the heels of Beatrice's memorial service; his late wife had not approved of the marriage; and above all else, Daisetz himself did not approve. It is also possible that there was something about Nobu that displeased Daisetz.

Confronted with these facts, one cannot blame anyone for thinking that Daisetz was a terrible father who was not concerned with his son's happiness. Defenders of Daisetz would probably take the position that Daisetz, who devoted himself to thinking deeply on behalf of all humanity, naturally did not have time to waste on his worthless son. However, what was deemed

---

47. *SDZ* 35, 26.

perfectly natural for Daisetz and what may have been necessary to disseminate Japanese Zen throughout the world may have caused the deterioration of the father-son relationship.

Nevertheless, Daisetz did keep Alan's marriage in mind. In a letter to Iwakura Masaji dated October 22, the day of Beatrice's one-hundred-day memorial service, Daisetz wrote, "Regarding Masaru's marriage, an intermediary is necessary, so may I ask you to undertake this duty?"[48] Daisetz himself would not attend the ceremony, but delegated the job of serving as a liaison between the two families to Iwakura. So Daisetz did make some effort to fulfill his obligation to his son and the Kubo family. Whether Iwakura actually acted as an intermediary is unknown. Alan married Nobu in defiance of his parents, but this did not end his relationship with Daisetz. From the "Daisetz Diaries," one can discern that during the year 1940 Alan typed up Beatrice's posthumous works for Daisetz and took the corrected proofs to the publisher. Also, while the reasons are unclear, Alan visited Daisetz frequently.

On July 4, 1940, Daisetz adopted Suzuki Ichio, the fourth son of Suzuki Ryōkichi (Daisetz's nephew) and his wife Hatsuko, and Hayashida Kumino's younger brother, as he had promised. There is no record of the intention behind this adoption, so we are forced to speculate. It is likely that Daisetz, feeling that he did not know how much longer he had to live, thought that leaving his estate (which included a massive volume of valuable books and documents) to someone like Alan was unwise. At the time, Ichio was nineteen years old and a student at the Yokohama Higher Vocational School.

What sort of a person was Suzuki Ichio? His name appears in the nonfiction novel *Mutsu bakuchin* (The Explosion and Sinking of the Battleship *Mutsu*; 1970)[49] by the novelist Yoshimura Akira (1927–2006). On June 8, 1943, the *Mutsu*, which was on standby in the Port of Hiroshima, mysteriously exploded and sank. Fearing the effect that this could have on the war effort, the military covered up the incident. Ichio makes his appearance in the novel at that time as an assistant to the commanding officer in charge of the strictly classified salvage work, and who prevented a secondary disaster

48. Iwakura, *Shin'nin Suzuki Daisetsu*, 113. In a traditional Japanese marriage, a man and woman are brought together by a matchmaker or intermediary (*nakōdo*). Even in cases where it was not an arranged marriage, it was customary to ask the head of one's company, a colleague, or a relative (often a married couple) to serve as the intermediary in the wedding ceremony.

49. Yoshimura Akira, *Mutsu bakuchin* (Tokyo: Shinchō Bunko, 1979). Originally published in 1970.

by relying on his calm judgment. However, since the book is a nonfiction novel, it is impossible to tell how truthful it is.

In reality Ichio worked in the domain of shipbuilding. During the war, he was a technical officer at the Kure Naval Shipyard and later worked at Ishikawajima-Harima Heavy Industries Company (today's IHI Corporation). Yoshimura Akira described the actual Suzuki Ichio as a person with "gentle eyes and urban manners."[50] Thirty years after his adoption, Ichio described what it was like when Daisetz adopted him.

> For us in the Suzuki family, the word "Shōden-an" conveyed a special feeling. On one hand there was a sense of pressure from the most influential member of the Suzuki family, who supported the family of his nephew after it lost its primary means of support, not once failing to send them seventy yen a month for more than ten years. On the other hand it also conveyed awe and admiration. For utterly ordinary people like us, the atmosphere created by the peculiar smell—a combination of cats, Buddhist incense, and the refreshing fragrance of flowers; Okono, with her personality concentrated solely on sincere, diligent service; and Daisetz's way of living, which was a complete fusion of Meiji-period thinking and modern Western rationality, was rather strange.[51]

Although Ichio thought that the Suzuki family was not normal, there was probably no way for him to refuse being adopted by his great-uncle to whom he owed so much. Even so, Ichio did not use the opportunity of his adoption to live with Daisetz or study Buddhism. Since Ichio was planning to become an engineer, he probably harbored no intention of carrying on Daisetz's research.

To Shanghai

After marrying Nobu, Alan moved to a new home close to her family's residence in Shirokane-sankō-cho, Shiba-ku (present-day Shirokane, Minato-ku). After graduating from Doshisha University, Alan worked for the *Japan*

---

50. Yoshimura, *Mutsu bakuchin*, 99.

51. Suzuki Ichio, "Shōden-an no Daisetsu," in Hisamatsu et al., *Suzuki Daisetsu*, 418. Originally published in *Suzuki Daisetsu zenshū geppō* (November 1969).

Times newspaper and later, in 1942, went to work for the Dōmei News Agency.[52] In March of the following year, a daughter was born to the young couple. As for Daisetz, the long-awaited construction of the Matsugaoka Bunko began in April in the mountains behind the Tōkeiji temple in Kita-Kamakura, and in June, Suzuki Hatsuko and Kumino came to live at the Suzuki home in Kyoto to look after him. It appears that starting in the autumn of that year, Alan's visits to Daisetz ceased for a while.

Since Alan had married against his parents' wishes, Daisetz was probably worried about Kumino, who, for a time he had considered as a potential wife for Alan. He entreated her to marry one of his disciples and carry on the Suzuki name. Kumino's older brother Rei also pressured her to do as Daisetz asked. However, this backfired and awoke in Kumino a spirit of resistance, and she politely declined Daisetz's request. Her mother arranged a meeting between Kumino and Hayashida Sueo to discuss the potential of marriage, and they subsequently got married.[53]

Meanwhile, Japan's international situation was worsening day by day. Finally, on December 8, 1941 (Japan time), Japan entered into war with the United States and the UK. For Alan, who spoke English and looked like a Westerner, and for Daisetz as well, who had been married to an American and whose strengths included his ability to express himself in English, Japan had become a difficult place to live. In the midst of this situation, the Dōmei News Agency dispatched Alan to Shanghai. The entry in the "Daisetz Diaries" on October 17, 1942, records the sudden news.

> The morning writing was broken up by Alan's visit, quite an unexpected one as he failed to come now for more than a year I think. He is going to Shang-hai next week as carrespondent [*sic*] of Domei Press where he has been working since last January. Stayed to lunch, and afterward a visit together to the Tokeiji grounds. Left after tea.[54]

Did father and son discuss the birth of Alan's daughter or his work at the Dōmei News Agency and the like? In any case, in the diaries and letters that have been made public, Daisetz does not mention his first grandchild on this occasion or any subsequent time.

---

52. *Asahi gurafu* (February 9, 1949): 15; Torii Hideharu, *Kokusaku tsūshinsha "Dōmei" no kōbō: Tsūshin kisha to sensō* (Tokyo: Kadensha, 2014), 729.

53. Hayashida, *Ōoji Suzuki Daisetsu kara no tegami*, 90–95.

54. *MBKN* 21, 126.

FOUR

"Tokyo Boogie-woogie"

Shanghai

Shanghai was a polyglot city, populated by people from myriad countries. The British were the first to build a settlement in the port city that had been opened at the end of the Opium War (1840–1842). They were followed by Americans, French, and people from nearly every country in Europe. The downtown streets were lined with cinemas, dance halls, and nightclubs, and at night the town reverberated with the sounds of jazz. The Japanese were late to settle in Shanghai, and at the beginning of the twentieth century were concentrated in the Hongkou district in the northern part of the International Settlement. The Japanese called it "The Devil's Capital": its public face was that of an international capital full of freedom that was not available in Japan, but its hidden face concealed opium dens and brothels. This was Shanghai's appeal. The Japanese military presence, however, made itself increasingly felt from the 1930s onward, and simultaneously with the attack on Pearl Harbor on December 8, 1941 (Japan time), the Japanese army placed the Shanghai International Settlement under its jurisdiction.

Alan and Nobu, with their six-month-old daughter, arrived in Shanghai in October 1942, almost a year after the Japanese military clampdown on American and British residents. According to the employee directory of the Dōmei News Agency, Alan and his family lived at the company dormitory, which was located at 580 Laobazi Lu (present-day Wujin Lu).[1] The main street, Haining Lu, filled with movie theaters, was one block south. For the cinema aficionado Alan, it must have been the perfect environment. In

---

1. Ariyama Teruo and Nishiyama Takesuke, eds., *Dōmei Tsūshinsha kankei shiryō*, vol. 10 (Tokyo: Kashiwa Shobō, 1999), 504.

Japan, all of the dance halls were shut down on October 31, 1940, but they remained active in the settlements, excluding the Hongkou district. There it was still possible to enjoy jazz, the music of the "enemy."[2]

Alan was employed in the English-language department of the Dōmei News Agency's China Office. The Dōmei News Agency was a wire service that existed from January 1936 to October 1945. It was formed as a matter of state policy from a merger between the Nihon Dempō News Agency (present-day Dentsu) and the Shimbun Rengō News Agency, and had a monopoly on the acquisition of foreign communications and the distribution of news domestically. It had branch offices all over the world and was responsible for gathering local information and transmitting news from Japan. As a result, there were accusations that it was a propaganda organ of the militaristic nation of Japan. One important mission of the Dōmei News Agency was intercepting information about the enemy. In 1942, Reuters transmissions from London could not be intercepted in Tokyo, but it was possible in Shanghai. Valuable information from Reuters was intercepted in Shanghai and telegraphed to Tokyo.[3] Since he was employed in the English department, it is likely that Alan was engaged in this sort of work, but no details are available.

During his time in Shanghai, Alan had an important encounter that would change the course of his life. This was his meeting with Hattori Ryōichi (1907–1993), a composer (under exclusive contract with the record company Nippon Columbia), who wrote a number of hits during the period spanning the prewar and postwar years. Some of his representative tunes are "Soshū yakyoku" (Suzhou Serenade; 1940), "Tokyo Boogie-woogie" (1947), and "Aoi sanmyaku" (Blue Mountains; 1949). As a composer who personified one era in Japanese popular music, Hattori was posthumously awarded the People's Honor Award.[4] He was the founder of a musical family that spanned four generations, continuing with his son Hattori Katsuhisa (1936–2020; composer and arranger), his grandson Hattori Takayuki (1965–; composer and arranger), and great-granddaughter Hattori Mone (1999–; violinist). In June 1944, Hattori Ryōichi was assigned to the Shanghai Army

2. Ueda Ken'ichi, *Shanhai bugiugi 1945: Hattori Ryōichi no bōken* (Tokyo: Ongaku no Tomo Sha, 2003), 99–101.

3. Tsūshin Shashi Kankōkai, ed., *Tsūshin Shashi* (Tokyo: Tsūshin Shashi Kankōkai, 1958), 607–8.

4. An award from the prime minister of Japan in recognition of those who are widely loved and respected by the Japanese people and who have made outstanding contributions to giving society a more optimistic outlook.

Press Bureau and was given the task of putting together cultural productions involving music.

In May of the following year, Hattori composed the symphonic jazz piece *Yelaixiang Rhapsody* for the singer Li Xianglan (Yamaguchi Yoshiko; 1920– 2014) and the Shanghai Symphony, and conducted it himself, receiving great acclaim. This piece was Hattori's homage to *Rhapsody in Blue* (1924) by his idol, George Gershwin (1898–1937). Alan frequented the Shanghai Army Press Bureau where Hattori worked and became friends with him.[5] Since Alan was thoroughly enamored of the entertainment world, he may have been a frequent attendee at Hattori's concerts.

These last dying embers of Shanghai's splendor, however, were soon extinguished. The war ended on August 15, 1945, three months after the premier of *Yelaixiang Rhapsody*, and the Shanghai Settlement was returned to the Kuomintang government. The property of foreigners was confiscated, and Chinese who had cooperated with the Japanese were labeled *hanjian* (traitors) and arrested and executed. The Japanese in the settlements lived in fear of Chinese vengeance.

According to comparative musicologist Enomoto Yasuko (1968–), after the war was over, approximately seventy thousand Japanese residents were isolated in Hongkou, and a further twenty thousand were rounded up from Nanjing and Hangkou and taken there as well. The Kuomintang allowed the Japanese to govern themselves inside the Hongkou district, and with no restrictions on their activities, the black market flourished. Repatriation to Japan began in December 1945 and by May of the following year, almost all of the Japanese residents of Shanghai had been repatriated.[6] Hattori Ryōichi was demobilized in December 1945, and Yamaguchi Yoshiko, who had posed as a Chinese under the name Li Xianglan, narrowly escaped execution as a *hanjian* and returned to Japan in April 1946.

The Chinese Bureau of the Dōmei News Agency continued operations for a short time after the war was over. Repatriation of its employees began in December 1945 and was completed in July of the following year.[7] Alan and his family returned to Japan at the start of the repatriation. Since they moved back into their former residence in Shirokane-sankō-cho, it appears that the house escaped the air raids.

---

5. Hattori Ryōichi, *Boku no ongaku jinsei* (Tokyo: Chūō Bungeisha, 1982), 205–11, 223.

6. Enomoto Yasuko, *Shanhai: Takokuseki toshi no hyakunen* (Tokyo: Chūkō Shinsho, 2009), 257.

7. Tsūshin, *Tsūshin Shashi*, 651.

Reunion with Ike Mariko

Shortly after leaving Shanghai, Alan came to be involved with the editing of the new monthly English-language magazine *Spotlight*, which was founded in June 1946. The mission of *Spotlight* was to be an "impartial publication aimed to presenting the views of leading writers in Japan."[8] It was a magazine that featured everything from articles on politics, economics, and the war crime trials, to reviews introducing the beautiful actresses who graced the stage and the silver screen. Judging from the fact that the magazine was in English, it appears that the objective was to present the current situation in Japan to the Occupation authorities. The founder of the magazine, Suzuki Takeshi (ca. 1910–) married the actress Takamine Mieko (1918–1990) in October 1946 after Spotlight Publishing Company was established. Alan made his appearance in *Spotlight* as the guest editor for the combined October–November 1946 edition. On the editorial page of that issue, Alan introduced the economic theories of Nobu's father, Kubo Hisaji. The gist of his argument was that public works investment in the manufacturing sector was necessary to put Japan back on its feet.[9]

At about the same time, Alan began frequenting Nippon Columbia. Both Spotlight and Columbia were located in the building that housed the main office of the old Toyo Takushoku Company. Alan was probably looking for work, using the connection with Hattori Ryōichi that he had cultivated during his time in Shanghai. It is also possible that he was interested in the pretty women who frequented the headquarters of this record company.

According to associates of Ike Mariko, Alan reconnected with Mariko in December 1945. Alan saw a woman who looked familiar in the hall at the Columbia office, and it was Ike Mariko. Turning around at the sound of a familiar voice calling her name, she saw that it was her old English tutor, Alan. They had a pleasant chat in Kyoto dialect about what each of them had been doing over the last eight years after they went their separate ways. After the Higashiyama Dance Hall was shuttered in 1940, Mariko was sent all around Japan and its settlements on condolence calls, first for the Japanese army during the war and then serving the Occupation forces after the war. After their chance meeting at Nippon Columbia, Alan and Mariko started seeing each other occasionally. Then, in March 1946, her song "Ai no suingu" (Swinging Love) became a huge hit, solidifying her position as the "Queen of Swing."

8. *Spotlight* 1: 1 (1946): 1.
9. Alan M. Suzuki, "Editorial Page," *Spotlight* 1: 5–6 (1946): 14.

In the December 1946 edition of *Spotlight*, Alan introduced Mariko in the feature "The Spotlight Album of Beauty."[10] Under his byline and with great enthusiasm, Alan wrote about her life, describing the first time he heard Mariko sing "St. Louis Blues" at the Higashiyama Dance Hall and her time with the Takarazuka Review. He also included details about her personal history, episodes with her family, and the fact that during the war she was unable to listen to the Western music that she loved. If Mariko had been able to read English, she would no doubt would have sensed Alan's feelings toward her.

Since it was a magazine that got started in the chaos following the war, we do not know how long it lasted. Judging from the issues that are extant, the only occasion on which Alan's name appears is the issue where he was the guest editor and introduced Ike Mariko. Alan and *Spotlight* did not have a deep relationship. I cannot help but think that Alan may have used news gathering for the magazine as a way to get close to Mariko. By that time, Alan had probably already forgotten about his wife and child.

"Tokyo Boogie-woogie" Is Born

After the end of the war, the Japanese popular music industry got off to a fresh start. Jazz and dance halls, which had been banned during the war, came back to life. The industry tried to bring back entertainment to the Japanese, who were living in a burned-out wasteland, and also provide diversion for the Occupation forces.

At this juncture, Kasagi Shizuko (1914–1985), who had been Nippon Columbia's marquee singer before the war, was leading a twilight existence, having been left with a child born soon after the death of her lover Yoshimoto Eisuke (ca. 1923–1947). Hattori Ryōichi was trying to engineer a comeback for Kasagi and wanted to write a happy song that would buoy people's spirits, thinking that "it might give the Japanese, who were mourning over Japan's defeat, the power and vitality we need for the future."[11]

As Hattori was pondering the issue of what constituted a bright, snappy tune, the boogie rhythm that he had used for test recordings before the war flashed through his mind. The melody suddenly came to Hattori as he was riding home one night on the Chūō Line and saw the swinging of the leather

10. A. M. Suzuki, "The Spotlight Album of Beauty: Mariko Ike, Moonlight and Roses," *Spotlight* 1: 7 (1946): 18–19, 30–31.

11. Hattori, *Boku no ongaku jinsei*, 221.

hand straps suspended from the ceiling. When the train stopped at Nishi-Ogikubo station, he rushed off the train into a coffee shop and wrote the melody down on a napkin before he forgot it. The tune for "Tokyo Boogie-woogie" was born.

Thinking that "for this new rhythm, a new lyricist with no preconceptions would be best,"[12] Hattori approached Alan, his friend from Shanghai days whom he regarded as a "literary youth." Hattori played the melody for Alan on the piano several times and said: "Since it's got this sort of dynamic rhythm, I need a snappy rhyme rather than lyrics that have any particular meaning. If you get stuck on the words, just keep repeating something along the lines of 'Tokyo Boogie-woogie, rhythm happy, happy.'"[13]

Alan leaped at the opportunity that Hattori was giving to him; however, he could not read music. Therefore Alan enlisted Mariko's aid: she played the piano and he tried to conjure up all sorts of lyrics that fit the tune. A few days later, upon seeing the lyrics Alan had come up with, Hattori was not too pleased: "Let's dance together / around the pond / Tokyo Boogie-woogie / a sweet love song." It was then that Hattori knew that Alan was head over heels in love with Ike Mariko.[14] Hattori did not like the lyrics, but the deadline for recording was approaching fast, so he got rid of "Let's dance together around the pond" and worked together with Alan to complete the words to the song.[15]

Thus "Tokyo Boogie-woogie" was presented as having music composed by Hattori Ryōichi and lyrics by Masaru Suzuki. Considering Hattori's reminiscence already cited, we cannot say that Alan was solely responsible for the lyrics. There is no way of knowing for sure to what extent Alan's original lyrics were changed as a result of his dialogue with Hattori; however, it seems clear that they reached an agreement to credit Masaru Suzuki as the lyricist.

"Tokyo Boogie-woogie" was recorded on September 10, 1947. Around the time the recording session was to start, American soldiers, some of whom were at the Occupation Forces Club for noncommissioned officers located next to the Toyo Takushoku (Oriental Development Company) Building, where the Nippon Columbia offices were located, started showing up at the studio in droves. The soldiers came because Alan had put out an announce-

12. Hattori, *Boku no ongaku jinsei*, 224.
13. Hattori, *Boku no ongaku jinsei*, 224.
14. The surname "Ike" means "pond."
15. Hattori, *Boku no ongaku jinsei*, 224–25.

ment about the recording session, but the number was far more than he expected, so that Alan was both pleased and embarrassed. It would not do to send them all away, so Hattori and Kasagi decided to go ahead with recording in front of the crowd of somewhat inebriated noncommissioned officers. The soldiers, who had been somewhat noisy up to that point, suddenly became silent once the performance began and started to sway back and forth in time with the music. Once the all-clear was given, they broke into loud cheers. They brought beer and chocolate from the officer's club, and a big celebration ensued with everyone singing the "Tokyo Boogie-woogie." Hattori and Alan savored the joy of knowing that the Americans had also understood the lyrics to the song.[16]

"Tokyo Boogie-woogie" (Music: Hattori Ryōichi, Lyrics: Masaru Suzuki, Singer: Kasagi Shizuko)

Tokyo boogie-woogie, rhythm happy happy
My heart thump thump, my heart giddy, giddy
It's the Tokyo boogie-woogie echoing across the sea
The boogie dance is the whole world's dance
Your dream and mine, that song
Whistle that tune, love and the boogie melody
Let's dance to the song for burning hearts
And the voice of sweet love
Dance with me tonight, under the moon
Tokyo boogie-woogie, rhythm happy happy
My heart thump thump, my heart giddy, giddy
The song of the century, the song of the heart.
Tokyo boogie-woogie, hey!

Let's boogie-woogie, beat that drum
Let's dance and sing like crazy
You and me and that cool Tokyo boogie-woogie
When we dance the boogie, the world is one
The same rhythm and the same melody
Clap to the beat and sing that boogie melody
Let's dance to the song for burning hearts
And the voice of sweet love

16. Hattori, *Boku no ongaku jinsei*, 225–27.

Dance with me tonight, under a shower of stars
Tokyo boogie-woogie, rhythm happy happy
My heart thump thump, my heart giddy, giddy
The world's song, a happy song, Tokyo boogie-woogie
Boogie-woogie, a cheerful song, Tokyo boogie-woogie
Boogie-woogie, the song of the century, sing and dance, boogie-
    woogie.

What deserves attention is the section in the second stanza that goes: "When we dance the boogie, the world is one / The same rhythm and the same melody." I think this is the heart of the song's message. These words do not fit Hattori's instructions for a "snappy rhyme,"[17] so there is a strong possibility that they are Alan's creation.

It was Daisetz's wish that the cultures of the East and the West would come to a mutual understanding. In order to accomplish that, Daisetz piled theories one on top of the other and discussed the cultures of the East and the West in the context of complete binary opposition. Alan's lyrics also sing of the fusion of cultures. In contrast to Daisetz, however, who was extremely long-winded, Alan simply said, "The world is one" and "Dance with me." Their styles were completely opposite, but the messages of father and son resonate with one another.

The "Tokyo Boogie-woogie" sung by Kasagi Shizuko went on sale in January 1948. In live performances, Kasagi would dance vigorously, using the whole stage, and at the end of the song she would let out a resound-ing "Yaahh!" that came straight from the depths of her diaphragm as she ran offstage.[18] Aided by Kasagi's performance, "Tokyo Boogie-woogie" was a phenomenal smash hit. Even today, its fame as a popular Japanese song representing the immediate postwar era is unshakable.

Which message reached the hearts of the Japanese people and which is remembered: Daisetz's Zen or Alan's "Tokyo Boogie-woogie"? On this point, in their home country of Japan, Daisetz is no match for Alan. Learned religious scholars and philosophers can laughingly dismiss popular songs as worthless, but that does not alter the facts in the slightest.

What did Daisetz think of his son's enormous success? The answer is

---

17. Hattori, *Boku no ongaku jinsei*, 224.

18. Kasagi's performance has been uploaded to YouTube. These clips are the extractions from a film *Haru no kyōen*, directed by Yamamoto Kajirō (1948); https://www.youtube.com/watch?v=_qXfgP8U1Mo

he ignored it almost completely. Looking through the materials that had been made public at the time this book was written, there is not a single mention of "Tokyo Boogie-woogie" in essays, diaries, or letters written by Daisetz. For Daisetz, who was totally immersed in Zen, popular music was simply not something he paid any attention to. However, there is one piece he wrote that touches upon this. In 1951, he contributed a short essay to the magazine *Sengenrei* titled "Uta o tsukutte sukuwareruka?" (Can One Be Saved by Writing Songs?). An excerpt:

> Regarding the question, can one be saved by writing just one song, religiously and scientifically, one can be saved. In art and all other things as well, one can be saved. However, there is the issue of *issekigan* (discerning eye). Without that, it is useless. If one has a discerning eye, one can be saved even just by hearing the sound of the rain. Taking art as an example, if someone who devotes his life entirely to art has an awareness and consciousness of the workings of the wisdom of the Buddha (one can also call this the will of God), whatever they do is fine. Looking at things with that awareness—that is *issekigan*.[19]

It all sounds very complicated. In dictionaries, *issekigan* is defined as "a special kind of discernment that has the power to perceive the nature of things. Superior insight." Perhaps what Daisetz means here is simply, "Whatever one is doing, writing a song or something else, one must have superior insight." Daisetz must have known that Alan had published some sort of song. This essay was directed at Alan. What Daisetz was saying to his son is, "I have heard that you have written lyrics that say 'Just sing, just dance.' What sort of insight could something like that possibly have?"

Second Marriage

Alan and Hattori Ryōichi had actually collaborated on writing songs before "Tokyo Boogie-Woogie." Taking their inspiration from the popular novel *Tokyo Romance* (1946)[20] by Earnest Hoberecht (1918–1998), Tokyo correspondent of the United Press, Alan wrote lyrics using the same title, Hat-

19. *SDZ* 35, 198–99. Originally published in *Sengenrei* 11 (1951).
20. Hōburaito Ānesuto, *Tokyo romansu*, trans. Ōkubo Yasuo (Tokyo: Kobarutosha, 1946). The English edition is Earnest Hoberecht, *Tokyo Romance* (New York: Didier, [1947]).

tori composed the music, and it was recorded in 1947 with Ike Mariko as the singer. *Tokyo Romance* told the story of a love affair between a foreign newspaper correspondent and a Japanese woman, and was the first postwar novel written by a non-Japanese with postwar Japan as the setting. The lyrics, however, were not credited to Alan but to the better-known Hoberecht.

We do not know whether Hoberecht and Alan first met each other at the time the song was recorded, whether they had a prior relationship, or whether they ever got together again afterward. Hoberecht was a handsome man; there is an anecdote about him in which he visited a movie set and instructed the popular actress Mimura Hideko (dates unknown) on how to kiss, causing her to faint. Alan and a man like that would probably have gotten along quite well. In July 1947, Hoberecht published the book *Ladies and Gentlemen: Democratic Etiquette* (1948),[21] directed at a Japanese audience. Alan did the Japanese translation, using his pen name, "Victor Bellwood."[22] From 1947 until 1948, in addition to this sort of work, Alan translated English-language magazine articles and English conversation course materials. In the "English Conversation Class" article published in the November 1, 1947, issue of the magazine *Keikō* under the name Victor Bellwood, Alan wrote: "Concerning English, it goes without saying that for those of you who have already had even a bit of contact with the Occupation forces, or have overheard their incomprehensible speech in passing them on the street, you can understand that English is not what you have read in your readers or studied via literary texts."[23] Many of the readers no doubt agreed with Alan's opinion.

Through his work on "Tokyo Romance" and "Tokyo Boogie-Woogie," Alan became closer to Ike Mariko and proposed marriage. According to those close to her, Alan lied, telling her that he had divorced his previous wife. Although Alan was estranged from Nobu, she was still listed in the family register as his wife. Their mutually agreed-upon divorce was not finalized until after the wedding ceremony of Alan and Mariko.

Mariko was seeing an employee of Nippon Columbia at the time of Alan's proposal. The man told Mariko that he was single, but in actuality,

---

21. Hōburaito, Ānesuto, *Shukujo to shinshi: Demokuratikku etiketto*, trans. Vikutā Beluwuddo (Tokyo: Rajio Shinbunsha, 1948). The original title is *Democratic Etiquette*.

22. This name is a play on Alan's Japanese name: "Masaru" is written with the Japanese character for "victory," and "Suzuki" is composed of two characters: *suzu*, meaning a kind of bell, and *ki*, or "wood."

23. Vikutā Beruwuddo, "Eigo kaiwa kōza dai 2 kō: Beigo no rekishi," *Keikō* 22 (1947): 7–8.

he had a wife and children. He said that he was going to get a divorce, but Mariko's grandmother persuaded Mariko to drop him, threatening to throw herself into the Lake Biwa Canal if Mariko stole a man away from his wife and children. Mariko broke up with him and accepted Alan's proposal on the condition she be allowed to continue her career as a singer. Of course Mariko's grandmother probably did not know that Alan also had a wife and a child. Moreover, it is highly likely that up until around the time of the wedding, Mariko was not aware that Nobu was still registered as Alan's wife. Mariko did not find out until after the wedding that Alan was adopted rather than being Daisetz's biological child. As far as Mariko was concerned, however, that was of no consequence.

Having decided to marry Alan, Mariko went with him to visit Daisetz in Kita-Kamakura. However, at the entrance to Shōden-an, they were met by the maid Okono, who greeted them coldly, saying: "Is your new girlfriend a singer? If you have a child, will she carry him piggy-back and sing him a song?" Mariko took much pride in being a popular singer, and she indignantly returned to Tokyo without meeting Daisetz. According to the "Daisetz Diaries," after a change of heart Alan and Mariko went to see Daisetz again, on May 26, 1948. It was at that time that Mariko became aware that Daisetz was a scholar rather than a priest.

There is an unexpected common point shared by Daisetz and Mariko: they both lived at a sub-temple of Tōfukuji in Kyoto at the same time. Perhaps it was fortunate that, unlike Nobu, whose intelligence was above average, Mariko came from an entirely different background than Daisetz. Doing a 180-degree turn from when Alan married Nobu, Daisetz welcomed Mariko with open arms. Alan had brought Nobu to meet Daisetz just after causing a scandal by getting another girl pregnant, so Daisetz had a reason for opposing the match. Daisetz would undoubtedly have opposed this match as well had he known that Alan's divorce from Nobu was not yet final. Alan had probably lied to Daisetz as well and told him that he had broken cleanly from Nobu.

Okono had been inhospitable when they first met, but now she began to look after Mariko, doing things like helping to search for a future new home for her and Alan near Engakuji. Unfortunately, Okono became ill in June and died on July 2 from acute pneumonia.[24] Daisetz and Alan must have been devastated by Okono's death, for she had served them for many years. In a letter to Kobori Sōhaku (Nanrei) of Ryōkō-in at the Daitokuji temple

---

24. Kusunoki Kyō, "Okono-san no tsuioku," 392.

dated August 7, Daisetz gave voice to his grief, saying: "When I think about it, I'm no longer certain that getting old is a good thing. My friends are dead, my wife is dead, the person who took care of me is dead. . . . Dear old Okono, she used to laugh a lot. That's what life is made of: all these trivial things piled one atop the other."[25]

In October 1948, Daisetz left the home in Kyoto where he had shared so many memories with Beatrice and Alan and returned it to Ataka Yakichi. From then on, Daisetz made the Shōden-an and the Matsugaoka Bunko in Kita-Kamakura his primary residence. His books and two large trunks of old letters from Kyoto were transported to the Shōden-an, but it is said that Furuta Shōkin burned most of the letters under orders from Daisetz. However, Furuta secretly kept the important letters,[26] which have been preserved to the present day as valuable research material. I owe a great debt to the publication of these letters for this book project.

On November 21, 1948, Asahina Sōgen officiated at Alan and Mariko's grand wedding ceremony, which took place in the Abbot's quarters of the Engakuji temple. Since the bride and groom were both involved in show business, many figures from the entertainment world, such as the famous actress Takamine Mieko, were invited. Reporters also flocked to the ceremony. The scholar of Japanese cinema Donald Richie (1924–2013), who had been invited to the wedding, said that the ostentatious ceremony with its loud music echoing through the temple grounds "made me angry."[27]

It appears that Alan and Mariko's marriage deeply moved Daisetz. In 1949, Daisetz published an essay entitled "Waga ko no kekkon" (My Son's Marriage) in the magazine *Fujin seikatsu* (Women's Life).[28]

I am eighty years old this year and "a grain of seed" (*hitotsubudane*) of mine, Masaru, married Ike Mariko, who is also "a grain of seed." They both wanted to marry, and since they can both make their own way in the world, I thought, fine, so I agreed to it. I am not concerned with whether or not Mariko is in the family register or the fact that she is a singer. So long as the two of them work things out for themselves, everything will be fine.

25. *SDZ* 37, 196–97.

26. Furuta Shōkin, "Ohimareru kotodomo," in Hisamatsu et al., *Suzuki Daisetsu,* 301. Originally published in *Suzuki Daisetsu zenshū geppō* (July 1971).

27. Hokkoku Shinbunsha Henshūkyoku, ed., *Zen: Suzuki Daisetsu botsugo 40 nen* (Kanazawa: Hokkoku Shinbunsha, 2006), 120.

28. *SDZ* 33, 323–36. Originally published in Suzuki Daisetsu, "Wagako no kekkon," *Fujin seikatsu* 3: 3 (1949).

Mariko is a songstress and is at the top of her field, and Masaru went to college in the United States and has been working with foreigners since his return, so I think that he knows what he is doing.[29]

Daisetz described Alan as his "grain of seed." One can read this as meaning that Daisetz continued to act as though Alan was his biological, rather than his adopted, child and that he still loved Alan as a parent. Daisetz also recognized Mariko's abilities as a singer. On the other hand, while Daisetz said that "Masaru went to college in the United States," in actuality Alan was never an exchange student. Daisetz probably just used the words to describe the fact that Alan had gone to the United States as a representative of the Japan-America Students Conference.

Mariko was delighted with having Daisetz as a father-in-law. Because her father had died when she was young, Mariko had no one she could call "father" for a long time. As his daughter-in-law, Mariko offered to help Daisetz, filling the gap caused by Okono's death. In order to do this, she began to turn down jobs that would take her to the provinces. For Daisetz, who had been traveling back and forth between Shōden-an and the Matsugaoka Bunko (established in 1942 with the support of Ataka Yakichi and located about 650 meters away from the Shōden-an), having a young daughter-in-law close by must have been a great help. Alan's marriage made Daisetz very happy, and Alan said that he would strive to make Mariko happy and do his best to put his father's mind at ease.

According to those close to her, when the three of them traveled to Kanazawa to visit the Suzuki family crypt, Mariko, seeing how solicitous Alan was of his father's feelings, thought to herself that he was a dutiful son. Daisetz gave Mariko a shawl that had been a keepsake of Beatrice's as well as some furniture. Mariko used the shawl to make a stage costume. Alan and Mariko called each other *ossan* and *obahan*, literally "uncle" and "aunt" but used to refer to middle-aged persons, and were the picture of happily married newlyweds.

Alan's work was going well. In databases of the National Diet Library of Japan and the Japanese Society for Rights of Authors, Composers and Publishers (JASRAC), one can find a number of popular songs from this time that are registered with Alan as the lyricist: "Kikyoraifu" (Going Home; music: Yamazaki Hachirō), "Sayonawa warutsu" (Goodbye Waltz; music: Reimondo Hattori; 1949), "Suingu musume" (Swing Girl; music: Hirakawa Hideo; 1950), "Bugi kakuteru" (Boogie Cocktail; music: Hattori Ryōichi),

---

29. *SDZ* 33, 323.

"Bugi kantāta" (Boogie Cantata; music: Hattori Ryōichi), and "Bésame Mucho" (music: Consuelo Velázquez; 1950). Among these, "Goodbye Waltz" and "Swing Girl" feature Ike Mariko as the singer. "Boogie Cocktail" and "Boogie Cantata" were probably reworkings of "Tokyo Boogie-woogie."

As for books, the Kyokutō Gakugei Tsūshin Shuppansha, which Alan himself was involved in founding, published his translation of *Amerikashiki kaseihō* (How to Run an American Household) in 1948.[30] In December of the next year, Alan's translation of *Baseball for Everyone* (1948) by the major leaguer Joe DiMaggio (1914–1999) was published under the name of Victor Bellwood.[31] The former was written by a Japanese and was a collection of instructions for women who were going to be working as maids for families of the Occupation forces; Alan supplied the side-by-side translation. The latter was an introduction to baseball written by a famous player for the New York Yankees that explains in simple prose how to enjoy baseball, concentrating on the role of each defensive position and the fundamentals of pitching, hitting, and running.

Blessed with work, from all appearances everything was smooth sailing for the newlyweds. The February 9, 1949, issue of the magazine *Asahi gurafu* (Asahi Graph), featuring popular songwriters, included a photo of Masaru Suzuki as the lyricist of "Tokyo Boogie-woogie" together with his wife Ike Mariko (fig. 4). Since they both appear to be relaxed and happy, from this picture it is hard to imagine that their happiness was about to come crashing down.

Alan's Drinking

Alan's work was going well. In normal circumstances, he was a handsome man with a gentle personality who was gallant toward women. However, he was notorious for his drinking habits. He had an office in Akasaka, and everyday he would drink late into the night with his office mates and then take the last train home to Kita-Kamakura. When their schedules coincided, Mariko would accompany Alan home. It was his habit always to take the last train, and the return trip would be noisy and lively as he would dis-

---

30. Kyokutō Gakugei Tsūshin Shuppansha, ed., *Amerikashiki kaseihō* (Tokyo: Kyokutō Gakugei Tsūshin Shuppansha, 1948).

31. Deimajio, Jō, *Hyakuman-nin no yakyū*, trans. Bikutā Beruwuddo (Tokyo: Hōmu Jānarusha, 1949). (Translation of Joe DiMaggio, *Baseball for Everyone: A Treasury of Baseball Lore and Instruction for Fans and Players* [New York: Whittlesey House, 1948].)

Fig. 4. The newlyweds
Alan and Mariko.
Source: *Asahi gurafu*
(February 9, 1949): 15.

cuss music and trade risqué stories with the riders he befriended on the
train. When Alan did not return home after the arrival time of the last train
had passed, Mariko often would find him asleep in the bamboo grove at
Engakuji. When Alan drank, he would quarrel over trifling matters, and
when drunk he would become violent, doing things like upsetting dinner
trays in front of Nippon Columbia VIPs and throwing a desk out of the
second-story window of his house. According to those close to Mariko, however, he would remember nothing the next day. Those who knew Alan all
said that even though he threw things, he never attacked anyone. Was he
able to control his actions even when he was dead drunk because his sober
self was somewhere inside?

Around this time Daisetz wrote two essays concerning drunkenness. It
is not stated whom he is writing about, but I think it is safe to say that he
was referring to Alan. The first essay is titled "Yopparai to shinjū to shūkyō"
(Drunkenness, Double Suicides, and Religion). It is unclear where the essay
first appeared, but it is included in *Zen: Zuihitsu* (Zen Essays; 1927).[32]

Among my acquaintances there is a man who knows and enjoys
liquor. Usually he is a very timid man, afraid of everything. He is
a truly gentle and exemplary (?) person. When he drinks, however,

---

32. Suzuki Daisetsu, "Yopparai to shinjū to shūkyō," repr. in Suzuki, *Zen. SDZ* 19, 563–
70.

he suddenly changes. When he reaches this state, his true nature is revealed in all its glory. Freed by drinking, an uninhibited being appears. A well-mannered man who was content to dwell humbly in the prison he had made for himself all of a sudden metamorphoses into a person with no limits. So long as he has no demonic or evil nature, bystanders go along with him. First of all, he transcends the duality of self and other; that is, he is free in space. He is not bound by time; the clock may tick off a minute or two minutes or up to an hour or two hours, but he does not care. That is, he gets lazy. He does not care if he misses his train; he is freed from the limitations of time. Even if he is drunk, he will say that he is not. He does not think about tomorrow, and he forgets his debts. He forgets how to behave in front of his superiors, completely trampling morality, convention, and retribution under his feet. What is such a person if not one who is free and without limits? Has it not always been true that sentimental people and those who bear the burden of hard work day in and day out are lovers of drink? The yearning to be free from limits is religion; and if it is also art, drinking is religion itself, art itself.[33]

From the fact that Daisetz deliberately inserts a question mark in the sentence "He is a truly gentle and exemplary (?) person," it can be surmised that the person Daisetz is referring to is someone close to him. Overall, he is criticizing this person's drinking habits; however, Daisetz concludes that "drinking is religion itself." Opinions will probably differ as to whether this was sarcasm or his profound philosophy.

The second essay is entitled "Sakenomi" (The Drinker) and appeared in the February 1949 issue of the magazine *Kamakura* shortly after Alan and Mariko were married.[34] I want to quote a passage from this essay since it contains some vital information suggesting Daisetz wrote it with Alan in mind.

There is something I think about sometimes: there is no greater idiot than a drinker. First of all, he just wastes his time. Second, precious rice is wasted to make his drink. Third, since drinking confuses his spirit and shortens his natural lifespan, he ruins the life that should be devoted to being useful to society and thereby puts a burden on others. Fourth, he has an adverse spiritual effect on his descendants (it

33. *SDZ* 19, 564–65.
34. *SDZ* 33, 320–22. Originally published in *Kamakura* 8 (1949).

is said that this has not been sufficiently proven in a biological sense, but leaving academic proof aside, actual everyday experience seems to indicate that the descendants of heavy drinkers inherit something undesirable). Fifth, drinking destroys a person's respectability. Sixth, drinking puts a burden on his family. Seventh, his nature becomes perverse. When a man drinks, he usually goes in this direction, leaving everything else aside. I am sure some examples could still be given, but even if we leave it at that, suffice it to say that drinking leads to great harm. It is a great question whether there is anything good about it at all.[35]

There is no need to dwell on this, but I would like to make one comment. In point number four, Daisetz wrote: "actual everyday experience seems to indicate that the descendants of heavy drinkers inherit something undesirable." Daisetz seems to have heard that Alan's biological parent was a problematic drinker, since in a letter to Alan dated July 27, 1960, he wrote: "Your inebriety I am afraid goes back to your heredity."[36] There is a possibility that Daisetz knew something about the origins of Alan's birth parents that he never divulged to anyone.

Though it appears that Daisetz was being critical of drinking, he concluded his essay with the following ambiguous statement.

If you want to drink, go ahead and drink; if you want to babble incoherently, babble incoherently. And then if you just drop dead one day, who is to say that would be strange? And if you want to write songs, go ahead. If, when you raise your cup, "cherishing the anxiety of a hundred years," and free yourself from the prison of time and intellect, thus tasting eternity in the present, what is wrong with letting a person do whatever he wants?[37]

The last part seems a bit perfunctory. Daisetz appears to be saying: "Drunkards are no good. This is sad, and if it weren't for that, Alan would have been a good son. However, Alan is a grown man and I am old. Let him do whatever he wants."

35. *SDZ* 33, 320.
36. *SDZ* 39, 224.
37. *SDZ* 33, 322.

The Meeting with a Psychiatrist

In 1949, Nippon Columbia put forward the idea of making a movie out of the essay *Nagasaki no kane* (The Bells of Nagasaki) written by the doctor Nagai Takashi (1908–1951), who had been a victim of the atomic bombing of Nagasaki. Koseki Yūji (1909–1989) and Satō Hachirō (1903–1973) would write the music and lyrics for the theme song, respectively, and Mariko would be the singer. Mariko accordingly put "The Bells of Nagasaki" into her repertoire and sang it on stage in preparation for recording. The intermediary for the film production was Shikiba Ryūzaburō (1898–1965), a psychiatrist and art critic who was friends with Nagai. Nagai was undergoing treatment, and when there were sudden changes in his condition, Mariko and Alan would go to Nagasaki with Shikiba to visit him. During this process, their relationship with Shikiba deepened. Since the lyrics of "The Bells of Nagasaki" are written from a man's viewpoint, in the end, the well-known popular singer Fujiyama Ichirō (1911–1993) was selected to do the recording. The resulting record was a smash hit. Even though Mariko was not able to be the singer for "The Bells of Nagasaki," meeting Shikiba turned out to be a fateful event that changed her life.

Shikiba Ryūzaburō was well versed in Western art. Not only he was famous as the psychiatrist who first noticed the talent of the outsider artist Yamashita Kiyoshi (1922–1971), he was also a leader in the campaign for sex education and birth control. His career alone was enough to attract Alan's interest. On top of that, Ryūzaburō had a beautiful daughter named Mikako, who was fluent in both English and French and was actively translating and publishing books on American etiquette. Mariko's becoming close with her supporter Ryūzaburō had the unfortunate result of bringing Alan and Mikako together, even thought Mikako was already married.

The March 1, 1948, issue of the magazine *Shufu to seikatsu* (Housewives and Life) features a roundtable talk called "Meiokusama bakari de kataru enman kokoroe uchiake kai" (Accomplished Wives Reveal Their Secrets for Harmony in the Home). In the article, Mikako discussed something that gives us a glimpse of her view of men.

> I am entering my fifth year of marriage, but I have decided that I want to have an ideal. As humans, men have something that is all their own and a certain manliness. I want a man who, for example,

projects an air of sophistication and breeding but is never ostentatious about it, a man who can lead his wife firmly, but not force her, as has been the way up to now.[38]

It is obvious that Mikako was dissatisfied with her husband. Her words give the strong impression that if a more attractive man were to make his appearance, she might immediately shift her feelings to him. Mikako would meet Alan about two years later.

In November 1949, Daisetz was awarded the Order of Culture in recognition of his contributions from the long years of his research into Zen. At the time of the presentation ceremony, Daisetz was participating in a conference in Hawaii and was unable to attend. Other honorees that year included the Kabuki actor Onoe Kikugorō VI (1885–1949), the historian Tsuda Sōkichi (1873–1961), and the novelists Tanizaki Jun'ichirō and Shiga Naoya (1883–1971). Daisetz was also recognized as a Person of Cultural Merit in 1951. He used all of the stipends from his awards for the Matsugaoka Bunko.

The year after Daisetz was awarded the Order of Culture, the Ike Mariko Supporter's Association was founded as a result of Alan's efforts. Shikiba Ryūzaburō was the chairman, and Daisetz was named as a founding member. In 1950, Mariko recorded the song "Sentimental Journey." The theme song from the American film *The Paleface* (1948) was to be on the B side of the record, and Alan was given the job of translating the lyrics. The record went on sale from Nippon Columbia in June and the B-side song, "Buttons and Bows," became a big hit. In 1950, Alan also translated the lyrics for the Mexican song "Bésame Mucho," sung by Kuroki Yōko (1921–1959).

With the establishment of Mariko's support group and a string of hits, things were going swimmingly for Mariko and Alan. Toward the end of 1950, Mariko realized she was pregnant, and in June of the following year she gave birth to a daughter. Alan and Mariko asked Daisetz to be the godfather, and Daisetz named her Maya after the mother of the Buddha. Upon recovering from the birth, Mariko went back to singing. Now a mother, she felt that it would lead to the opening of new frontiers in her art.

---

38. "Meiokusama bakari de kataru enman kokoroe uchiake kai," *Shufu to seikatsu* (March 1, 1948): 36.

A Sudden Parting

One day, Mariko heard a disturbing rumor about her husband.[39] Someone saw Alan go into the Tokyo Imperial Hotel, the most prestigious accommodation in Tokyo, accompanied by a foreign-looking woman in a fur coat. When Mariko asked Alan about it, he told her it was Shikiba Mikako. Alan explained himself by saying that he and Mikako were working together. Mariko completely believed Alan's story and, so placated, replied how nice it was that he had found a good colleague. Being busy with her own career, Mariko had been paying less and less attention to her husband. Alan set up an office in the Sanshin Building in Yūrakuchō and began to work on translations with Mikako as his partner. After the war, the Sanshin Building was used as living quarters for noncommissioned officers in the Occupation forces, but it was derequisitioned in June 1950. Alan moved in as a tenant, though Mariko did not have a clear idea what he was doing there.

Among Daisetz's letters from this period, there are some that ask Alan to serve as a guide and interpreter for Cornelius Crane (1905–1962) and another foreign visitor[40] and others refusing Alan's requests to borrow money.[41] Daisetz trusted Alan's abilities as an interpreter. As for Alan, he wanted to be able to rely on Daisetz for financial support, but Daisetz resisted lending him money. On the other hand, Daisetz continued to provide monetary assistance to his relatives and those close to him, which must have been a source of discontent for Alan.

Alan and Mariko's marriage was officially entered into the family register on November 20, 1951. The certificate of Maya's birth was submitted on the same day, giving the impression that registering the marriage was unavoidable when finally submitting the birth certificate, five months after Maya was born.

At the end of that year, Alan left the house in Kita-Kamakura, saying he had to go out and buy stamps for New Year's cards, but when evening came, he still had not returned. With a six-month-old baby in her care, Mariko spent an uneasy New Year. Later, she learned that a friend of hers had discovered that Alan was living in a hotel with a woman. On January 3, 1952,

---

39. The information in the succeeding account is all from personal interviews with people close to Ike Mariko that took place several times between July 2010 and November 2014.

40. *SDZ* 37, 305. Cornelius Crane was an American philanthropist who supported Daisetz's lecture at Columbia University in the 1950s. See Richard M. Jaffe, "D.T. Suzuki and the Two Cranes: American Philanthropy and Suzuki's Global Agenda," *MBKN* 32 (2018): 29–58.

41. *SDZ* 37, 314.

Mariko took part in the second annual NHK Kōhaku Uta Gassen (Red and White Singing Contest) television special.[42] However, the sleepless nights caused by her anxiety prevented her from singing at her best.

A month passed, but Alan still did not return home. One day while Mariko was out, Alan and Mikako showed up at the house and removed all of the furniture and household goods. Mariko sent Alan letter after letter asking what she had done wrong and begging for a meeting. She finally received a reply in the third month after Alan had left, and a meeting with Alan in Ginza was arranged. Mariko went to the restaurant where the meeting was to take place, accompanied by her cousin's husband, but Alan was not there. Instead of Alan, Shikiba Ryūzaburō and Mikako were waiting. Ryūzaburō said that he was sorry that his daughter had stolen Mariko's husband from her, but seeing as how they were both adults, there was nothing that he could do as a parent. Mariko begged Mikako to give Alan back to her, but Mikako retorted that if he had been so important, she should have kept him tied up. Ryūzaburō offered to adopt Maya, but Mariko said that she would raise Maya herself, even if she had to become a prostitute to do it. Mariko felt sorry for her daughter, who was now bereft of one of her parents. She lost weight, and her milk production suffered. One day, she received an invoice demanding repayment of significant debts that Alan had incurred. She was astonished to see that the loan agreement listed the house as collateral and was signed with her signature and personal seal. Naturally, Mariko did not know anything about taking out such a loan.

Utterly ignorant of the situation to which he was returning, Daisetz came back to Japan for a temporary visit from his extended stay in the United States. Mariko went to see Daisetz and, in a flood of tears, told him what had happened over the last six months. Daisetz, who had been hopeful that Alan had finally settled down, was disappointed to learn about the collapse of their marriage. Daisetz comforted Mariko, telling her that Alan was no good after all and that she should part ways with him and that he was willing to adopt her as his daughter. According to the "Daisetz Diaries," Daisetz met with Alan numerous times from July to August 1952. While having him type up his manuscripts, he discussed Alan and Mariko's divorce. On August 24, Mariko visited Daisetz with her mother to discuss the divorce. Mariko had made up her mind to leave Alan. The September 12 entry in the "Daisetz Diaries" reads, "Alan house ownership transferred to me by paying his

---

42. A musical show that is very popular with Japanese people, taking place on December 31 each year and nationally broadcast by NHK. At this time, it was held in early January.

debt . . . ," making it clear that Daisetz had arranged to take care of Alan's debts. It was agreed that Mariko would receive a monthly childcare allowance from Alan; however, she did not demand any compensation money.

Daisetz's Anxiety

Daisetz left Japan again on September 14 for the United States. In a letter to Suzuki Rei dated September 21, he wrote: "Please let me know how Alan is getting along from time to time. And Mariko as well,"[43] showing he was worried about them. In a letter to Furuta Shōkin dated October 12, he wrote: "How is Ike Mariko doing?" and "I saw Shikiba-san over here for a while."[44]

Alan and Mariko's divorce was finalized in November. Mariko began to think about performing in the United States, which had been her dream since she was young. In a letter to Furuta Shōkin dated November 25, Daisetz wrote: "Regarding the [text redacted] issue, has he been working hard since then? I met Shikiba-san over here, but of course he didn't tell me anything. What about the plan for [text redacted] to come over here? Will [Nippon] Columbia come up with the money?"[45] The two redactions are by the editor of *The Complete Works of D.T. Suzuki, Expanded New Edition.* The first is probably "Alan," and the second is no doubt "Mariko." In a letter to Suzuki Ichio dated December 18, Daisetz wrote: "Is Alan standing firm? Drinking is the worst thing he can do, but if this is a psychological problem, in the end, this has something to do with something very fundamental."[46]

On January 2, 1953, Mariko appeared in the third annual NHK Red and White Singing Contest. There were some who said that her art had deepened after giving birth and then going through a divorce. Her dream of going to the United States had hit a snag over the acquisition of a passport. At that time it was not possible for Japanese to freely travel abroad. Mariko was hoping to be able to rely on Daisetz, who had since become an instructor at Columbia University in New York. She undoubtedly conferred with Daisetz about him serving as her guarantor there, and probably discussed finances as well. In a letter to Hayashida Kumino dated January 20, Daisetz

43. *SDZ* 37, 369.
44. *SDZ* 37, 373.
45. *SDZ* 37, 379.
46. *SDZ* 37, 381.

explained that he would be Mariko's guarantor but that he could not provide any funding: "Regarding Mariko's trip to America, I believe that my inviting her here is just for form's sake. I won't be able to provide any funds; Mariko will pay for everything. I'm sure she's doing quite well, but for myself, I'm just barely getting by."[47]

It appears that Alan had some sort of objection to Mariko going to the United States. In the entry in the "Daisetz Diaries" dated January 16, Daisetz wrote that he received a letter from Alan, the first since the previous summer and added, "Poor boy, very much upset over the aftermath of divorce." Later, in a letter to Furuta dated February 6, Daisetz wrote: "I heard that [text redacted] is very angry about [text redacted] going to the United States, but I hope he doesn't do anything stupid."[48] It is not unreasonable to read the first redaction as "Alan" and the second as "Mariko."

Shikiba Mikako was entered into Alan's family register in February 1953. They had a perfunctory wedding ceremony; Hattori Ryōichi was invited to attend, but he refused. It is not known when or in what manner Mikako separated from her previous husband. She had had a son with her first husband, but there is nothing to indicate that Mikako's son lived with her and Alan. It appears that they lived by themselves.

In letters from the United States dated April and May, Daisetz expressed concern about what had been happening with Alan after the divorce and about Mariko's US trip. These sections are excerpted below.

> April 10: What's the news on Mariko's US trip? I heard that a wonder lasts but nine days; in any case, if Alan is sticking to the straight and narrow, that would be the best of all.[49]

> April 12: This brings the Alan affair to a conclusion; now, nothing would be better than for him to dedicate himself to his work. I pray that he does.[50]

> May 23: I have heard that Alan has been doing well. It is great news, and I hope that it continues indefinitely. If he keeps his drinking within limits and does not indulge in luxuries, he's a good person.[51]

47. *SDZ* 37, 384.
48. *SDZ* 37, 386.
49. *SDZ* 37, 393.
50. *SDZ* 37, 396.
51. *SDZ* 37, 403.

May 26: It appears that it will not be easy for Ike Mariko to get a passport. It goes without saying that she won't be able to get one before I travel to Europe; if she comes to the United States, it will probably be in the autumn.[52]

According to documents housed at Columbia University, Daisetz prepared certificates testifying to his status and income for the arrangements for his daughter-in-law's trip to the United States.[53] Despite Daisetz's efforts, Mariko's trip did not materialize and had to be postponed. In sum, the period from 1945 to 1953 was one in which Daisetz, Nobu, and Mariko were all victims of Alan's selfishness. In 1951, Nobu married an American she had met in Japan and went to America with her daughter and husband. She never saw Alan again and died in 2009 at the age of ninety-three. Mariko went on to establish an unshakable reputation as the "Queen of Swing" in the world of Japanese popular music.

52. *SDZ* 37, 404.

53. Letters between Daisetz T. Suzuki and Richard Herpers, Secretary of the University, on April 15 and 21, 1953, in Dr. Daisetz Teitaro Suzuki, Historical Biographical Files, Columbia University Libraries Archival Collections.

FIVE

Daisetz and the Beat Generation

American "Comrades"

The middle of the 1950s was a very important period for Daisetz, and the Zen that he introduced took the general public in the United States by storm. One of the driving forces behind this was the young writers and poets known collectively as the Beat Generation. The Beats were antisocial and wild and were searching for a way of living different from the prevailing social order. Since Alan and the Beats were close to each other in age, Alan may have shared the same view of the times. If we follow the interchange between Daisetz and the Beats from that perspective, perhaps we can understand how Daisetz viewed an "Alan-like phenomenon" in the mid-1950s when there was little contact between father and son because Daisetz was in the United States. Furthermore, I would venture to say that if this issue is examined from perspective of the father-son relationship, the interaction between Daisetz and the Beats can be seen in a different light. If I may be permitted to consider Beat literature as "literature," then we will see how Daisetz and Alan's relationship cast a shadow over an "incident" in the history of American literature in which the Beat Generation grew close to and then severed its relationship with Zen. So, then, who and what was the Beat Generation?

> I saw the best minds of my generation destroyed by madness,
>   starving hysterical naked,
> dragging themselves through the negro streets at dawn looking for
>   an angry fix . . . [1]

1. Allen Ginsberg, "Howl for Carl Solomon," in Ann Charters, ed., *The Portable Beat Reader* (New York: Penguin Classics, 1992), 62–70.

On October 7, 1955, at the Six Gallery on 3119 Fillmore Street in San Francisco, the culture of 1950s America was approaching a sort of climax. On that evening, several novelists and poets such as Allen Ginsberg (1926–1997), Jack Kerouac (1922–1969), Gary Snyder (1930–), and Philip Whalen (1923–2002) were at the Gallery, and Ginsberg recited his poem "Howl." Ginsberg dedicated the poem to Carl Solomon (1928–1993), whom he had met in a psychiatric hospital. People at that time with "good sense" frowned at such verses studded with references to drugs, sex, and homosexuality, and the manager of the City Lights bookstore who published "Howl" was later arrested, charged with obscenity, and put on trial.

The public reading had been planned by the poet Michael McClure (1932–2020). According to McClure, the 150 people in the audience felt "at the deepest level that a barrier had been broken, that a human voice and body had been hurled against the harsh wall of America and its supporting armies and navies and academies and institutions and ownership systems and power-support bases."[2] He declared that the crazy ones were not the people who had been put in mental institutions but those who put them there. It was the society controlled by the government, authorities, academics, and army that dropped the atomic bomb, engaged in the hysterical "Red Purge," and, being unable to halt the Cold War, continued to manufacture weapons of mass destruction. It was the society that was crazy.

The young talent that gathered to hear the recitation were collectively called the "Beat Generation." The sources of their inspiration were drugs and Buddhism, in particular the Zen of Daisetz. The Beat writers, who did not have steady jobs or fixed domiciles, abandoned themselves to the pleasures of sex with both genders and gave birth to "immoral" literature composed with senses that had been sharpened by the use of drugs. Their literature turned its back squarely on the ideal of the wrapped-up-in-love "American family," with its home in the suburbs, a television, and two cars. What the Beat Generation was looking for was a "new consciousness"; however, the American mainstream did not accept the Beats, and even today there are still some people who detest them. Nevertheless, the Beat Generation played a vital role in disseminating Buddhism in one segment of American society.

Of course, Alan was not the same as the Beats; there is no evidence that he indulged in the use of illicit drugs. However, he shared something in common with them in that he was influenced by Daisetz and used lyrics

---

2. Ann Charters, "Introduction: Variations on a Generation," in Charters, *The Portable Beat Reader*, xxviii.

to put out his message to society at large in Japan. One could imagine that from Alan's point of view, the Beats were his "brothers." What did these "brothers" learn from Daisetz, and how did they position his thought? How did Daisetz relate to his "American sons"? Before discussing Zen and the Beat Generation, however, I will give a brief overview of the history and the background of how Zen reached the United States. Without explaining how the thread of culture between Japan and the United States came to be connected, the discussion cannot go forward. For a moment, I would like to turn the clock back to the mid-nineteenth century.

The Basis of Transcendentalism

For a foreign culture to be accepted in a new environment, it needs a seed-bed that can assimilate it. Interpreting a foreign thing by saying "X from the other country is like Y in our land" allows one to feel close to a foreign culture and makes it easier to approach. In nineteenth-century America, the philosophy of such thinkers as Ralph Waldo Emerson (1803–1882) and Henry David Thoreau (1817–1862)—"Transcendentalism"—was one of the things that allowed for the assimilation of Zen.

Transcendentalism is a philosophy that was developed by Unitarian theologians in the Boston area who had studied German idealism and were influenced by Indian philosophy. The Transcendentalists looked deeply into the interconnection of all living things, believed in man's innate goodness, and regarded ideas as having more weight than experience. Emerson was one of the central thinkers of Transcendentalism, and his book *Nature*[3] is considered to be the pinnacle of Transcendentalist thought.

Thoreau, who was a colleague of Emerson's, built a log cabin on the shore of Walden Pond in Concord, not far from Boston, and lived a self-sufficient life there for two years and two months. In the record of his experience, *Walden*,[4] Thoreau described an ascetic life that seems very much like that of a Zen monk. He continues to exert a powerful influence, from the writers who came after him to present-day environmentalists. In addition to Emerson and Thoreau, the author of *Little Women*[5] Louisa May Alcott (1832–1888), whose parents were Transcendentalists, can be considered to be part

---

3. Ralph Waldo Emerson, *Nature* (Boston: James Munroe and Company, 1836).
4. Henry David Thoreau, *Walden; or, Life in the Woods* (Boston: Ticknor and Fields, 1854).
5. Louisa May Alcott, *Little Women* (Boston: Roberts Brothers, 1868).

of the second generation. These three all lived in Concord and shared their thoughts as they interacted on a regular basis.

Daisetz was very well acquainted with Transcendentalism; for example, in his book *Ichi shinjitsu no sekai* (The World of One Truth; 1941),[6] he introduced the primitive life of Thoreau and stated that the Transcendentalists had studied Eastern philosophy, especially that of India. Daisetz read Emerson when he was young and wrote, "I felt something that touched close to my heart."[7] Later he realized that the reason for this was that Eastern philosophy was at the roots of Transcendentalist thought. In 1896, shortly before Daisetz went to the United States to work for Carus, he published an essay entitled "Emāson no zengakuron" (Emerson's Theory of Zen)[8] in which he went so far as to say, "I venture to say that Emerson is talking about Zen, or, at least, Zen-like practice."[9]

In light of these words, how close were Transcendentalism and Daisetz's Zen? The final chapter of Emerson's *Nature* contains the following passage.

It will not need, when the mind is prepared for study, to search for objects. The invariable mark of wisdom is to see the miraculous in the common. What is a day? What is a year? What is summer? What is woman? What is a child? What is sleep? To our blindness, these things seem unaffecting. We make fables to hide the baldness of the fact and conform it, as we say, to the higher law of the mind. But when the fact is seen under the light of an idea, the gaudy fable fades and shrivels. We behold the real higher law.[10]

I want to be careful about judging this too lightly, but it seems that "to see the miraculous in the common" is similar to the state of Zen satori. One can understand how this resonated with the young Daisetz and led him to say that "Emerson is talking about Zen." Furthermore, from his experiences at Walden Pond, Thoreau realized that "[i]n proportion as he simplifies his life, the laws of the universe will appear less complex."[11] Thoreau's life was also Zennish.

---

6. *SDZ* 16, 92–97. Originally published in Suzuki Daisetsu, *Ichishinjitsu no sekai*.

7. *SDZ* 16, 96.

8. *SDZ* 30, 42–50. Originally published in *Zenshū* 14 (1896).

9. *SDZ* 30, 43.

10. Emerson, *Nature*, chapter 8. Cited from Project Gutenberg. http://www.gutenberg.org/files/29433/29433-h/29433-h.htm

11. Thoreau, *Walden*, conclusion. Cited from Project Gutenberg. http://www.gutenberg.org/files/205/205-h/205-h.htm

Surveying these statements, it appears as though the philosophy that started in India made its way westward, where it influenced Emerson and Thoreau, and went eastward to Daisetz, whereupon Daisetz then took it even further east and back to the United States, where the two streams blended. This view, however, should be regarded with caution, because the words that Daisetz used to explain Zen were themselves influenced by Transcendentalism. I am sure that Daisetz struggled with what sort of terms he should use to explain Zen, which professed *furyū monji* (not relying on words and letters), to the West with its different language, thought, culture, and religion. At that time, it is conceivable that the style of Emerson and Thoreau, with which Daisetz was familiar from his youth, came out in Daisetz's explanations, whether consciously or unconsciously.

For example, Daisetz described life after satori as follows: "All your mental activities will now be working to a different key, which will be more satisfying, more peaceful, and fuller of joy than anything you ever experienced before. . . . The spring flowers look prettier, and the mountain stream runs cooler and more transparent."[12] He also described the state of *mushin* (lit. no-mind) as follows: "He thinks like the showers coming down from the sky; he thinks like the waves rolling on the ocean; he thinks like the stars illuminating the nightly heavens; he thinks like the green foliage shooting forth in the relaxing spring breeze. Indeed, he is the showers, the ocean, the stars, the foliage."[13] One could be forgiven for mistaking statements like this as being Transcendentalist.

In a paper that Daisetz published in 1948 entitled "Meiji no seishin to jiyū" (Spirit and Freedom of the Meiji [Period]),[14] Daisetz wrote that he was "deeply moved" by the following statement by Emerson: "Do not hesitate to express what moves in your heart. Even a person who is said to be a great man does not possess anything over and above what is in his heart. Here, now, a ray of light shines (through a gap in the window) and falls upon your head. No matter how faint it may be, the one witness to this light is no one other than you alone. You do not need anyone's permission to proclaim this

12. Daisetz Teitaro Suzuki, *An Introduction to Zen Buddhism* (New York: Grove Press, 1964), 97–98. Originally published in 1934.

13. Daisetz T. Suzuki, "Introduction," in Eugen Herrigel, *Zen in the Art of Archery*, trans. R.F.C. Hull (New York: Vintage Spiritual Classics, 1989), ix. The English edition with D.T. Suzuki's introduction was published in 1953 by Pantheon Books.

14. *SDZ* 21, 210-19. Originally published in Suzuki Daisetsu, *Tōyō to seiyō* (Tokyo: Tōri Shoin, 1948): 63–80.

to the world."[15] Perhaps Daisetz inherited the spirit of freely expressing what is in one's heart without hesitation from Emerson.

Emerson dedicated one of the chapters of his book *Representative Men*[16] to Swedenborg. Considering the fact that Daisetz had long been familiar with Swedenborg and had even attempted to translate some of his more important works, it is likely that philosophically these three men shared some perceptions. In addition to Swedenborg, Emerson, and Thoreau, one should mention the medieval German mystic Meister Eckhart (ca. 1260–ca. 1328) and the American philosopher William James (1842–1910) as Western thinkers who also influenced Daisetz.

There is still room for research into how these thinkers influenced Daisetz as he was formulating his philosophy and learning how to express it in English. What can be said at the present point in time is that there was turbulence around the "Zen" that Daisetz transmitted to the United States, generated by the collision of the currents of Eastern and Western culture. It is not just a simple matter of Japanese Zen being accepted in the United States because it embodied sublime concepts.

Early Preaching

The book *How the Swans Came to the Lake*[17] by Rick Fields presents a useful explanation of how Buddhism came to the United States I would like to summarize how the process played out up until the 1930s, following the outline of this book.

If one views Transcendentalism, with its aura of Eastern thought, as having flowed from the East Coast of the United States westward, then Buddhism itself entered the United States from the West Coast starting in the mid-nineteenth century, brought by Chinese and Japanese immigrants. Western intelligentsia, however, came to know of Buddhism and Zen primarily from books.

The first World's Parliament of Religions was held on the occasion of the

---

15. *SDZ* 21, 213–14. This excerpt is reportedly Daisetz's vague account of Emerson's *Essays, First Series* (1841). See Takanashi Yoshio, "Emason to Suzuki Daisetsu: 'Tōyōteki na mikata' o chūshin to suru hikakuteki kōsatsu," *Nagano-ken Tanki Daigaku kiyō* 70 (2015): 89.

16. Ralph Waldo Emerson, *Representative Men* (Boston: Phillips, Sampson and Company, 1850).

17. Rick Fields, *How the Swans Came to the Lake: A Narrative History of Buddhism in America*, 3rd edition (Boston: Shambhala, 1992). The first edition was published in 1981.

World's Columbian Exposition in Chicago in 1893. Representatives from the various religions were invited and gave speeches regarding their respective faiths. The participants from Japan were Ashizu Jitsuzen (1850–1921) of Tendai esoteric Buddhism, Doki Hōryū (1855–1923) of Shingon esoteric Buddhism, Yatsubuchi Banryū (1848–1926) of Jōdo Shinshū, and Shaku Sōen of the Rinzai sect of Zen. Sōen's speech was actually given by an English speaker standing in for Sōen. It was the first time that Zen was introduced in a public setting to an audience comprising members of the Western intelligentsia. I have already mentioned how translating the draft of Sōen's lecture in Japan became the impetus for Daisetz's long stay in the United States.

The increasing numbers of immigrants led to the founding of Chinatowns and Japantowns in major cities. Buddhist temples were built, and the various sects officially sent preachers. Meanwhile, priests and laymen who existed on the margins of denominational organizations in Japan worked hard to spread their religions in the new world of the United States. In 1905, Shaku Sōen went to the United States a second time at the invitation of the San Francisco businessman Alexander Russell. Sōen spent nine months in the Russell home and taught Mr. and Mrs. Russell the Zen way of life while delivering lectures in various locations. Daisetz took a temporary leave from the Open Court company, where he was working as a translator, to help Sōen by serving as an interpreter during his stay. In this way, Mr. and Mrs. Russell became the first Americans who studied Zen koan.

Sōen brought his disciple Senzaki Nyogen (ca. 1876–1958) with him on this trip. Nyogen had an aversion to the ultranationalism that was becoming widespread in Japan, and he decided to remain behind in San Francisco to pursue missionary work after Sōen returned to Japan. He took a job at a hotel to support himself while studying English, read books on Western philosophy at the public library, and did zazen by himself in Golden Gate Park.

In 1906, Sōen's disciple Shaku Sōkatsu (1871–1954) arrived in San Francisco accompanied by six disciples, including the sculptor Sasaki Sōkei-an Shigetsu (1882–1945). In Japan, Sōkatsu presided over the Ryōbō Kyōkai layman's Zen group, and he founded a branch in San Francisco's Japantown. To Sōkatsu's dismay, however, the majority of the people who came there to study Zen were of Japanese descent. His attempts to spread Zen did not go well, and after four years he returned to Japan, leaving Sōkei-an to take over. Sōkei-an lived on the West Coast and was working to restore Buddhism there, but in 1916 he moved to New York. There he contributed sketches of New York to the magazine *Chūō kōron* and devoted himself to his Zen training under Sōkatsu's guidance, while sculpting and writing poetry as he traveled back and forth between Japan, Seattle, and New York. Subsequently, in 1928 he received permission from Sōkatsu to teach Zen even though he was only a layman. Regrettably, few Americans were willing to listen to Zen instruction from someone who was not a priest. Sōkei-an realized that there was only so much he could do in spreading Zen while he was still a layperson, and so he decided to become a priest. His teacher Sōkatsu, however, was opposed to his idea. Unable to accept his master's decision, Sōkei-an parted ways with Sōkatsu and became a monk at the Daitokuji temple in Kyoto. Sōkei-an suffered many hardships after returning to New York, but he finally found a patron. In 1930, he established the Buddhist Society of America (later the First Zen Institute of America), and the number of his disciples increased.

Meanwhile, Senzaki Nyogen left the hotel business by 1922 and began working to disseminate Zen teachings. His teacher Sōen had died three years earlier, and Sōen and Nyogen had not seen each other after their parting in the United States in 1906. With nothing but a picture of the bodhisattva Manjusri that he had borrowed from an antique art dealer, Nyogen traveled from place to place operating a "floating Zendo" (floating Zen meditation hall). He eventually attracted donations and was finally able to open his own Zendo, first in San Francisco (by 1927), followed by a second one in Los Angeles in 1931.

Sasaki Sōkei-an Shigetsu and Senzaki Nyogen both can be considered as having rendered distinguished service in propagating Zen on the East Coast and the West Coast, respectively. What the two shared was that while they were devoted lay disciples of Zen, they were not officially dispatched by any religious organization. Sōkei-an was a sculptor by trade, and while Nyogen was a priest, he began his work of teaching Zen after spending seventeen years as a businessman. In this way Zen Buddhism transcended the barrier of the Pacific Ocean, though questions lingered regarding the authenticity of the lineage of transmission.

Zen in English

Along with missionary work by religious persons, scholarly publications on Zen written in English began to appear, eventually having a huge impact worldwide. Of course the pioneer of this effort was D.T. Suzuki. In 1921, Daisetz founded the English-language magazine *Eastern Buddhist* with the assistance of Beatrice. Even though this magazine was published by Otani

University, which was associated with the Shin sect, it transcended sectarian borders and had as its objective discourse on Mahayana Buddhism. Most religious scholarship is concerned with interpreting doctrines and researching the history of the sect to which the author belongs. By straddling the divide between the Zen and Shin sects, Daisetz had the foresight to expand the possibilities of religious scholarship and introduce Buddhism to the world.

Daisetz published paper after paper on Zen in the *Eastern Buddhist.* These articles were gathered together for the volume *Essays in Zen Buddhism,* published by Luzac and Company of London in 1927.[18] Three volumes of *Essays in Zen Buddhism* were published and have been reprinted by numerous publishing houses. In addition, *An Introduction to Zen Buddhism,* in which the contents were adapted for a general audience, was published in Kyoto in 1934. It is not an exaggeration to say that up until the 1940s, the intelligentsia of the English-speaking world learned about Zen relying exclusively on these books by Daisetz as their primary source of information.

In 1929, Ruth Fuller Everett (later Ruth Fuller Sasaki; 1892–1967), the wife of a prominent lawyer in Chicago, visited Japan on a family trip during which Daisetz taught her how to do zazen. Because of the publication of *Essays in Zen Buddhism,* Daisetz had become known as the person who introduced Zen to the West. Foreigners who wanted to learn about Zen started to come to visit him, and Mrs. Everett was one of them. She apparently met the thirteen-year-old Alan during her trip. According to a letter dated August 10, 1929, Daisetz wrote to Beatrice that Mrs. Everett took Alan to Kamakura and Alan had liked her.[19] Even after Mrs. Everett returned to the United States, she did not lose her interest in Zen. Daisetz recommended to her that if she wanted to pursue Zen, she should come back to Japan. She returned to Japan in 1932, and Daisetz introduced her to a Zen master at the Nanzenji temple. With Daisetz's help as interpreter, she seriously trained in Zen for several months before returning home.

This is something of a digression, but Daisetz once coldly rebuffed Beatrice when she started to show an interest in Zen. Beatrice appears to have been extremely upset at this and in a letter to Daisetz, she could not hide her jealousy of Mrs. Everett: "You very unkindly say that I am doing this in imitation of Mrs. Everett" and "You always immediately respond to other

---

18. Daisetz Teitaro Suzuki, *Essays in Zen Buddhism, First Series* (London: Luzac and Company, 1927).

19. *SDZ* 36, 518–19.

people, such as Mrs. Everett for example, who come to you for help, but when I come to you for help, you seem not to be interested and seem to neglect me completely. Why is that? Do you believe her to be more sincere than I?"[20] I would like to know how Daisetz faced or did not face his wife over this issue.

Another person who came to Zen through Daisetz was the Englishman Alan Watts (1915–1973). When Daisetz was invited to the first World Congress of Faiths that took place in London in July of 1936, Watts participated in the discussions along with Mrs. Everett and her daughter Eleanor (1918–). At the end of the year Watts published *The Spirit of Zen*, which presented the contents of *Essays in Zen Buddhism* reworked for a general audience, thus beginning the process of solidifying his position as a native English-speaking interpreter of Zen.[21]

In 1938, Mrs. Everett moved to New York and became a patron of Sōkei-an. Alan Watts married her daughter Eleanor and moved to New York in the same year. At first Watts started practicing Zen with Sōkei-an, but they parted ways immediately because of differences in their outlook. Mrs. Everett's husband died in 1940, after which she deepened her relationship with Sōkei-an.

Unfortunately, with the outbreak of war between the United States and Japan in 1941, Sōkei-an, Mrs. Everett, and the First Zen Institute of America drew the attention of the FBI. The following year, Sōkei-an was placed in an internment camp. Mrs. Everett hired a talented lawyer and got him released. Sōkei-an then divorced his wife, from whom he had long been separated, and he and Ruth Everett were married in 1944. Their marital life, however, did not last long. Sōkei-an had always been in poor health, and the harsh conditions in the internment camp took their toll. He died from an illness in 1945, thus depriving the First Zen Institute of America of New York of its teacher. Senzaki Nyogen had also been interned, but he survived those years and reopened a "floating Zendo" in Los Angeles after the war. In this way, due to the efforts of people like Daisetz, Sōkei-an, and Nyogen, Zen was already present in the United States before World War II. However, it was only known to a small circle of practitioners, intellectuals, and artists, and was still unknown to the American public at large.

---

20. Suzuki Biatorisu Rēn, "Saiai naru Tei-sama," 82. Since the original English text is not published, the letter was translated from the Japanese rendition of it.

21. Alan Watts, *The Spirit of Zen: A Way of Life, Work and Art in the Far East* (New York: Dutton, 1936).

Art Encounters Zen

In all times and places, the fastest way to communicate ideas is not through words or practice, but through visual expression. One can get inspiration from a single piece of paper without any need for explanations or interpretations. After Ernest Fenollosa (1853–1908) enthusiastically promoted Japanese art in the West, works classified as "Zen art" began to attract the attention of American collectors and museums. This subsequently led to the appearance of artists who had been influenced by the "Zen art" they saw in the United States.

Georgia O'Keeffe (1887–1986) and Mark Tobey (1890–1976) were probably the first American artists whose works reflected this trend. O'Keefe was an admirer of Fenollosa and in 1916 exhibited works that had been influenced by *sumie* (ink painting). Tobey was a painter based in Seattle. While he was in England between 1931 and 1933, he associated with Arthur Waley (1898–1966), who translated *The Tale of Genji*, a lengthy Japanese novel from the eleventh century, and the ceramic artist Bernard Leach (1887–1979), which led him to deepen his ideas about East-West exchange.

After traveling with Leach to Hong Kong and Shanghai in 1934, Tobey spent a month at a Zen temple on the outskirts of Kyoto, where he came into contact with Zen paintings, haiku, calligraphy, and other Japanese arts. It is thought that the temple Tobey stayed at was Enpukuji in the city of Yawata in Kyoto prefecture. At the time, Enpukuji had a Zendo for foreigners, and Daisetz would often give lectures there. There is no proof that the two of them had any in-depth exchange, but Tobey had probably read Daisetz's books, and it seems likely that they met while Tobey was in Kyoto. Immediately after his return to Seattle, Tobey developed an abstract style of painting featuring calligraphic lines and symbols, often overlaid one on top of the other. His paintings were reportedly inspired by Zen calligraphy, and Tobey called this new style "white writing," which eventually solidified his fame as an artist. The collections of Zen art in the United States and works done by American artists influenced by Zen all helped to form the seedbed that would give birth to the postwar Beat Generation.

The Birth of the Beat Generation

Jack Kerouac entered Columbia University as a promising football player, but after some injuries and a fight with his coach, he dropped out of school.

After leaving Columbia in 1942, he became a sailor in the US Merchant Marine and was on the crew of a ship that transported supplies to war zones. However, because of his rebellious attitude, words, and actions toward his superiors, which made him appear to be deranged, he was discharged the following year. Kerouac then moved in with his girlfriend in New York and led a carefree life, supported by the allowance she received from her parents.

In the winter of 1943, Jack Kerouac was living the life of a playboy in New York. He had been heavily involved with liquor, drugs, and prostitutes from the time he was a student. In May 1944, a friend introduced him to Allen Ginsberg. They felt an instant rapport, and Ginsberg, who was a homosexual, was apparently smitten with Kerouac. However, Kerouac was a heterosexual, so it appears that their sexual relationship did not go well.

Another important personage in the Beat Generation at this time whom Kerouac and Ginsberg both knew was William S. Burroughs (1914–1997). Burroughs was older than Kerouac and Ginsberg, and was a dyed-in-the-wool drug addict who had tried every possible narcotic and stimulant. He was also a homosexual and was in love with Ginsberg. They lived a communal life together with several other men and women, and while indulging themselves in drugs and sex, they relentlessly pursued creative activities in search of a "new consciousness."

It is said that it was Burroughs who first described this generation as the "Beats."[22] The word "Beat" is slang that was used by jazz musicians and hustlers, meaning down and out, poor, and tired. Kerouac liked Burroughs's expression and in 1948 dubbed himself and his friends the "Beat Generation." An article by writer and poet Clellon Holmes (1926–1988) titled "This Is the Beat Generation" appeared in the November 16, 1952, issue of the *New York Times*, establishing the usage of the term. Holmes has been called the first Beat writer, and he heard the term in conversations with Kerouac and Ginsberg. According to the article, the Beats had an instinctive individuality, an eccentric way of expressing themselves, and while they distrusted collectivity, "they have never been able to keep the world out of their dreams."[23]

The religious backgrounds of the Beats varied widely. Kerouac was a Catholic; Ginsberg was Jewish (though his parents were Communists and atheists); and the poet Gary Snyder had a close relationship with Native American religion.[24] Among the Beat writers, the person who had the ear-

---

22. Charters, "Introduction," xvii–xix.
23. Clellon Holmes, "This Is the Beat Generation," *New York Times* (November 16, 1952).
24. Stephen Prothero, "Introduction," in Carole Tonkinson, ed., *Big Sky Mind: Bud-*

liest encounter with Buddhism was the poet Philip Whalen. Whalen was raised in a Christian Science household, and he is said to have become aware of Buddhism when he was in high school, which would be in the 1930s. That evolved into an interest in Zen after meeting Snyder when he was in college. Whalen read Daisetz's books that Snyder introduced him to and together they studied the haiku translated by Reginald Blyth (1898–1964).[25] Whalen was a very interesting person who in fact later became a Zen priest. Burroughs became aware of Zen Buddhism fairly early on, and Kerouac and Ginsberg seem to have discovered it in the 1940s.[26] In 1951, Kerouac began reading the *Lankavatara Sutra*, which Daisetz had translated into English,[27] and then turned to Thoreau's *Walden* in the winter of 1953–1954.[28]

When Ginsberg met Kerouac and Burroughs, he was a student at Columbia University. He had originally intended to study law; however, troubled by the fact that he was a homosexual, he honed his skills as a poet rather than devoting himself to his college coursework. The apartment that he was renting had become a gathering place for thieves, and in 1949 he was placed in a detention house. With that as a stimulus, he followed the advice of a friend and checked into a mental hospital. It was there that he met Carl Solomon, to whom he would later dedicate the poem "Howl." Another pivotal event in Ginsberg's life was seeing a painting titled *Sakyamuni Descending the Mountain* at the New York Public Library in April 1953. The painting depicts Sakyamuni walking down the mountain, having been unable to attain enlightenment even after a long period of ascetic practice. The emotional excitement he felt upon seeing this painting propelled Ginsberg even more toward Buddhism. His encounter can be viewed as a consequence of the collecting of Asian Art in the United States that had begun with Fenollosa. At about the same time, Ginsberg was reading Daisetz's *An Introduction to Zen Buddhism*.[29]

dhism and the Beat Generation (New York: Riverhead Books, 1995), 13–14; Ginzubāgu Aren, "Watashi ni totte Tōyō to wa," trans. Katagiri Yuzuru, in *Gendaishi techō tokushūban: Sōtokushū Aren Ginzubāgu* (Tokyo: Shichōsha, 1997), 180.

25. Prothero, "Introduction," 2–3; Tonkinson, *Big Sky Mind*, 193–94.

26. Prothero, "Introduction," 15.

27. Ginzubāgu, "Watashi ni totte Tōyō to wa," 180.

28. Prothero, "Introduction," 1.

29. Ginzubāgu, "Watashi ni totte Tōyō to wa," 181; Endō Tomoyuki, ed., "Aren Ginzubāgu nenpu," in *Gendaishi techō tokushūban*, 306–10.

Daisetz's Name Recognition Increases

At the beginning of the 1950s in America, Daisetz was "only known to those in the know." In the early twentieth century, it seems he was completely unknown to society at large. This is shown clearly by the following article in the April 8, 1906, issue of the *Washington Post*.

> Mr. Suguki [*sic*] is interpreter for Sakhu Soyen, the lord abbott [*sic*] of the Temple of Kumurgaji, at Kamakura, Japan, who is visiting the country. Mr. Suguki's address demonstrated his thorough familiarity with the English language, as well as his comprehensive grasp of the subject, which was forcibly presented.[30]

In 1906, people did not even know how to spell his name correctly. This changed with the republication of *An Introduction to Zen Buddhism* in London in 1948, the new edition of which included a foreword by the psychologist Carl Gustav Jung (1875–1961). In the review featured in the June 19, 1949, issue of the *Washington Post*, Daisetz's name was spelled correctly: "Dr. Suzuki . . . presents an introduction to the speculative mysticism of Zen."[31] In the same year, *Essays in Zen Buddhism, First Series* was republished in London and New York.

In recognition of the fact that he was making a significant contribution to the gradual spread of interest in Zen in the United States, Daisetz received support from organizations such as the Rockefeller Foundation and began to give lectures at universities throughout the United States in 1949, including Columbia University.[32] Aside from some temporary return visits to Japan, Daisetz spent most of his time until November 1958 in New York. In 1949, however, many difficulties still lay ahead for Daisetz. In a letter sent to a friend in Hawaii on October 22, Daisetz wrote: "Wherever one looks, Buddhism is not thriving. People are struggling just to get by. It is very sad. It seems to me that people should understand our work at least a bit, but I suppose this is just the way the world is. Still I will do my best."[33] The March 11, 1950, issue of the *Los Angeles Times* featured an article about a lecture that Daisetz had given at Claremont College, even quoting some of his words.

---

30. Roberta V. Bradshaw, "Clubs and Club People," *Washington Post* (April 8, 1906).

31. "In a Nutshell," *Washington Post* (June 19, 1949).

32. Regarding support from the Rockefeller Foundation, see Jaffe, "D.T. Suzuki and Two Cranes."

33. *SDZ* 37, 236.

"'When an American goes for a walk,' the bespectacled scholar said, 'he is going from some place, to some place. When the Oriental goes for a walk it is to commune with his soul and with his God.'"[34] Here we can see the rhetoric that Daisetz liked to use, where the East and the West are presented as being in binary opposition.

There were also some articles around this time that were critical of Zen. For example, the June 4, 1950, issue of the *New York Times* featured a review of *Essays in Zen Buddhism* by the historian and philosopher Gerald Heard (1889–1971). In this article, Heard wrote that while Zen was a good psychological method, or religion, for freeing oneself and knowing oneself, it has two dangers. The first is that "this shock system of insistent paradox may not work. This forcing of the mind to face and accept an alogical proposition may not take it into a consciousness." The second is that "[t]he individual may be freed from his personal greed and fear only to become the selfless tool of some insane national, class, or sectarian fanaticism."[35] Heard was deeply interested in the development of consciousness, and was one of the first people to take an interest in the effects that LSD had on human consciousness. Some people looked upon his discourse with skepticism, but his second point has a ring of truth to it. The reason for this is that in Japan during the war, Zen was used in spiritual training to make soldiers go willingly to their deaths, and according to Brian Victoria (1939–), is being used similarly today in the United States as well.[36]

In January 1952, Daisetz became an instructor at Columbia University. According to records preserved at the university, Daisetz's first post was as a visiting lecturer in Chinese; in June of that year his title was Associate in Religion; he was appointed Adjunct Professor of Religion in May 1957; he declined reappointment in July of the same year, citing illness as the reason.[37]

At Columbia University Daisetz lectured on "Kegon Philosophy," and as New York was a mecca for avant-garde art, a large number of young artists who were looking for an alternative to Western culture came to listen. The Beat writers did not know that Daisetz was in New York at that time; nei-

---

34. "Famed Buddha Scholar Finds Sanctuary Here," *Los Angeles Times* (March 11, 1950).

35. Gerald Heard, "On Learning from Buddha," *New York Times* (June 4, 1950).

36. Brian Victoria, "The Emperor's New Clothes: The Buddhist Military Chaplaincy in Imperial Japan and Contemporary America," *Journal of the Oxford Centre for Buddhist Studies* 11 (2016): 155–200.

37. "Suzuki, Dr. Daisetz Teitaro," Historical Biographical Files, Columbia University Libraries Archival Collections, Box 301, Folder 23.

ther Kerouac nor Ginsberg attended his lectures at Columbia University,[38] although they would meet Daisetz several years later. Among those who did attend, however, was the avant-garde composer John Cage (1912–1992). He is known for the silent piano composition *4'33"* (1952) that he "composed" having been inspired by Zen. Cage describes Daisetz's lectures as follows:

> The room had windows on two sides, a large table in the middle with ash trays. These were always filled with people listening, and there were generally a few people standing near the door. The two or three people who took the class for credit sat in chairs around the table. The time was four to seven. During this period most people now and then took a little nap. Suzuki never spoke loudly. When the weather was good the windows were open, and the airplanes leaving La Guardia flew directly overhead from time to time, drowning out whatever he had to say. He never repeated what had been said during the passage of the airplane. Three lectures I remember in particular. While he was giving them I couldn't for the life of me figure out what he was saying.[39]

Daisetz was encouraged by the fact that young Western artists, philosophers, and psychotherapists were responding to Zen. In a letter to the philosopher Hisamatsu Shin'ichi (1889–1980) dated May 20, 1954, Daisetz wrote: "Recently, not only at Princeton, bit by bit people who find our way of thinking congenial have begun to appear, which is encouraging. There is something of a response from the young students as well."[40] Also, in a letter to Furuta Shōkin dated August 13, Daisetz wrote: "Since the interest in Zen will continue to spread in Europe and the United States, Japanese scholars and practitioners will have to exert increasing efforts on this point. In particular, one hopes that the priests will be strict in their observance of the precepts."[41]

---

38. Ginzubāgu Aren, "Intabyū: Ginzubāgu to bukkyō," ed. and trans. Shigematsu Sōiku, in *Gendaishi techō tokushūban*, 258.

39. John Cage, *Silence* (Hanover: Wesleyan University Press, 1973), 262. First published in 1961.

40. *SDZ* 38, 35.

41. *SDZ* 38, 69.

A Change in the Life of the Great Scholar

Daisetz began living by himself outside of Japan after he was eighty years old. Even accepting that his physical endurance was superhuman, it certainly would have been a great help if he had had a companion to help with his daily needs, since it was ten years since Beatrice had died. Such a person—a young woman—suddenly appeared. The precise date is unclear, but it was at the end of a term in 1952. A Japanese girl who had been diligently attending Daisetz's lectures at Columbia University approached the lectern one day and asked a question. Her name was Okamura Mihoko, and she was fifteen years old. Mihoko's parents were Japanese and her father, Okamura Frank Masao (1911–2006), took care of the Japanese garden at the Brooklyn Botanical Gardens. Mihoko had been born in the United States and had never seen Japan at an age where she would have known what she was seeing. Her question was that it seemed that ultimately all of the world's religions were saying the same thing. Daisetz invited Mihoko to his apartment near the university for afternoon tea. Subsequently, Mihoko started visiting Daisetz's apartment frequently; she typed his manuscripts and cooked his meals while further discussing with him the meaning of life.[42] It was almost as though she forced herself on him.

The letter that Daisetz wrote to Hayashida Kumino dated January 20, 1953, is very telling. Daisetz was giving voice to his weakening resolve in the face of his single life in New York.

> Recently, I have taken to eating at home as much as possible; even if I go out, it is unsatisfying when one is alone. Also, I usually eat the same thing, so I've gotten sick of it. A lot of strange things happen when I cook my own food. When one gets old, traveling is not easy. Sometimes I wonder why I have to do this, but when I tell myself that I must see it through, the feeling goes away. Nothing would be better than to have someone to help me, but that would just increase my expenses, so I guess I'll just go on as I have been going for now.[43]

Daisetz was revealing to Kumino how he would like to have someone to help him. If one reads this in combination with the "Daisetz Diaries," one

---

42. Okamura Mihoko, "Daisetsu-sensei ni oai shite," in Ueda and Okamura, *Suzuki Daisetsu to wa dareka*, 29–31. Originally published in *Chichi* (September 2001).

43. *SDZ* 37, 384.

can see that it was a foreshadowing. Looking through the "Daisetz Diaries" from the beginning, one can sense how the mood of the writing changes around January 20, 1953. From this date onward, Mihoko appears in the diary almost every day, and Daisetz's writing becomes colorful and happy, as follows:

February 17, 1953: Miho-ko came about noon-time. Prepared lunch for us. Yes, when a young girl is here, the whole atmosphere changes, talked about many subjects, will come regularly after this, helping me in typing letters and articles.

March 2: Mihoko, when I told her about the Buddhist bell, especially at Engakuji, she got excited and expressed her deep longing for Japanese life in connection with Buddhism. Yes, Mihoko will visit Japan, if possible, next year, with me.

March 27: After lecture Mihoko cooked dinner (Japanese) which both enjoyed. She was in a talkative mood and talked much about herself— her inner feeling, her lack of knowledge, her mind filled with superficialities, &c. Here is not probably a scholarly mind. She wants to be sincere to herself.

April 28: Mihoko typing and lunching as usual. She is helpful in various ways. Glad that I have her now.

If one did not know that the people in question were a scholar and a girl acting as his secretary, between whom there was a gap in age of sixty-five years, one could read this diary in a completely different way. The two of them had gone beyond a public relationship and were communicating on a deep spiritual level. Mihoko subsequently kept close to Daisetz and continued to support him in his studies up to the end. If Mihoko had not considered Daisetz to be an attractive man, such an intelligent woman would not have served him so devotedly and dedicated many years of her young life (from her midteens into her twenties) to him.

The author Iinuma Nobuko (1932–2018) recorded the following episode from an interview she conducted with Mihoko.

How did Daisetz respond to this pure devotion from Mihoko, who loved him as a father and revered him as a master?

In response to Mihoko's words at our parting, "He was a wonderful man," the thought "Yes, I know" came unbidden to my mind. Her statement, "He was a wonderful man," not "He was a wonderful sensei," made sense to me.[44]

Perhaps one should call it "women's intuition"; it is impressive that Iinuma divined the meaning of the single word that Mihoko chose: "man." Of course people will be curious when they see a young, pretty secretary at the side of an aged scholar. When Mihoko became Daisetz's secretary, her relationship with him was scrutinized by those around them. When Mihoko could not bear it and came to Daisetz for advice, he is reputed to have acted in a very aloof manner, saying: "Well, of course. You're a woman and I'm a man. What about it?"[45]

Mihoko did not conceal her memories of her close relationship with Daisetz. She spoke about how he would take her hand and say things like "You have such pretty hands. Look. They're the hands of Buddha."[46] She also recounted how he would tease her, stroking her youthful forehead and saying: "It will be interesting when this area gradually becomes wrinkled. I would like to live long enough to see it."[47]

Mihoko went to Daisetz's house every day to help, and she also accompanied him on his travels to Europe from June to September 1953. In January 1954, Daisetz moved into the apartment where the Okamura family lived. In September of that year, just before he made a brief return trip to Japan accompanied by Mihoko for the first time, Daisetz wrote the following letter to Hayashida Kumino dated August 31, 1954. It shows his consideration of Kumino's feelings, not wanting to surprise her by just suddenly showing up with a young girl. One can see Daisetz's human side in this.

A daughter of Okamura will be accompanying me. She is a second-generation Japanese-American, very intelligent and quick on the uptake. She has been very helpful to me, writing letters and typing.

---

44. Iinuma Nobuko, *Noguchi Hideyo to Merī Dājisu: Meiji Taishō ijintachi no kokusai kekkon* (Tokyo: Suiyōsha, 2007), 241.

45. "Hito: Suzuki Daisetsu no omoide o shuppan shita moto hisho Okamura Mihoko-san," *Asahi Shimbun* (June 27, 1997).

46. Okamura Mihoko, "Myōyō," in Nishitani Keiji, ed., *Kaisō Suzuki Daisetsu* (Tokyo: Shunjūsha, 1975), 120. Originally published in *Daihōrin* (September 1, 1966), and *Tosho* (January 1, 1971).

47. Okamura, "'Shi'nin' Daisetsu," 372.

Since she is a girl, it might be a bit inconvenient, but she wants to learn about Japan and I want her to see as much as possible.[48]

At this time, Mariko's daughter Maya was three years old. She had begun to realize that she did not have a father, and Mariko had told Maya that her father was in the United States on business. According to people close to Mariko, Mariko was disconcerted when, upon seeing Daisetz, Maya asked her mother why she had married such an old man. Later, Maya learned that Daisetz had taken on the role of her father out of compassion for his daughter-in-law and grandchild.

Daisetz's sojourn in Japan lasted for about four months, after which he went back to the United States and continued lecturing at Columbia University. With Mihoko's expert secretarial help, Daisetz's work progressed smoothly and his name recognition in the United States steadily increased.

San Francisco Renaissance

By 1954, Kerouac and Ginsberg had moved to California, where they met Gary Snyder. Together they became the core members of what would later be called the "San Francisco Renaissance." Different from the conservative East, there they found the kind of freedom that they were searching for. Kerouac intensified his study of Buddhism and in 1953 began to write *Some of the Dharma*, a record of his personal research. He and Ginsberg both studied the haiku that Blyth had introduced. Snyder was living a rather primitive life close to nature in the Sierra Nevada while studying Asian languages and culture at UC Berkeley. With financial assistance from Ruth Fuller Sasaki, in May 1956 he left for Japan to undergo Zen training in Kyoto.

During this period, on October 7, 1955, a reading by the leading writers and poets of the San Francisco Renaissance took place at the Six Gallery in San Francisco, where Ginsberg presented "Howl," dedicated to Carl Solomon. Ginsberg's voice was the first cry of the birth of new American culture. "Howl" was published in August of the following year by City Lights bookstore in San Francisco. On September 2, an article lauding "Howl" titled "West Coast Rhythms" by the poet Richard Eberhart (1904–2005) appeared in the *New York Times*: "It is a howl against everything in our mechanistic

---

48. SDZ 38, 78.

civilization which kills the spirit."[49] In May 1957, however, US Customs confiscated a collection of poems containing "Howl," claiming it was obscene material that had been printed in England and imported into the United States, and the San Francisco police arrested the manager of City Lights (who had imported the book) on charges of distributing obscene material. It led to the "Howl" trial, which was a clash over the definition of obscenity, freedom of expression, and censorship of printed material. A decision was handed down in October of the following year, and it was at this time that Daisetz got his big break in the United States.

Daisetz's Big Break

It started with a small article in the "People Are Talking About" corner in the January 15, 1957, issue of the woman's magazine *Vogue*.

> PEOPLE ARE TALKING ABOUT . . . The Columbia University classes of the great Zen Buddhist teacher, Dr. Daisetz Suzuki, who sits in the centre of a mound of books, waving his spectacles with ceremonial elegance while mingling the philosophical abstract with the familiar concrete: "To discover one is a great achievement, to discover zero, a great leap"; or another time: "Have no ulterior purpose in work, then you are free."[50]

Vogue was famous as a fashion and lifestyle magazine for women who were au courant with the times, and even though the article was a short one, clearly Daisetz was already of a stature that attracted the attention of the editor. Two weeks later an article on Zen appeared in the weekly magazine *Time*. An excerpt from that article follows:

> In the centuries since the death of its founder in 483 B.C., Buddhism has had little direct impact on the Christian West. Today, however, a Buddhist boomlet is under way in the U.S. Increasing numbers of intellectuals—both faddists and serious students—are becoming interested in a form of Japanese Buddhism called Zen. . . . And the current issue of *Vogue* tips off its readers that People Are Talking

---

49. Richard Eberhart, "West Coast Rhythms," *New York Times* (September 2, 1956).
50. "People Are Talking About," *Vogue* (January 15, 1957).

About "the Columbia University classes of the great Zen Buddhist teacher, Dr. Daisetz Suzuki, who sits in the center of a mound of books, waving his spectacles with ceremonial elegance while mingling the philosophical abstract with the familiar concrete." . . . Columbia's 87-year-old Dr. Suzuki, whose weekly lectures attract a well-packed but mixed bag of serious students and cult shoppers, is one of the most respected religious leaders in America. His classes are drawing a wider variety as well as a larger number of students since the war. Painters and psychiatrists seem especially interested in Zen, he finds. Psycho-analysts, says Dr. Suzuki, his tiny eyes twinkling under wing-like eye-brows, have a lot to learn from Zen: "They go round and round on the surface of the mind without stopping. But Zen goes deep." The main difficulty Westerners have with Zen, says Suzuki, is their habit of thinking dialectically—either-or, subject-object, positive-negative. Zen sees only one instead of two. "Westerners analyze things," says Dr. Suzuki, "but in the East we see a thing all at once and with our whole bodies, instead of just our minds."[51]

One can see how the reports spread from the earlier article in *Vogue*. *Time* was enormously influential, and with the *Time* article as the impetus, all sorts of inquiries came Daisetz's way. In a letter dated March 18, Daisetz reported on this new development to Furuta Shōkin, who was taking care of Shōden-an:

I'm sending you my recent publications sometime soon. The most recent issue of *Time* came out yesterday and was favorably received, and I have been dumbfounded at the flood of requests for lectures and the letters that have come. They may write something for a New York magazine. Probably, Zen will become fashionable.[52]

What Daisetz called the "New York magazine" was the *New Yorker*. A fifteen-page article introducing Daisetz in great detail, accompanied by a drawing of Daisetz with his bristling eyebrows, appeared in the August 31, 1957, issue (fig. 5). It was written by Winthrop Sargeant (1903–1986), a music critic and violinist. Since no other general interest magazine wrote about Daisetz in such a thoroughgoing fashion, I would like to include an excerpt from the article, even though it is a bit long.

---

51. "Religion: Zen," *Time* (February 4, 1957): 65–66.
52. *SDZ* 38, 491.

PROFILES

GREAT SIMPLICITY

Dr. Daisetz Teitaro Suzuki

ON Friday afternoons, in a lecture room in the northwest corner of Philosophy Hall, at Columbia University, a small, wiry, and very aged Japanese named Dr. Daisetz Teitaro Suzuki regularly unwraps a shawlful of books in various ancient Oriental languages and, as he lovingly fingers and rubs them, delivers a lecture in an all but inaudible voice to a rapt and rather unusual-looking group of graduate students. On one wall of the room is a framed photograph of the American philosopher John Dewey, who, peering over his spectacles, appears to be viewing the scene with some misgivings, as well he might. For Dr. Suzuki is the world's leading authority on Zen Buddhism—a subject of considerable mystery to the relatively few people in this country who have heard of it at all, and a philosophy (if it can properly be called a philosophy) of extremely anti-philosophical, or at least methodically irrational, character to the even fewer people who have studied it. Dr. Suzuki, however, does not look anywhere near as worried as Mr. Dewey. Despite his great antiquity—he is eighty-seven—he has the slim, restless figure of a man a quarter of his age. He is clean-shaven, his hair is closely clipped, and he is almost invariably dressed in the neat American sports jacket and slacks that might be worn by any Columbia undergraduate. The only thing about him that suggests philosophical grandeur is a pair of ferocious eyebrows, which project from his forehead like the eyebrows

of the angry demons who guard the entrances of Buddhist temples in Japan. These striking ornaments give him an added air of authority, perhaps, but the addition is unnecessary. Dr. Suzuki is obviously a man who thought everything out long ago and has reached a state of certainty. The certainty, it appears, is so profound that it needs no emphasis, for it is expressed in quiet, cheerful phrases (marked here and there by the usual Japanese difficulty with the letter "l") and punctuated by smiles and absent-minded rubbings of his forehead. Now and then, he bounces up from his desk to make his certainties even more certain by drawing diagrams on a nearby blackboard, or chalking characters in Chinese or Sanskrit. To the uninitiated, these characters, and the talk that accompanies them, are likely to be enigmatic indeed. "So, as you see," he said at the conclusion of a recent lecture on the ancient Kegon Sutra, one of the great metaphysical documents of Mahayana Buddhism, "at this point, zero equals infinity and infinity equals zero. The result is emptiness." With that, Dr. Suzuki carefully wrapped his books in his shawl again and took his departure, leaning gently on the arm of his secretary and constant companion, a very pretty and very young Japanese-American girl named Mihoko Okamura.

Dr. Suzuki's lectures by no means explore all the ramifications of the mystical doctrine that he concerns himself with, nor do his tireless writings, which in English alone have filled a score of volumes with remarkably lucid prose. Dr. Suzuki is, in fact, merely the most celebrated and most eloquent international commentator on a branch of Buddhist thought that is followed, in a popular form, by millions of laymen in Japan (where it has more adherents than any other Buddhist sect except the Shin-shu, or Pure Land, branch of Japanese Buddhism), and, in a more advanced form, is practiced with rigorous austerity by thousands of monks and acolytes in various secluded Japanese monasteries. Moreover, Zen has recently been spreading, in a modest way, through the United States and Europe, where it has attracted the attention of artists, philosophers, and psychologists, in particular, and is enjoying the status of what some might call an intellectual fad but what many seri-

ous thinkers regard as a religious—or, at any rate, cultural—movement of considerable importance. Dr. Suzuki has himself been responsible for a good deal of this Occidental interest in Zen, and those who have given his ideas more than passing notice have included, besides the usual array of specialized scholars and addicts of the occult, a rather imposing list of well-known figures, among them Arnold Toynbee, Aldous Huxley, Martin Heidegger, C. G. Jung, and Karen Horney. American writers and musicians, ranging from J. D. Salinger to the composer John Cage and the jazz trumpeter Dizzy Gillespie, have at one time or another come under the influence of Zen, and on a different, purely religious level it has invaded both New York and Los Angeles, where small, dedicated groups of individuals are busy practicing its rites.

In New York, the center of these activities is a Japanese temple that occupies the top floor of a brownstone building, known as the First Zen Institute of America, on Waverly Place. Though the First Zen Institute at present lacks an accredited Zen master to conduct its meditations (the Institute's founder, a Japanese Zen monk named Sokei-an, died a few years ago), its disciples, about twenty-five in number, do their best to keep up the prescribed rituals of the order while awaiting the arrival of a new master, who is expected to come from Japan as soon as he learns English, and who, in the words of the Institute's secretary, Mrs. Nicholas Farkas, has a "sufficiently irascible" personality to get the group's discipline back into proper shape. Mrs. Farkas is not joking. The disciplines that the First Zen Institute hopes to resume are modelled on those of the Japanese Zen monasteries, and though they may strike the innocent observer as somewhat bizarre, there is no doubt about their severity. They involve very little in the way of verbal communication. Books—even Dr. Suzuki's books—are forbidden, since logic and rationality are regarded by orthodox Zen students not only as frivolous but as a positive bar to the perception of truth. The Zen student meditates in silence, facing a wall (the word "Zen" derives from the Japanese "zazen," meaning to sit and meditate), or occupies himself with humble and useful household tasks,

Fig. 5. Sargeant, "Profiles" column from *New Yorker* (August 31, 1957): 34.

On Friday afternoon, in a lecture room in the northwest corner of Philosophy Hall, at Columbia University, a small, wiry, and very aged Japanese named Dr. Daisetz Teitaro Suzuki regularly unwraps a shawlful of books in a various ancient Oriental languages and, as he lovingly fingers and rubs them, delivers a lecture in an all but inaudible voice to a rapt and rather unusual-looking group of graduate students. . . . He is clean-shaven, his hair is closely clipped, and he is almost invariably dressed in the neat American sports jacket and slacks that might be worn by any Columbia undergraduate. The only thing about him that suggests philosophical grandeur is a pair of ferocious eyebrows, which project from his forehead like the eyebrows of the angry demons who guard the entrances of Buddhist temples in Japan. . . . "at this point, zero equals infinity and infinity equals zero. The result is emptiness." With that, Dr. Suzuki carefully wrapped his books in his shawl again and took his departure, leaning gently on the arm of his secretary and constant companion, a very pretty and very young Japanese-American girl named Mihoko Okamura.[53]

According to the article, Zen had been quietly spreading in the United States and Europe in recent years. In particular it was drawing the attention of artists, philosophers, and psychologists, and had taken on the flavor of an intellectual fashion. The article went on to state that the teacher at the First Zen Institute of America in New York (Sōkei-an) had died several years earlier, and although the institute no longer had a teacher, it apparently eschewed verbal communication, even going so far as to ban the reading of Daisetz's books.

Sargeant went on to write about what a koan is. At times his words are somewhat harsh; for example, he said that while the teachings of Zen transcend logic, Daisetz has strayed from the correct path in that his interest is in explaining Zen logically.

The fact that he has written a large number of books on the subject is enough to disqualify him as a strict Zen practitioner, since the written word is regarded by the orthodox as more or less taboo. Dr. Suzuki's approach to Zen is, in fact, more like that of a Western philosopher than like that of a true Zen disciple. . . . Dr. Suzuki often depreciates his own elaborate ventures into philosophical speculation, describing his works as "my sins."[54]

---

53. Winthrop Sargeant, "Profiles: Great Simplicity," *New Yorker* (August 31, 1957): 34.
54. Sargeant, "Profiles: Great Simplicity," 36.

The article also introduced Daisetz's life at the Okamura home, discussed the history of Zen and its teachings and how Zen has affected the lives and the art of the Chinese and the Japanese, and gave an outline of Daisetz's life history. Sargeant went on to say, "As a personality, he radiates not only the general glamour that attaches to aging Oriental men of wisdom but a special serenity that makes him a magnificent living example of the doctrine he preaches."[55]

It appears that Daisetz was pleased with the *New Yorker* article. On September 6, instead of reporting on recent events, Daisetz sent Furuta a copy of the magazine. The accompanying letter reads as follows:

> Here in America, Zen has become sort of fashionable. Real Zen will come later, I guess. In any case, this is a bit of publicity for it. I'm sending you a copy of a weekly magazine called the *New Yorker* that has a "Profile" of me. I believe this will show you what my situation is. The reporter is a man named Sargeant who has been diligently gathering material since spring. It seems to be some sort of entertainment magazine, and it always contains at least one subject of interest. It appears that "Profiles" is one of the hallmarks of the magazine.[56]

The fact that the reporter Sargeant had been gathering information since the spring suggests that he started research on this article after reading *Vogue* and *Time*. A published chronology of Daisetz's life shows that on March 12, 1957, he received a visit from a reporter from the *New Yorker* after *Vogue* and *Time* had come out.[57] These articles are all connected by the thread that started from *Vogue* and "People Are Talking About."

On the Road

On September 5, 1957, immediately after the piece featuring Daisetz appeared in the *New Yorker*, Kerouac's *On the Road*, considered to be the epitome of Beat literature, was published.[58] The book describes a trip that Kerouac actually took from 1947 to 1950, and the individuals who appear are all modeled after actual people. The protagonist is Kerouac himself and

---

55. Sargeant, "Profiles: Great Simplicity," 53.
56. *SDZ* 38, 572.
57. Kirita, *Suzuki Daisetsu kenkyū kiso shiryō*, 206.
58. Jack Kerouac, *On the Road* (New York: Viking Press, 1957).

characters that seem to be Ginsberg and Burroughs make their appearance. The original manuscript was made into the form of a horizontal hand scroll by taping pages of typing paper together, totaling 36.5 meters in length. Kerouac purportedly typed the entire thing in three weeks in April 1951. Leaving aside the credibility of that story for a moment, his style of writing, which is bursting with speed and energy, captured the hearts of the American youth. The *New York Times* featured a review of *On the Road* three days after it was published. Quoting John Aldridge in *After the Lost Generation*, the reviewer described the approach Kerouac has taken.

> assertion "of the need for belief even though it is upon a background in which belief is impossible and in which the symbols are lacking for a genuine affirmation in genuine terms." . . . There are sections of "On the Road" in which the writing is of a beauty almost breathtaking. . . . And, finally, there is some writing on jazz that has never been equaled in American fiction, either for insight, style or technical virtuosity. "On the Road" is a major novel.[59]

Written by *New York Times* reporter Gilbert Millstein (ca. 1916–1999), the review gave the book the highest praise possible. *On the Road* immediately became a bestseller, and conservatives responded by mounting a counterattack. In the September 8 issue, three days later, the *New York Times* published a very different review that stated: "'On the Road' is a stunning achievement. But it is a road, as far as the characters are concerned, that leads nowhere—and which the novelist himself cannot afford to travel more than once."[60] Later, a review in the October issue of the *Atlantic Monthly* commented: "It disappoints because it constantly promises a revelation or a conclusion of real importance and general applicability, and cannot deliver any such conclusion."[61]

In the midst of the controversy over *On the Road*, the decision on the trial involving the publication of Ginsberg's "Howl" was handed down in a San Francisco court, which proclaimed that the book was not obscene and all of the defendants were declared innocent. Thus the legal battle between the conservatives and the Beats ended in complete vindication for the Beats.

---

59. Gilbert Millstein, "Books of the Times," *New York Times* (September 5, 1957).

60. David Dempsey, "In Pursuit of 'Kicks,'" *New York Times* (September 8, 1957).

61. Phoebe Adams, "The Atlantic Bookshelf: Reader's Choice," *Atlantic Monthly* 200, no. 4 (October 1957): 180.

The attacks on the Beats, however, did not cease. In the November 16, 1957, issue of *The Nation*, a leftist opinion magazine, the novelist Herbert Gold (1924–) wrote in his review of *On the Road*, titled "Hip, Cool, Beat–and Frantic," that "Jack Kerouac's book is a proof of illness rather than a creation of art, a novel."[62]

> Despite its drag race of words and gestures, *On the Road* does nothing, thinks nothing, acts nothing, but yet manages to be a book after all . . . they run 110 miles an hour in order to stand still. It's a frantic book, and for that reason there is hope for Jack Kerouac. Pseudo-Hipster, You Can't Run Further. Meta-Hipster, You Can't Yell Louder. Hipster, Go Home.[63]

Rather than a book review, the text reads as being quite repressive. In this way, in the context of the overwhelming support of Beat literature by the young and attempts at suppression of that literature by the "adults," the Zen that had influenced the Beat Generation was accepted wholeheartedly by the "adults." Let's try to untie the Gordian knot of the complicated relationship of Beats and Zen a bit more.

America's Dharma Year

From the end of 1957, the year that the Beat Generation became a topic of discussion into 1958, magazines all over the United States presented special features on Zen. For example, the November 16, 1957, issue of the *Saturday Review* featured an article entitled the "Search for Inner Truth" that asked, "What is Zen Buddhism, the philosophical way of life currently being widely discussed in this country?"[64] Kerouac, who sensed the growing popularity of Zen, predicted in a letter to Philip Whalen on January 7, 1958, that "58 is going to be dharma year in America."[65]

Around this time, the woman's fashion magazine *Mademoiselle* published

62. Herbert Gold, "Hip, Cool, Beat—and Frantic," *The Nation* 185: 16 (November 16, 1957): 350.

63. Gold, "Hip, Cool, Beat–and Frantic," 355.

64. Daniel J. Bronstein, "Search for Inner Truth," *Saturday Review* (November 16, 1957): 22.

65. Jack Kerouac, *Selected Letters, 1957–1969*, ed. Ann Charters (New York: Viking, 1999), 97.

a lengthy special feature in its January 1958 issue called "What Is Zen?" *Mademoiselle* was the second women's magazine after *Vogue* to publish an article introducing Zen, but *Vogue's* short essay could not compare to *Mademoiselle's*, which was quite lengthy and substantial. The special feature began with the following sentence.

> A young New Yorker telling a friend about a cocktail party she had attended described the conversation as uncommonly stimulating, even "fascinating." Everyone present, she said, had been "talking about Zen."[66]

The article was written by the novelist and critic Nancy Wilson Ross (1901–1986), who had long been interested in Zen Buddhism and is known for later editing the anthology *The World of Zen*.[67] Ross's article dealt with such subjects as how Zen had influenced Kerouac and Ginsberg; the relationship between Zen and the "white writing" of Mark Tobey; koan and satori; and the history of Zen. Ross lived in Seattle in the 1930s and had lectured there on Zen and painting, and so it is possible that she had some interaction with Tobey, who was residing in Seattle at that time.[68] Her article prominently featured a photograph of the *Seated Pensive Bodhisattva* statue housed at the imperial convent Chūgūji in Nara prefecture and explained that this photograph was on the wall of Dr. D.T. Suzuki's room in New York.

Ross's posthumous papers (hereafter the "Ross Papers") are almost all preserved at the Harry Ransom Center at the University of Texas at Austin. Among these papers is a memo concerning the planning within the *Mademoiselle* editorial department that discusses its intention to publish a special feature on Zen. The memo says, "Now that 'Zen,' as it's cozily called, has become one of the most popular cocktail party conversation topics . . ."[69] From this, one can see that Ross borrowed the text of the planning memo to begin her article. The Ross papers also contain a letter from an editor advising Ross to open the article with an episode from a cocktail party.[70] This

---

66. Nancy Wilson Ross, "What Is Zen?," *Mademoiselle* (January 1958): 64.

67. Nancy Wilson Ross, *The World of Zen: An East-West Anthology* (New York: Random House, 1960).

68. Ross's lecture notes are archived in Nancy Wilson Ross Papers 1913–1986, held by the Harry Ransom Center, University of Texas at Austin.

69. "Street & Smith Publications Inter Office Memorandum; From MW to CA; Subject: article on Zen Buddhism," dated June 19, 1957, Nancy Wilson Ross Papers 1913–1986.

70. Letter from Cyrilly Abels to Nancy Wilson Ross, dated October 4, 1957, Nancy Wilson Ross Papers 1913–1986.

memo backs up the fact that the radar of the editors of women's magazines had locked in on Zen.

Did Ross herself sell the idea to *Mademoiselle?* The Ross papers invalidate that hypothesis, since among the letters that Ross sent to the editors is one that inquired about who the author of the planning memo was and asking for clarification of some of the unclear points.[71] If Ross herself had been pushing the plan, she would not have asked about the author of the memo or its contents.

The Ross Papers do not tell us anything about the details of how Ross was chosen to write the article. In 1953, however, Ross had contributed an article to *Mademoiselle* on Eastern religions, and it appears that the editor had faith in Ross's writing abilities in that area.[72] In addition, Ross had been in contact with Daisetz up until 1952.[73] In response to a request from Daisetz, Ross made a separate printing of the article nine months after its publication and sent it to him.[74] Along with the *New Yorker*, perhaps Daisetz liked this article as well.

Meanwhile, what did the general public in the United States think of the Beat Generation in early 1958? The answer can be divined from an article called "The Beat Mystique" that appeared in the February issue of *Playboy*.

> The term Beat Generation is an apt coinage to characterize the angry, roving youngsters whom writers like Kerouac have caught in print. But beat is a national phenomenon which knows no barriers of age— or economic or social status. From the dope-addicted frigid cat to the baby-faced imitator wistfully wishing he were vicious, the beat attitude infiltrates all levels of our society.[75]

In contradistinction to this assessment, an entirely negative view of the Beats was spreading elsewhere in the English-speaking world. An example is the article "A Road with No Turning" that appeared in the July 3, 1958, issue of *The Listener*, a magazine published by the BBC.

---

71. Letter from Nancy Wilson Ross to Cyrilly Abels, dated July 17, 1957, Nancy Wilson Ross Papers 1913–1986.

72. Letter from Blythe Morley to the Editors, *Mademoiselle*, dated December 17, 1953, Nancy Wilson Ross Papers 1913–1986.

73. Letter from Mrs. Stanley Young (Nancy Wilson Ross) to Dr. Suzuki, dated December 20, 1952, Nancy Wilson Ross Papers 1913–1986.

74. Letter from Mrs. Stanley Young (Nancy Wilson Ross) to Dr. Suzuki, dated October 16, 1958, Nancy Wilson Ross Papers 1913–1986.

75. Herbert Gold, "The Beat Mystique," *Playboy* 5: 2 (February 1958): 20.

I do not foresee a great future for the Beat Generation. Their empty vitalism, their hatred for the balanced human intelligence may give a short useful shock to some of the conventional writers who take their own bourgeois prejudices for granted as the props of a sensible community. But the beat have nothing to say, not even a protest to make. Their writing is like signwriting scrawled on the air. It catches the attention for a moment, and then the wind blows it away.[76]

In the midst of the pro and con views it generated, the Beat Generation became the keynote of the American popular culture of 1957–1958. I would like to reemphasize the fact that the Zen that put down roots in the United States at this time was not the Japanese religion with its disciplined practice, but as it became interwoven with the Beat Generation, it transformed into a kind of American "Zen culture."

The Context of the *Chicago Review* Special Issue on Zen

The year 1958 was when the arts magazine *Chicago Review*, put out mainly through the efforts of University of Chicago students, devoted its summer issue to a special feature on Zen. One look at the table of contents shows the connection between Zen and the Beats.

Alan W. Watts, "Beat Zen, Square Zen, and Zen"
Daisetz T. Suzuki, "Rinzai on Zen"
Jack Kerouac, "Meditation in the Woods"[77]
Shinichi Hisamatsu (Hoseki), "Zen and the Various Acts"
Philip Whalen, "Excerpt: Sourdough Mountain Lookout"
Ruth Fuller Sasaki, "Chia-shan Receives the Transmission"
Nyogen Senzaki, "Mentorgarten Dialogue"
Gary Snyder, "Spring Sesshin at Shokoku-ji"
Harold E. McCarthy, "The Natural and Unnatural in Suzuki's Zen"
Akihisa Kondo, "Zen in Psychotherapy: The Virtue of Sitting"
Paul Wienpahl, "Zen and the Work of Wittgenstein"[78]

---

76. Alan Pryce-Jones, "A Road with No Turning," *The Listener* 60: 1527 (July 3, 1958): 16.
77. Excerpt from Kerouac's *The Dharma Bums*.
78. *Chicago Review* 12: 2 (Summer 1958).

Prior to this, the spring edition of the *Chicago Review* was a special issue on San Francisco, featuring poems by Kerouac and Ginsberg and a portion of Burroughs's *Naked Lunch*, which was still unpublished.[79] The editors of the *Chicago Review* also saw Zen and the Beats in a single context. One of the articles, "Beat Zen, Square Zen, and Zen" by Watts, is often quoted. "Square" means old-fashioned, behind the times, and rigid. Watts's thesis was that the "Beat Zen" that was popular in the United States was different from the "Square Zen" passed down in Japan. Watts did not by any means dismiss "Beat Zen" but said that both were ways that could lead to enlightenment and that each person was free to choose as he or she saw fit. As the first essay, it perfectly set the tone of the special edition.

The Zen special edition of the *Chicago Review* was well received, being featured in the July 21 issue of *Time* in an introductory article entitled "Zen: Beat & Square."[80] In a conversation featured in the March 1960 issue of the magazine *Kiitsu*, Daisetz praised the special edition: "The Beats are featured in the *Chicago Review* (the 1958 Summer edition). It is a magazine put out by the students, who are graduate students, I think, and it is very well put together. It is quite well known in certain circles."[81]

Following the *Chicago Review*'s special Zen issue, however, the publication of the autumn 1958 issue of the magazine exposed the context of the Zen fad in the United States. Conservatives fiercely attacked an excerpt from Burroughs's *Naked Lunch* that was included in the magazine, and the following comment appeared on the front page of the October 25 issue of the *Chicago Daily News*.

> A magazine published by the University of Chicago is distributing one of the foulest collections of printed filth I've seen publicly circulated.
>
> I DON'T recommend anyone buying the thing out of curiosity, because the writing is obscure to the unbeat generation, and the purple prose is precisely what you can see chiseled on washroom walls.
>
> I'm not naming the magazine because I don't want to be responsible for its selling out. . . . If the obscenity in the magazine were read in

79. *Chicago Review* 12: 1 (Spring 1958).

80. "Zen: Beat & Square," *Time* 72: 3 (July 21, 1958).

81. Suzuki Daisetsu and Tsuji Sōmei, "Bīto zenerēshon sono ta no koto," in Furuta Shōkin, ed., *Suzuki Daisetsu zadanshū 5 zen no sekai* (Tokyo: Yomiuri Shinbunsha, 1972), 62. Originally published in *Kiitsu* (March 1960).

a public performance as a literary presentation, the performers would be arrested and charged with indecency, in my opinion.[82]

Faced with this negative public opinion, the administration of the University of Chicago intervened in the editorial affairs of the *Chicago Review* and ordered the staff to scrap plans for the next issue. The editor resigned and started up another magazine, where he continued to introduce the Beat literature that had been blocked from publication in the *Chicago Review*.[83] This was the sort of struggle that young people in the United States who were attracted to Zen were waging.

The Dharma Bums

In the midst of the pro and con views it generated, Kerouac's *On the Road* was a roaring success. I imagine many readers and publishers were hoping for a sequel. In October 1958, Kerouac published *The Dharma Bums*,[84] which was a novel about his post–*On the Road* experiences. The main character was modeled on Gary Snyder. As Kerouac and Snyder walked around the Sierra Nevada, their minds were filled with fantasies of Zen.

The Dharma Bums describes a vision of a "rucksack revolution," referring to a carefree life of constant movement in lieu of settling down in a stable environment. Kerouac's vision clearly was colored by his image of Zen. However, it does not appear that his new book received much praise. In fact, like *On the Road*, it was met with scornful criticism. For example, the review in the October 6, 1958, issue of *Time* stated: "This [rucksack revolution] vision helps to illustrate Author Kerouac's unhappy faculty for confusing freedom with irresponsibility, for abusing the Zen Buddhist idea of the inseparability of good and evil by using it as an excuse for self-indulgence."[85]

Daisetz was aware of how Zen was beginning to be "misunderstood" on the West Coast. In an essay titled "Zen in the Modern World" that appeared in the October–December 1958 issue of the *Japan Quarterly*, he wrote as follows:

82. Jack Harley, "Jack Rips Magazine," *Chicago Daily News* (October 25, 1958).

83. Ann Charters, "Foreword," in Ann Charters, ed., *Dictionary of Literary Biography*, vol. 16: *The Beats: Literary Bohemians in Postwar America. Part 1: A–L* (Detroit: Gale Research, 1983), xi–xii.

84. Jack Kerouac, *The Dharma Bums* (New York: Viking Press, 1958).

85. "The Yabyum Kid," *Time* 72: 14 (October 6, 1958).

Zen is at present evoking unexpected echoes in various fields of Western culture: music, painting, literature, semantics, religious philosophy, and psychoanalysis. But as it is in many cases grossly misrepresented or misinterpreted, I undertake here to explain most briefly, as far as language permits, what Zen aims at and what significance it has in the modern world, hoping that Zen will be saved from being too absurdly caricatured.[86]

Judging from the month of publication, when he wrote this essay Daisetz had not yet read *The Dharma Bums*, which emphasized Zen even more than *On the Road*. Even if had read it, however, it probably would not have changed his views. In his essay Daisetz directly criticized the Beat Generation, writing that "[t]hey must grow up as human beings."[87] When Daisetz wrote this phrase, he was probably visited by recurring thoughts of Alan, a bohemian like the Beat Generation.

A Once-in-a-Lifetime Conversation

At around this time, Kerouac, Ginsberg, and another Beat writer named Peter Orlovsky (1933–2010) got a once-in-a-lifetime opportunity to meet Daisetz. It was in October 1958 when Kerouac and the others were in New York for the book launch party for *The Dharma Bums*. They somehow heard that Daisetz was interested in them, and so they went to a phone booth and called him. Speaking through Okamura Mihoko, they managed to arrange for a meeting with Daisetz before the day was out. Kerouac later described the meeting in 1960 in a magazine called the *Berkeley Bussei* as follows:

> I rang Mr. Suzuki's door and he did not answer—suddenly I decided to ring it three times, firmly and slowly, and then he came. . . . Doctor Suzuki made us some green tea, very thick and soupy—he had precisely what idea of what place I should sit, and arranged—he himself sat behind a table and looked at us silently, nodding—I said in a loud voice (because he had told us he was a little deaf) "Why did Bodhidharma come from the West?"—He made no reply—He said

---

86. Suzuki T. Daisetz, "Zen in the Modern World," *Japan Quarterly* 5: 4 (October–December 1958): 452.
87. Suzuki T. Daisetz, "Zen in the Modern World," 454.

"You three young men sit here quietly and write haikus while I go make some green tea"—He brought us the green tea in cracked old soupbowls of some sort—He told us not to forget about the tea—When we left, he pushed us out the door but once we were out on the sidewalk he began giggling at us and pointing his finger and saying "Don't forget the tea!"—I said "I would like to spend the rest of my life with you"—He held up his finger and said "Sometime."[88]

It seems almost like a dialogue between a Zen master and pupil (*zen mondō*), but the story seems a little too glib. Since this appeared in a magazine more than a year after the encounter took place, I think it is safe to view the article as a dramatization on Kerouac's part. The story has five main points occurring in the following order: (1) Daisetz served tea; (2) Daisetz did not answer the koan Kerouac had posed, "Why did Bodhidharma come from the West?";[89] (3) Daisetz had them write haiku; (4) Daisetz told them, "Don't forget the tea!" when they left; and (5) in response to Kerouac, who said, "I would like to spend the rest of my life with you," Daisetz held up one finger and said, "Sometime." In particular, the scene where Daisetz holds up one finger is reminiscent of the koan "Gutei's Finger" in *The Gateless Gate*.[90] Kerouac had previously related this story in a letter to Philip Whalen. Since the letter was written immediately after the meeting in November 1958, I think it is safe to assume that Kerouac was honestly expressing something closer to what actually happened. Let us read part of the letter and then compare the two descriptions.

Finally I rang three times deliberately and then he famously came, walking downstairs, a small bald Japanese man of 80 and opened the door. Then he (he had paneled walls, ancient tomes) (and eyebrows that stick out an inch like the bush of the Dharma that takes so long to grow but once grown stays rooted grown) led us upstairs to a room where he picked out three special chairs and made us sit just there and picked his own chair facing us behind a huge bookpiled desk. So I wrote him out my Koan, "When the Buddha was about to speak a horse spoke instead," and he had a funny look in his eye and said, "The western

---

88. Jack Kerouac, [no title,] *Berkeley Bussei* (1960): [unpaginated].

89. *The Gateless Gate*, Case 37.

90. Case 3; the story of the Zen master who answers every question simply by holding up one finger.

mind is too complicated, after all the Buddha and the horse had some kind of understanding there." I didnt [*sic*] remember your own answer to that Koan. Then he said, "You young men sit here quietly and write haikus while I go and make some powdered green tea." . . . and when Allen said it tasted like shrimp he answered, "It tastes like beef" then he said "Dont [*sic*] forget that it's tea." . . . I wrote a haiku for him:

"Three little sparrows
on the roof,
Talking quietly, sadly"

. . . I said, "I would like to spend the rest of my life with you, sir," and he said "Sometime." And he kept pushing us out the door, . . . when we were out on the street he kept giggling and making signs at us through the window and finally said "Dont [*sic*] forget the tea!" And I said "The Key?" He said "The Tea."[91]

Compared to the description cited earlier, the latter gives more details about the meeting. The story here transpires as follows: (1) Kerouac challenged Daisetz with his own koan, which Daisetz answered; (2) Daisetz had them write haiku; (3) Daisetz served tea; (4) in response to Kerouac, who said, "I would like to spend the rest of my life with you," Daisetz said, "Sometime"; and (5) when they were leaving, Daisetz gestured to them and said, "Don't forget the tea!" Kerouac also talked about the meeting with Daisetz in an interview in the March 19, 1959, issue of the *New York Post*, but the story was as related in the letter.[92] Thus it appears that Kerouac made up the scene where Daisetz held up one finger and said "Sometime" by combining scenes (4) and (5) from the letter to Whalen. Ginsberg also described the meeting in an interview, reminiscing about how Daisetz had said, "Don't forget the tea" while "waving his hand."[93] In other words, Daisetz did not "hold up one finger"; he just "waved his hand."

It appears that Daisetz actually did make matcha (powdered green tea) for them. In that case, what reason did Daisetz have for serving the three of them matcha? In a roundtable discussion that was published in March

---

91. Letter from Jack Kerouac to Philip Whalen, dated early November 1958, in Kerouac, *Selected Letters, 1957–1969*, 164–65.

92. Alfred G. Aronowitz, "The Beat Generation," *New York Post* (March 19, 1959).

93. Ginzubāgu, "Intabyū," 258.

1960, Daisetz talked about the Beat Generation, saying that in the United States they had the reputation of rebelling against traditional things as they engaged in free creation. He was not praising Kerouac and the others by any means, but he was not being harshly critical of them either, as the conservatives in the United States were doing. He even went so far as to express his regrets over their recklessness, which was similar to Alan's, saying: "If they were properly instructed, there would be some who really wanted to sit zazen. Some really interesting people might appear, you know."[94]

In the same discussion, Daisetz used the Zen term *kissako* (to drink tea). *Kissako* means to guide a person to enlightenment just by the simple act of drinking tea. Daisetz was not explicitly talking about his meeting with the Beat writers, but judging from the context, it seems as though the memory of having served matcha to Kerouac and his friends flashed through his mind as he was discussing the Beat Generation.

> For a Zen person, *kissako* means to serve a person a cup of tea, but I want to point out that we can see the social nature of Zen here. Going to the United States a lot, I wonder what is going to happen with Zen in a social sense: I wonder if it will just be nothing more than personal enlightenment and things like that. That's not it; if guests come, how do you treat them? Having guests has social meaning, and it is there one finds the roots of compassion.[95]

By serving Kerouac and his friends matcha, Daisetz was trying to teach them about the social nature of Zen. Zen is not just for individuals; when a guest comes, how does the host treat the guest? While this is a social matter, it is, at the same time, a Zen matter. What Daisetz probably wanted to say was, "Not fitting into society and rebelling against it is all well and good, but it is within society that humans are truly alive."

In this discussion, Daisetz perhaps was questioning exactly how "social" Buddhism actually is. Since early modern times, Japanese Buddhism has neglected its relationship to the actual conditions of society to such an extent that it has been sarcastically labeled "funeral Buddhism." With earthquakes and disasters as the impetus, in recent years the participation of Buddhism in society has become the theme of scholarly research and symposia because

---

94. Suzuki and Tsuji, "Bīto zenerēshon sono ta no koto," 63.
95. Suzuki and Tsuji, "Bīto zenerēshon sono ta no koto," 70.

it has seemingly become detached from the real world. What Daisetz was looking for was a Buddhism that took the middle way, not isolated from society but also not rebelling against it. At the same time, the passage cited above also reveals Daisetz's awareness that his personal position was on par with the majority.

I think that concealed behind the tea that Daisetz served to Kerouac and his friends was the difficult relationship that Daisetz had with the wild and reckless Alan, who resembled the Beats in so many ways. It would not have been strange for Daisetz to have superimposed his son on Kerouac, who was six years younger than Alan. Daisetz's "parental love," however, did not reach Kerouac as it did Alan. It was precisely because Kerouac could not understand the meaning of the tea that Daisetz served him that he could so blithely dramatize the incident as a seemingly profound Zen *mondō*.

The Beats and Zen: Parting of the Ways

America's "Dharma Year" began with the *Mademoiselle* special issue on Zen in 1958, continued with the *Chicago Review* special edition and the publication of *The Dharma Bums*, and ended with the *kissako* between Daisetz, Kerouac, and Ginsberg. It would be more accurate to say that the relationship between Kerouac and Buddhism ended for good. Kerouac became aware of the critical attitude of "orthodox" Zen, represented by people such as Daisetz and Ruth Fuller Sasaki, toward *The Dharma Bums*. Even Gary Snyder, the model for the protagonist who had lived and practiced Zen in Japan, did not think very highly of the book. In a letter to Snyder dated February 23, 1959, Kerouac wrote as follows:

> Meanwhile, since Dharma Bums came out I feel that you've been silent
> and disappointed about me. I dont [*sic*] think the book was as bad as
> you think. . . . For Mrs. Sasaki to say that "it was a good portrait of
> Gary but he doesn't know *anything* about Buddhism" is just so fuckin
> typical of what's wrong with official Buddhism and all official reli-
> gions today. . . . Even Suzuki was looking at me through slitted eyes
> as tho I was a monstrous impostor of some kind (at least I feel that, I
> dunno). . . . I don't want ANYTHING to do with Official Zen and their

monasteries. There are no Hui Nengs[96] around there, left, I'll bet. But I do want to meet the old hillsmen thinkers and haiku writers and also lay some pretty girls and drink saki.[97]

Kerouac's attitude toward Zen had cooled down, almost like the tide going out. In a letter to Whalen dated March 15, he even went so far as to say, "[F]uck Suzuki, fuck Sasaki, fuck em all."[98] In an interview with the *New York Post* that appeared on March 19, Kerouac said, "I quit Buddhism because it preaches against entanglement with women," and that "Buddhism is also just words. And wisdom is heartless." "To me," he said, "the most important thing in life is sexual ecstasy."[99] It was a declaration of a final break with Buddhism coming only about five months after Kerouac had said to Daisetz, "I would like to spend the rest of my life with you, sir."

The following passage that appeared in the February 6, 1960, issue of *Saturday Review* is helpful for understanding the relationship between the Beat Generation and Zen as seen from the standpoint of "good citizens."

But though the Beats have cried loud the name of Zen, the boys and girls have never been close to adopting Zen discipline. The last thing they want on earth is a discipline. They have, rather, raided from Zen whatever offered them an easy rationale for what they wanted to do in the first place.[100]

Insofar as there were people like Snyder, who lived at Daitokuji in order to undergo Zen training, it is a bit much to say that "the boys and girls have never been close to adopting Zen discipline." There is even the issue of whether or not it is proper to include Snyder in the Beat Generation at all. The point the author makes, however, is that the Beat Generation found in Zen a rationale that whatever they wanted to do was acceptable. What did the Beats themselves think about this? Snyder offered the following dispassionate analysis in an essay appearing in the January 1960 issue of *Chūō kōron*.

96. Chinese Chan master Huineng (638–713).

97. Letter from Jack Kerouac to Gary Snyder, dated February 23, 1959, in Kerouac, *Selected Letters, 1957–1969*, 186.

98. Letter from Jack Kerouac to Philip Whalen, dated March 15, 1959, in Kerouac, *Selected Letters, 1957–1969*, 190.

99. Aronowitz, "The Beat Generation."

100. John Ciardi, "Epitaph for the Dead Beats," *Saturday Review* (February 6, 1960): 12.

When his [Kerouac] novel *On the Road* was published in 1957, the word *beat* became famous and overnight America became aware that it had a generation of writers and intellectuals on its hands that was breaking all the rules. This new generation was educated, but it refused to go into academic careers or business or government. It published its poems in its own little magazines, and didn't even bother to submit works to the large established highbrow journals that had held the monopoly on avant-garde writing for so long. . . .

What was the reaction of the newspapers and the public to this? They were either outraged or a little jealous. It is one of those few times in American history that a section of the population has freely chosen to disaffiliate itself from "the American standard of living" and all that goes with it—in the name of freedom. . . . But both the left-wing intellectuals and the newspaper editors of America see this as heresy of the worst sort, and both sides shout "irresponsible." . . .

In a way one can see the beat generation as another aspect of the perpetual "third force" that has been moving through history with its own values of community, love, and freedom.[101]

Snyder was obviously drawing a line between himself and the Beat Generation. While he presented himself, who had gone to Japan and gotten close to real Zen, as different from the Beats, at the same time he was also defending the crazy Zen-inspired spirit of Kerouac.

It cannot be doubted that the Beat Generation, under the influence of Daisetz, changed American culture. It also appears that Daisetz saw Alan's lifestyle reflected in the way the Beat Generation lived. Without Alan, it is impossible to understand Daisetz's attitude toward the Beat Generation.

101. Gary Snyder, "Notes on the Beat Generation," in Ann Charters, ed., *Beat Down to Your Soul: What Was the Beat Generation?* (New York: Penguin Books, 2001), 518–20. Originally published in *Chūō kōron* (January 1960), in Japanese.

SIX

The Undutiful Son

Alan during the 1950s

A life like that of Kerouac, always on the move and never settling down in a stable position or fixed abode—that was Alan's life as well. What sort of a father-son relationship did Daisetz and Alan have between the year 1955, when the Beat Generation burst onto the scene, and the "Dharma Year" of 1958? Unfortunately, we do not know what Alan was up to during those years. It appears that he did translations, magazine editing, and the like—what one could call freelance work. He also did some work for the Yashika Camera Company. Alan loved photography, and in that sense he was following firmly in Daisetz's footsteps.

After marrying Shikiba Mikako, Alan probably relied on financial support from his wife's family. On June 18, 1955, however, a catastrophe struck: a fire broke out in the Shikiba Hospital, where Shikiba Ryūzaburō was the director, and eighteen patients burned to death. At the time Alan was visiting New York and was hoping to see his father, but the timing coincided with a trip by Daisetz, and they were not able to meet. Alan was probably traveling between Japan and the United States trying to do some business. Just at that time, his wife's family was greatly shaken by the fire, and Alan was probably unable to secure the financing he was hoping for. It appears that he wrote another letter to Daisetz asking for money. The reply to that request, dated July 24, is a matter of public record.

You seem to have too many things to accomplish while in America. How long do you expect to be in this country? You will be fortunate if you could accomplish one of your several tasks. / As to your kozukai [allowance], how much are you likely to need? I can't give you very much because I myself am not very much provided with. Let me have your detailed plans. / You may have all your passages payed [paid] both ways coming and going back but the Japanese Foreign Office is very strict since last year about getting dollar support in America which means who will pay your hotel bills and other expenses. How are you managing this; did you get any supporter? If you have one he has to notify the Japanese authorities on all the necessary datas [data] concerning his business, income, etc. . . . / As to my own income, it is not enough to get the necessary official sanctions because the income is to be far above mine which is only $4,000 a year and I have no bank account large enough to back any dollar support for others.[1]

It appears that Alan, in addition to starting up a new magazine, was planning to make a movie about life in a Zen monastery. In a letter to Alan dated August 31, Daisetz wrote: "As to making films about Zen monastery life, I once thought of the enterprise myself. I suppose it requires a great deal of money to carry out your plans. As far as I am concern[ed], I do not know of anybody who will advance the money."[2] Daisetz also wrote: "Before yours there have been attempts made but no one so far has succeeded, although this does not of course mean that yours will not bear fruit,"[3] showing that, as always, Daisetz supported Alan's business ideas. No matter what kind of trouble Alan caused, he never completely gave up on him.

In September 1955, members of the Tokyo Metropolitan Physician's Association were called upon to investigate a religious group called Shinreikyō that reportedly could perform miracles. There is a record indicating that the person who presided over the roundtable discussion at that time was "Mr. Masaru Suzuki, the son of the philosopher and Zen teacher Daisetz Suzuki; his wife transcribed the discussion."[4] We can see here that the appellation "the son of Daisetz Suzuki" was Alan's selling point. The pressure of being Daisetz's son must have weighed heavily on Alan and probably sometimes drove him to drink.

The novelist Mizukami (Minakami) Tsutomu (1919–2004) wrote that Alan and Mikako lived in a rented house in Tomisaka, Bunkyō-ku, Tokyo,

---

1. *SDZ* 38, 226.
2. *SDZ* 38, 241.
3. *SDZ* 38, 242.
4. Shinreikyō Shinja Ichidō, *Shinreikyō nyūmon* (Tokyo: Isuto Puresu, 2000), 165.

where he also lived from 1956 to the following year. His brief description of them follows:

> Yoshikatsu is the oldest son of Daisetz Suzuki sensei. His wife is Mikako, the oldest daughter of Dr. Shikiba Ryūzaburō, who was a psychiatrist as well as an art critic. . . . Mr. Suzuki typed all day and his job was writing the subtitles for foreign movies. He drank a lot and was always inviting us to his room.[5]

Mizukami mistakenly wrote Alan's name, "Masaru," not with one character, but with two, which he rendered as "Yoshikatsu."[6] Moreover, it is most likely that Alan was not writing subtitles for foreign movies but rather English subtitles for Japanese movies. The reason is that it is hard to imagine that Alan had a Japanese typewriter or the specialized skill to use it. Japanese typewriters of that time had a character platen on which were arranged about two thousand Japanese characters, and only a skilled professional could operate one. Alan's skill, on the other hand, was typing English. Perhaps because he was writing a lighthearted piece for a serialized newspaper column, Mizukami could be forgiven for this sort of lack of concern for accuracy.

The 1950s were the golden age of Japanese cinema, and Alan worked part time for the movie studio Tōhō Company. Tōhō produced a number of films that are well known in the English-speaking world, such as *Shichinin no samurai* (Seven Samurai; 1954) and *Gojira* (Godzilla; 1954). It may very well be that while his name was not recorded, Alan made a contribution to the export of Japanese cinema to foreign countries. Unfortunately, there is no way of knowing which films Alan worked on. More documents need to be brought to light to determine the facts.

In September 1956, Alan visited Daisetz in New York many times.[7] It is not clear if this happened during those visits, but according to those close to Ike Mariko, Alan tried to convince Daisetz to allow him to inherit the foreign rights to his books. Alan's father-in-law, Shikiba Ryūzaburō, who

---

5. Mizukami Tsutomu, *Watakushiban Tōkyō zue* (Tokyo: Asahi Bunko, 1999), 114. Originally published in the *Asahi Shimbun* (Tokyo and Tama district edition; June 5, 1994, to September 10, 1995).

6. "Masaru" and the *katsu* of "Yoshikatsu" are written with the same Chinese character: "Masaru" is the native Japanese pronunciation, whereas "katsu" is the Sino-Japanese pronunciation.

7. *SDZ* 38, 407.

had witnessed Daisetz's popularity in Europe with his own eyes, apparently advised Alan and Mikako to approach Daisetz about the rights. Daisetz scolded Alan and refused his request since he intended the royalties to be used for research on Zen culture. As far as Daisetz was concerned, he had done more than enough for Alan. Despite all that Daisetz had done, Alan continued to haunt the gaudy entertainment world, and had gotten a woman pregnant and then abandoned her. His habit of quarreling when drunk had not changed. As a father in his late eighties, Daisetz had probably reached the end of his rope. His feelings toward Alan are summed up in a letter to Suzuki Rei dated August 4, 1956.

> While Alan himself is a talented person, drinking has caused him to lose his way. He can't seem to apply himself to anything, and wherever he goes, he gets into arguments and ruins his future prospects. It is really quite regrettable.[8]

Daisetz Returns Home

It appears that Daisetz had been thinking about returning to Japan beginning in early 1958. During his absence, Hayashida Kumino had taken charge of the Matsugaoka Bunko, together with her husband and two children in January 1955.[9] In two letters to Kumino dated January 19, 1958, Daisetz wrote that one never knows when death will come and that there were things he wanted to research in Japan and friends he wanted to meet, and so he had decided to return, at least for a while. He also wrote that he would be inconvenienced in his daily life and work if he did not bring Mihoko with him, and since she was still young, he wanted to give her the opportunity to learn as much about Japan as she could.[10] In November 1958, Daisetz returned to Japan accompanied by Mihoko and made the Matsugaoka Bunko his sole workplace. Daisetz probably intended to compile all of his research with her help. In order to do that, he needed someone to keep away all the visitors who would disturb him, and so Mihoko took over that duty, which had previously been performed by Okono.

There are few if any records about what Alan was doing around 1960. It

8. *SDZ* 38, 393.
9. Hayashida, *Ōoji Suzuki Daisetsu kara no tegami*, 102.
10. *SDZ* 39, 6–7.

appears that he continued to do work for the camera maker Yashika. There are no signs that he wrote any more lyrics for popular songs, so it is unclear how he made his living. It is assumed that he received a certain amount in royalty payments for his big hits such as "Tokyo Boogie-woogie" and "Buttons and Bows." Among Daisetz's letters from this period is one that he sent to Alan on July 27 from the summer resort town of Karuizawa.

Dear Alan, / I am in receipt of your strong "indictments," most of which I do not deserve. You seem to be badly excited. What you state is mostly due to your misunderstanding, facts are misrepresented, situations are not grasped in their proper bearings. I am, however, not in the mood of explaining myself, at least for the present. / I never realised that an [redacted by editor] of your class was treated by the Japanese in the same manner as an [redacted by editor]. Perhaps the first surroundings in which you were brought up in Kyoto were not good, though we were quite innocent of all this. / The one thing I regret very much about you is that you have unfortunately not made full use of your talents so far. No doubt in many ways you are a gifted person. / Your inebriety I am afraid goes back to your heredity. I am however in full sympathy with you in whatever way you may turn. We are all more or less victims of "karma." / Do not talk about "fame"—which is a most despicable thing. I never aspired ofr [for] it. / I am now in Karuizawa. I am reminded of many things we both experienced together with mother. [sic] here. / When the summer is over and I am back in Kamakura, I hope you will visit me at the Library with your wife. Let us have a dinner together in a pleasanter mood. I hope you will accept my invitation. I will let you know at an early date. / In conclusion I wish to assure you of my not having any ill-will towards you, however much you may blame me. I always have a fatherly feeling for you. / Affectionately yours,[11]

We do not know what sort of trouble with Alan that Daisetz was referring to in this letter, but we can divine that, as always, Alan was a problematic son. We can also see that no matter what happened, Daisetz was a parent who would never abandon his adopted son.

Upon his return home, Daisetz began the onerous task of translating the *Kyōgyō shinshō* (Teaching, Practice, Faith, and Enlightenment; ca. 1224) by

---

11. *SDZ* 39, 224–25.

Shinran, the founder of Jōdo Shinshū (Shin sect) into English. It was also the earnest wish of the Jōdo Shinshū institution as well, and there was no one other than Daisetz who could do it. Daisetz temporarily shelved his translation of Zen-related works and, after three years, completed a draft translation of the *Kyōgyō shinshō* in July 1961.[12] For those who regard Daisetz as a "Zen" person, his translation of the *Kyōgyō shinshō* might seem odd. However, Daisetz made significant contributions to research on Jōdo Shinshū, beginning with his study of *myōkōnin*, a term that refers to worshippers of this sect and their deep faith.

Consequently, the perception that Daisetz was simply a Zen man is mistaken. He was a scholar of Buddhism whose interests included Zen, the Shin sect, and mysticism. The breadth of Daisetz's research must have seemed heretical to those Buddhist scholars who were devoted to their own sect. On a doctrinal level, the Zen sect, which disavows "life after death" and aims for enlightenment through *jiriki* (self-power) and the Shin sect, which relies on the *tariki* (other power) of Amitabha Buddha in the hopes of rebirth in paradise (*gokuraku ōjō*), must seem like oil and water. Because the doctrines of Shin and mysticism contradicted Zen, people who wanted to applaud Daisetz's research as contributing to the spread of Zen downplayed his interest in the Shin sect and mysticism.[13]

Ike Mariko continued to work in the entertainment world. She appeared in the NHK Red and White Singing Contest a total of six times by the time of its eighth broadcast in 1957. There was a man to whom she was considering getting married, but she did not want to make her daughter call a man who was not her actual father "Papa," so she remained single. Her daughter Maya continued to believe that Daisetz was her birth father. According to one of my interviews with Maya,[14] in response to her question to her mother about why she had married an old man, Mariko said: "Because he is a great man." Daisetz was devoted to both Mariko and his granddaughter Maya.

---

12. Okamura Mihoko, "Hongan ga nobotta," in Ueda and Okamura, *Suzuki Daisetsu to wa dareka*, 187–94. Originally published in *Zen bunka* 181 (July 2001).

13. In recent years there have been attempts to reevaluate Daisetz's legacy not just as it relates to Zen, but as seen through the totality of his work. An example of this is the conference "Reflections on D.T. Suzuki: Commemorating the 50th Anniversary of His Death," held at the International Research Center for Japanese Studies, Kyoto, December 5–6, 2016. See John Breen et al., eds., *Beyond Zen: D.T. Suzuki and the Modern Transformation of Buddhism* (Honolulu: University of Hawai'i Press, 2022).

14. My interviews with Ike Maya (in person, telephone, and email) took place between July 2010 and November 2014.

Maya was also a mischievous child. Daisetz would always tell Mihoko, "I'm afraid that Maya is going to be too much for Mariko to handle." Reminded of Alan when he was young, Daisetz must have been worried about Maya's future. One day Maya asked Daisetz, "What is Zen?" In reply, Papa Daisetz said, "Zen is things just as they are. So Maya should just be Maya." Maya, being a child, had no idea what Daisetz was talking about, but the conversation stuck with her.[15]

In one interview Maya told me that she was taken to meet her actual father when she was a child. Mariko's mother and Alan had an unusually simpatico relationship; when Alan and Mariko were first married, he would often say that even if he and Mariko parted ways, he would never sever his relationship with her mother. True to his words, Maya's grandmother remained friendly with Alan, and on several occasions took Maya with her to join Alan for lunch at the Hilltop Hotel in Tokyo. At the time, however, Maya did not know that the Western-looking man was her biological father. Alan was tall and handsome, and Maya referred to him as "the man at the hotel."

Mariko was not selected to appear on the NHK Red and White Singing Contest in 1958 and the following year. Although she had not been invited to the first broadcast in 1951 and the fifth broadcast in 1954, this was the first time she had been passed over two years in a row. For singers, being selected to appear in this contest was a very serious matter. Mariko realized that she had reached a turning point, and she decided to study jazz anew in the United States, its place of origin.

Mariko went to the United States with Maya in August 1960 at the urging of an old American friend. Mariko was worried about living in a country where she did not understand the language, but she decided to take up the challenge. She enrolled Maya in an elementary school in Oregon while she pursued music in New York. While in the United States Mariko also studied Latin music and broadened her performance style. She returned to Japan in April of the following year. Originally she intended to have Maya continue her education in the United States, but Maya's host family was worried that she would forget Japanese, and so Mariko had Maya return to Japan one month after she herself arrived.

Maya was on the verge of turning ten. She was always asking why her father was an old man, and so Daisetz decided that it was time to tell her the truth. Daisetz was probably reproaching himself for waiting until Alan was

---

15. Ike Maya, "Daisetsu papa to watashi," in Kaneko Tsutomu, ed., *Tsuisō Suzuki Daisetsu: Botsugo 40 nen kinen kikōshū* (Kamakura: Matsugaoka Bunko, 2006), 6–7.

twenty-two before telling him about his birth parents. Perhaps thinking that he should not repeat the same mistake, he summoned Mariko and Maya to the Matsugaoka Bunko.

The Incident

According to those close to Mariko, she received an urgent phone call from Mihoko on the day before she was to go with Maya to the Matsugaoka Bunko. Apparently, Alan had done something and reporters from newspapers and magazines had besieged the Bunko. As a result, Daisetz wanted her to know that it would be better not to come. With no idea of what had happened, Mariko went out, and at a newsstand in Shibuya station, she saw a headline in a sports newspaper saying something about "the ex-husband of Ike Mariko." I did an exhaustive search of the sports newspapers published in the Kantō region that are housed at the National Diet Library, but was unable to find such an article printed around that time. Instead, I located a short article in a mass-circulation newspaper. The *Yomiuri Shimbun* of June 5, 1961, relates the following incident.

> Waitress Jumps from a Third-Story Window and Is Injured—Confined and Beaten
>
> At around 6:20 pm on the 4th, at the Andōzaka Apartments 3F, 34 Suidō-cho, Bunkyō-ku, Tokyo, someone saw a woman jump from the apartment of Masaru Suzuki (44), a part-time employee of the Foreign Department of Tōhō Co. Ltd., to the garden eight meters below. The woman was taken to a nearby hospital with bruises on her left lower back and arms that will require three weeks to heal fully.
>
> According to the investigation by the Tomisaka police station, Miss T, an eighteen-year-old waitress at a bar in Jūnisō, Shinjuku-ku went with a friend, a U.S. Army corporal named Mogalin, to Suzuki's apartment in the afternoon, but once she was inside the door was locked and they took nude photos of her. After Mogalin left Suzuki attacked her, so she jumped out of the window. Suzuki was arrested and taken to the Tomisaka police station on suspicion of rape and false imprisonment. The investigation is ongoing.[16]

---

16. *Yomiuri Shimbun* (Tokyo edition; June 5, 1961).

The *Asahi Shimbun* from the same day carried essentially the same report. While it is not clear if these reports were accurate, this was the story that was circulated. According to my interview with Maya, Mariko was afraid that she would hear the story. Fortunately, Maya was attending the American School, and she did not hear about any Japanese current events while she was there.

Not long after, the June 26 issue (on sale June 19) of *Shūkan shinchō*, a popular weekly magazine, featured a seven-page article entitled "The Most Undutiful Son of the Shōwa Period: How the Son of a Recipient of the Order of Culture Went Wrong."[17] It was treated as a top story in newspaper advertisements for the magazine, so it is possible that the headline Mariko saw at Shibuya station was promotion for *Shūkan shinchō* (fig. 6).

Of course this article can be categorized as a "gossip feature" in a weekly mass-circulation magazine so the contents must be taken with a grain of salt. While the entire article should not be regarded as fact, I want to introduce it here just from the perspective that such a report was actually circulated. The article is replete with testimonies from the people involved, and these are backed up by other documentation. At the very least, it is much more reliable than the pieces written by Shiroyama Saburō and Mizukami Tsutomu that I introduced earlier, which have obvious factual mistakes regarding the most basic information, such as names.

After giving the outline of the incident, the *Shūkan shinchō* article includes a statement by Daisetz's disciple Shimura Takeshi (1923–1989), acting as Daisetz's spokesman. According to Shimura, Daisetz's position on the matter was as follows:

> Alan is already past forty years of age. As far as I am concerned, I have already given him a proper university education. Consequently, I can say that from whatever angle you look at this, Alan is his own person. Since he is already an independent member of society, even though I am his father, I am not in a position to say this and that over every little thing. For example, the daughter of Churchill [the prime minister of the UK] lives a very flamboyant life, but in foreign countries, they do not bring the parents into it on every occasion.[18]

---

17. "Shōwa saidai no fushō no musuko: Bunka kunshō jushōsha no chōnan ga guredasu made," *Shūkan shinchō* 6: 25 (June 26, 1961): 30–36.

18. "Shōwa saidai no fushō no musuko," 33.

Fig. 6. Advertisement for *Shūkan shinchō* from the June 19, 1961, issue of *Yomiuri Shimbun*

In addition to this "official" comment, the same article quotes Daisetz's remarks to Shimura.

> Alan is a very talented man. Even though this incident occurred, he could live an honorable life if he just stopped drinking. Society at large should not ignore a person of Alan's talents. My most fervent desire is to find some way to get Alan to stop drinking. Shimura, what can we do to get Alan to give up drinking? He's a good, upright person, but he lacks willpower.[19]

In his "official" statement, Daisetz distanced himself from Alan, but reading what Daisetz reputedly said to Shimura, Daisetz has still not lost his love for Alan. He was like the father in the New Testament waiting for the return of the Prodigal Son.

The article also contains the following account from a relative, Mr. X: Daisetz and Beatrice had no children. However, Beatrice wanted to raise a child following her own ideal and communicated that desire to Okono. Alan is the child that Okono found, and so far as the family register is concerned, he was raised as Daisetz and Beatrice's natural child. Beatrice's educational

---

19. "Shōwa saidai no fushō no musuko," 33.

ideal followed the American style and was very strict. Therefore, Alan was instructed to stay in his room at times designated by his parents, and compared to normal children, I felt sorry for him. Daisetz was so devoted to his study that he hardly spent any time with Alan; for example, if Alan said, "I want to go to Karuizawa," Daisetz's attitude was "How will that benefit your life?"[20]

Reading the "Daisetz Diaries" and Daisetz's letters, the assertion that Daisetz did not concern himself with raising Alan does not correspond with reality. Even though he often took action after Alan had caused some trouble, Daisetz performed his duty as a father at each important juncture. It appears that this relative was not aware of Daisetz's efforts.

Alan's Loneliness

The *Shūkan shinchō* also solicited a comment from Iwakura Masaji, who spoke about the time when Alan was young and Daisetz asked him to look after Alan for a summer in Iwakura's home prefecture of Toyama. Iwakura related that "Alan was intelligent and uncommonly daring. I felt strongly that he was different from the average child. He gave me the hope that if everything worked out, he could be an outstanding person. However, he possessed individuality, which in the formal and hypocritical educational environment of the time no one could understand, and therefore he could not develop normally."[21] Iwakura also said that as he spent time with Alan, "I gradually came to understand Masaru's loneliness."[22] Iwakura was moved by the love that Daisetz lavished on Beatrice, in particular how he shared her pain in caring for her when she was ill. "However, I never saw him express that kind of love to Masaru. It may be my limited view, however."[23]

This article obviously was published while Daisetz was still alive. Knowing full well that Daisetz might see the article, his disciple Iwakura is apparently taking a critical position vis-à-vis Daisetz regarding Alan. The article also introduces comments from an old friend of Alan, a Mr. F, regarding Alan's history with women.

---

20. "Shōwa saidai no fushō no musuko," 34.
21. "Shōwa saidai no fushō no musuko," 35.
22. "Shōwa saidai no fushō no musuko," 35.
23. "Shōwa saidai no fushō no musuko," 35.

In any case, he was tall and very handsome, and so he was extremely popular with the college girls. Because of that, even in middle school, there were always women problems (note: Alan transferred from the Kyoto Municipal Number Three Middle School to the Mt. Kōya Middle School midterm). . . . His graduation thesis was on the American playwright Eugene O'Neill, and I heard that it was outstanding and well regarded in the school (note: Mr. Ueno, the dean of Doshisha University, said that "he only did what the professor required of him; one cannot say that it was particularly good").

In 1937, he went to San Francisco as a representative for the Japan-America Students Conference, and that's where he came to know K, his first wife (note: K was a representative from Tokyo Woman's Christian University).

K was a remarkably talented woman, but he ensnared her on the spot. He was really good at that. He would frown a bit and flatter them.

So it was like this: after he got tired of K, he moved on to Ike Mariko (singer) and then he came back to the intelligentsia (note: his present wife). His tastes may change, but all of the women are exemplary. He possesses something that makes the top-level women fall for him. He knows exactly which buttons to push. . . .

Looking from that point of view, this latest incident was a mistake. The woman involved was from a different class compared to the women he'd been involved with previously.

He had already gotten a girl pregnant when he was in college, and he's gotten one girl after another pregnant since then. I think there have been three or four of them by now, and each time it's a different woman.

Anyway, back then, Daisetz and Okono had already washed their hands of him, and on the occasion of his first wedding, Daisetz didn't attend; except for one of his relatives, no one from his family attended.

I thought he would settle down, but he got together with Ike Mariko, whom he had known from when they were young, and dumped K. Then he got together with his present wife, who was working with him when he had a translation office in the Sanshin Building in Hibiya, and dumped Mariko. During that time there were a lot of rumors.

After all, he's pleasant and he's generous with his money.

Anyway, he went from wife to wife to wife without meaning anything good or bad by it. He's a man without a single shred of the sense of duty that ordinary Japanese have.[24]

Not only does this describe Alan's history accurately, one can see how carefully the magazine gathered its facts, even going so far as to get a comment from a university professor regarding Alan's thesis. According to Mr. F, Alan fathered three or four children, including Nobu's daughter and Maya. The article concludes with a statement from Yamaguchi Susumu (1895–1976), a former president of Otani University.

I think that as far as his son was concerned, he thought that a person's strength has its limits and that no matter how you look at it, the limit is the limit and there's nothing one can do. . . .

Sensei gave lectures on theology up until 1945, but the sensei was such a great man that he was beyond any evaluation the students could give. Sensei definitely felt that if he gave lectures to the best of his ability, whatever the students wanted to make of them was entirely up to them and of no concern to him.[25]

The article leaves the reader with the impression that, as a father, Daisetz was on a higher plane, out of reach by his son and others around him. Readers can judge for themselves whether such a banal evaluation is accurate or not.

Branded as an "Undutiful Son"

It appears that as a result of the extensive coverage in the weekly magazine, Alan lost his social position. It is not known how the affair was settled, whether Alan was sued or whether he came to a private settlement with the victim. Bringing that to light would have little meaning. Even if Alan had been found innocent, just being arrested by the police leaves an indelible stain on a person's life. Thereafter, Alan became an untouchable subject for the people in Daisetz's circle. They just wanted to forget about what happened. As proof of this, scholars and people connected with the Zen sect, as well as Hayashida Kumino, who wrote in detail about Alan and the inner

---

24. "Shōwa saidai no fushō no musuko," 36. All of the notes in the text are included as they appear in the original article.

25. "Shōwa saidai no fushō no musuko," 36.

workings of the Suzuki family in *Granduncle*, never mentioned a single thing about this incident in their writings. I was also unable to find any clues other than the statement that Daisetz gave to *Shūkan shinchō* that would inform us of his reaction. Among the letters that have been made public, there are none that refer to the incident. Additionally, as I mentioned previously, the diaries from Daisetz's later years are missing. There is no way of knowing Daisetz's true suffering over what his son had done.

I would like to think a bit about the "undutiful son" label that got pinned on Alan. There three ways this characterization can be used: when parents use it, when a son uses it on himself, and when society at large applies it to him. In all of these cases, the "undutiful son" label will be applied when the actions of the son are greatly inferior to those of the father. There are probably few cases where parents will say "that undutiful son of ours . . . ," since by doing so they put themselves on a pedestal. If the parents are universally recognized as being superior to the son, however, they might refer to their "undutiful son." If the son calls himself "undutiful," this expresses humility and respect for the parents; however, if a son is truly undutiful, he will probably not refer to himself in that way. As it was in Alan's case, on occasion this label is used by the general public.

There is no absolute standard for defining an "undutiful son." So long as he does not do something drastic, a son raised by normal parents will not be called undutiful. Whether a child is undutiful or not is determined by the relative relationship between the parent and child. Moreover, even if a child is superior to ordinary people, if the direction the child takes is not what is expected by society at large, he will be labeled as an undutiful son after all. Alan showed his talents in writing the lyrics to popular songs and translations in nonacademic fields. If Alan had not been Daisetz's son, his accomplishments probably would have earned him the label of "a son to be proud of."

However, this comes with a condition: if Alan had not been a drinker. Daisetz grieved over it time and again—Alan's drinking was nothing to be proud of. So we must ask ourselves: what was it that drove Alan to drink? It is necessary to objectively examine just how much of a "juvenile delinquent" Alan actually was. Leaving aside his early youth, I have found no record of Alan being violent to others other than the incident involving the waitress. I spoke with many people who knew Ike Mariko well, and they said that there was never any domestic violence. It does not appear that Alan resorted to Machiavellian tactics at work, and if one leaves aside his relationships with women, there is nothing to indicate that he ever did anything that would incur someone's wrath. He enjoyed drinking, but there are no indications that he gambled. He importuned Daisetz for money a number of times, but in all those cases, Alan was asking for capital for his business ventures, to pay off his drinking bills, and for consolation money to a woman (at least once).

It is true that Alan caused many problems, but he was not extraordinarily "bad." However, precisely because he was raised by D.T. Suzuki, society judged him severely. For Alan, this was probably stressful enough to lead him to turn to alcohol.

The Death of Daisetz

Daisetz continued his scholarly pursuits after the incident. He had much unfinished business such as completing an English translation of the *Kyōgyō shinshō*, the compilation of an English-language dictionary of Zen terms, and English translations of such fundamental Zen texts as *The Record of Linji* and *The Blue Cliff Record*. He had already begun translating *The Blue Cliff Record*, but it was not a task that even someone of Daisetz's talents would be able to complete easily. Daisetz was also busy with lectures, roundtable discussions, and dealing with visitors from foreign countries.

He had become very hard of hearing, but overall Daisetz was in good condition, and his sturdy legs were up to the task of going up and down the 150 steps between Tōkeiji and the Matsugaoka Bunko. After turning ninety he underwent regular health screenings at St. Luke's International Hospital in Tokyo, and other than hearing loss and having high blood pressure and cataracts, there was nothing wrong with him.[26] Daisetz sometimes spoke of how little time he had left. Mihoko wrote that she once said to Daisetz, "It's probably a bother for you, but I will follow you wherever you go." Daisetz, appearing to be nonplussed, instantly replied, "Oh, no bother. Follow me anywhere." Mihoko said that this conversation "put my mind at rest."[27]

The Angel of Death, however, appeared suddenly. In the early morning hours of July 11, 1966, on the day that he was to travel to Karuizawa to escape the summer heat, as was his annual custom, Daisetz was stricken by severe abdominal pains. Greatly concerned over Daisetz's unusual physical distress, Mihoko and Kumino asked a local doctor to make a house call and sent someone to the pharmacy to buy medicine. Around noon, a doctor from St.

---

26. Hinohara Shigeaki, *Shi o dō ikitaka* (Tokyo: Chūkō Shinsho, 1983), 79.
27. Okamura, "Myōyō," 109.

Luke's Hospital arrived; Daisetz was placed in a sleeper taxi and transported from Kita-Kamakura to Tokyo with a police car leading the way.[28]

On the way, the taxi got stuck in traffic, and it took three hours to get Daisetz to St. Luke's. Dr. Hinohara, who examined Daisetz, concluded that it was too late to put him through the dangerous procedure of opening up his abdomen. When Hinohara told Daisetz, who was still conscious, "Your condition is very grave," Daisetz indicated that he understood. Daisetz's blood pressure had begun to drop, so Hinohara administered morphine to ease the pain as well as a pressor agent and a blood transfusion, and placed him in an oxygen tent from the chest up to help him breathe.[29] Hearing of the emergency, many of Daisetz's associates came to the hospital to see him, but Hinohara refused all visitors aside from Mihoko and a minimal number of people.[30]

Kumino remembers Alan coming to Daisetz's sickbed, even though visitors were severely restricted. When Mihoko said to Daisetz, "Sensei, it's Alan," Daisetz crawled to the edge of the oxygen tent and murmured "Ohh, ohh," while moving his hands.[31] It was the final conversation between father and son in this world.

As Daisetz's conditioned further deteriorated, the following conversation took place between Mihoko and Daisetz.

"Would you like something?"

"No, nothing. Thank you."[32]

Thus, one of the great men of the twentieth century, who had left to posterity a veritable mountain of words, took his leave at 5:00 a.m. on July 12, 1966, with the simple phrase "No, nothing. Thank you." The cause of death was listed variously as thrombosis of the mesenteric artery or strangulation of the ileus.

The exchange that Mihoko remembers has taken on mythical status as "Daisetz's last words." "Nothing" has the meaning of *mu* (nothingness). The idea that the final state of consciousness of D.T. Suzuki was *mu* is the perfect tool for eulogizing the life of a "Zen man." Even if we believe Mihoko's recollection, that interpretation needs to be treated cautiously, because if

28. Hayashida, *Ooji Suzuki Daisetsu kara no tegami*, 130–37.

29. Asahina Sōgen, "Daisetsu sensei iku," in Nishitani, *Kaisō Suzuki Daisetsu*, 182. Originally published in *Engaku* (September 1, 1966).

30. Hinohara, *Shi o dō ikitaka*, 84.

31. Hayashida, *Ooji Suzuki Daisetsu kara no tegami*, 141.

32. Satō Taira, "Taikō," in Nishitani, *Kaisō Suzuki Daisetsu*, 146. Originally published in *Daihōrin* (September 1, 1966).

one reads this conversation straight, it is, after all simply his secretary asking Daisetz if he wants anything done for him and Daisetz responding, "No, nothing in particular."

Zen people focus on the "Nothing." However, the psychiatrist Kondō Akihisa (1911–1999), who rushed to Daisetz's bedside, remembers his last words as "Don't worry. Thank you, thank you."[33] Ōtani Kōshō (1925–1999), the newly appointed head priest of the Ōtani sect of Jōdo Shinshū, who was close friends with both Daisetz and Kondō, maintains that Daisetz's last words were not "nothing," but "Thank you," as related to him by Kondō.

I heard that he comforted everyone, saying, "Don't worry" and then said, "Thank you, thank you." It is my feeling that this "Thank you," filled with the sensei's unique nuance, was heard from him more and more as sensei's empathy for Shinshū deepened. No, for the sensei, who was born in Kanazawa, where Shinshū flourishes, if the sharpness and unbending spiritual strength of Zen was the father, this Shinshū-like feeling of gratitude was in the shadow as the mother, sometimes in the shade, sometimes in the sun, contributing to the harmonious creation of the unique person known as Daisetz Suzuki, permeating his entire life.[34]

It goes without saying that "nothing" is *mu*, which embodies the essence of Zen, whereas the word "thank you" is representative of the Shin sect and is akin to *go'on hōsha* (Indebtedness to Amitabha Buddha). Looking at all of this, one cannot help but feel how different people's life view can be according to their faith. However, an interpretation that favors "nothing" or "thank you" is incorrect. What Daisetz said was simply either, "No, nothing. Thank you" or "Don't worry. Thank you." and nothing more than that should be read into it.

Daisetz's funeral was held on July 14 at the Tōkeiji temple. Asahina Sōgen was the officiating priest, and of course Ike Mariko and Maya attended. According to Mariko's associates, Mariko saw Alan at the funeral, and while they nodded in greeting, no words were exchanged. I can imagine that it must have been excruciating for Alan to have been glared at by the other

---

33. Kondō Akihisa, "Jōshū shakkyō—Suzuki hakase to seishin bunseki," in Nishitani, *Kaisō Suzuki Daisetsu*, 288. Originally published in *Eastern Buddhist* (August 1967).

34. Ōtani Kōsho, "'Tenkan' no taiken," in Nishitani, *Kaisō Suzuki Daisetsu*, 140. Originally published in *Daihōrin* (September 1, 1946).

mourners, who must have wondered how he had the gall to attend. He must have realized quite clearly that he was reaping what he had sown. Daisetz's ashes were divided into three parts and were interred at Tōkeiji, the Suzuki family crypt in the Nodayama cemetery in Kanazawa, and the Shin'nō-in on Mt. Kōya. In all three places, Beatrice was there waiting for him.

Reconsidering the Parent-Child Relationship

Last, I would like to reconsider what sort of relationship Daisetz and Alan had as father and son. Daisetz registered his adopted son Alan as his natural child. He sometimes saw in the young Alan a purity that was similar to the state of satori. Daisetz no doubt hoped that Alan would become a scholar. When Alan became old enough to understand what was going on around him, he became an active child. He neglected his studies and told lies without compunction. While Daisetz was at a loss as to how to handle Alan, as a father he did not close the door to communication, and in the hope of putting his son on the right path, Daisetz tried to enroll Alan in a school with strict rules and sent him to live with a disciple in the countryside, imploring him to help educate Alan.

When Alan reached puberty, he started getting into trouble with girls. As a handsome, half-Japanese young man, he was quite popular. When he reached college age, he started frequenting dance halls and the like and was selected to be a representative to the Japan-America Students Conference, which was full of gifted students. While Daisetz worried about Alan's problematic relationships with women, he did not show any particular interest in Alan's hidden talents. Daisetz concealed from Alan the fact that he was an adopted child, but Alan became aware of the truth. He saw through the fact that his father, who had told him not to lie, was lying. I am sure that Alan's friends must have teased him about being a "half-breed."

When he reached young adulthood, Alan got a girl pregnant and Daisetz had to run hurriedly to clean up the mess. Immediately after that, Alan married another girl with whom he was having a relationship, but Daisetz chose not to acknowledge the marriage. Before long, the Pacific War broke out and it became increasingly difficult for Alan with his Western appearance to stay in Japan. He worked for the Dōmei News Agency in Shanghai until the war ended.

After being repatriated to Japan, the connections he had made in Shanghai made it possible for him to get work in the entertainment industry, where he wrote the lyrics to the "Tokyo Boogie-woogie." The lyrics resonated with the philosophy of his father, who hoped to be able to build a bridge between the East and the West. Later, Alan got remarried to the singer Ike Mariko, whom he knew from his student days. Daisetz had no interest in popular songs such as "Tokyo Boogie-woogie," but he welcomed Alan's marriage to Mariko. The marriage did not last long, however, for Alan had an affair and later married yet another woman. While criticizing Alan's moral laxity in his relationships with women and his drunkenness, Daisetz continued to take responsibility for Alan's debts and send work his way. Alan slowly but surely built up a work portfolio by composing lyrics and doing translations. However, Alan eventually got involved in a scandal that became grist for a weekly mass-circulation magazine. Daisetz published a statement washing his hands of what Alan had done, and it appeared that the father-son relationship had come to an end. Five years later, however, when Alan rushed to his deathbed, Daisetz tried to move close to him, murmuring "Ohh, ohh."

As we can see from these facts, Daisetz's attitude toward Alan was not consistent. At times, Daisetz loved his child; at times he pushed him away. It is not a matter of which of these acts represented his true feelings. All of these attitudes that changed from time to time belonged to Daisetz and him alone. But we should not reproach Daisetz for his lack of consistency. Declaring that a person's statement is "inconsistent" is nothing more than a convenient term used by the mass media when they want to attack a politician. The world around one continually changes and is full of things that do not go as one wishes. In such situations, there is little value in never vacillating. The minds of real people with blood running through their veins waver, and suffer distress from the interplay of love and hate. Daisetz was a father who had suffered through raising a child. He was human after all.

Actually, Daisetz reveals a variable side even in his academic writings. For example, the German philosopher Eugen Herrigel (1884–1955) wrote a book called *Zen in der Kunst des Bogenschiessens* (Zen in the Art of Archery; 1948)[35] in which he presented his experience of training in archery in Japan from a Zen point of view. In the introduction to the English version (1953), Daisetz gave it the imprimatur of his authority, writing: "Through his expression, the Western reader will find a more familiar manner of dealing with what very often must seem to be a strange and somewhat unapproachable Eastern

---

35. Eugen Herrigel, *Zen in der Kunst des Bogenschiessens* (Munich: Otto Wilhelm Barth-Verlag, 1948).

experience."[36] However, in a roundtable discussion that appeared six years later in the journal *Zen bunka*, Daisetz said: "He [Herrigel] is trying to get to Zen, but he hasn't understood real Zen" and "I was just asked to write the 'Introduction,' so I did."[37]

Even if the introduction that Daisetz wrote for the book contained a certain amount of lip service, when his statements intended for a foreign and a Japanese audience are this different, readers might find it difficult to understand his true intentions. Not being attached to one thing or approach—perhaps that is a Zen way of living. However, the general public did not show any interest in closely examining the inconsistency but only looked at one aspect of his attitude, talking about how Daisetz had disowned Alan, which was not true. In order to make Daisetz into the perfect "great man," it was necessary to cut Alan out of the picture.

In his later years, Daisetz talked about things that showed his love for the freedom of children. I would like to quote from the transcript of a lecture Daisetz gave at Otani University in 1963.

I think it was five or six years ago, or perhaps seven or eight years ago, but there was a book like this that was one of the best sellers that appeared in the *New York Times* in the United States. It was a children's story. A child goes out to play in the morning, and when he comes back in the afternoon because he's hungry, his mother asks him, "Where did you go?" and he answers, "I went outside." His mother asks, "What did you do?" and he says "Nothing." Now, that's interesting. I don't remember if the title of the book was *I Went Outside* or *I Didn't Do Anything*, but in any case, the child said, "I went outside, but I didn't do anything." However, that's not true; it goes without saying that he engaged in all sorts of children's activities. He ran and jumped around, and that's why he got hungry and came home. That's what's interesting. No matter what he does, it's the same as not doing anything. Running and jumping around is a big activity, but from the standpoint of a child, there is nothing great or special about it. It's nothing. It's free play.[38]

36. Daisetz T. Suzuki, "Introduction," in Herrigel, *Zen in the Art of Archery*, x.

37. Suzuki Daisetsu and Hisamatsu Shin'ichi, "Taidan: Amerika no zen o kataru," *Zen bunka* 14 (1959): 28.

38. *SDZ* 6, 434. Originally published in *Shinran kyōgaku* 7 (December 1965).

Daisetz remarked that this was a story from a best seller, but surely he must have recognized the image of the child presented in the book as none other than Alan. When Alan was young and came back home after running around outside, I am sure that Daisetz must have asked him, "What were you doing?" However, if Alan had replied "Nothing," I am sure that Daisetz would not have said, "That's interesting." He would have scolded him and told him, "Don't lie." The story quoted above can be read as a statement expressing Daisetz's critical self-reflection on his own actions: if I had only valued Alan's free play more when he was young, perhaps he would have become a different person.

Meanwhile, how did Alan feel about his father? Hidden in the text of the few records Alan left behind, we can see words and actions apologizing to his father for the unfilial ways in which he acted in response to his father's kindness. Was Alan hoping for more love from his father, who was completely devoted to scholarly pursuits? Alternatively, was he tormented by loneliness, uncomfortable in the family because he had a different nature from his parents, to whom he was not biologically related? According to people who had direct knowledge of the everyday Alan, he was a truly gentle person, and they are unanimous in saying that it is unbelievable that he could have been involved in an incident such as that reported in the mass-circulation magazine. However, Alan was aware that being publicly castigated had caused his dear father a loss of face, and he must have deeply regretted it.

Great Wisdom and Great Compassion

Another, perhaps somewhat surprising, clue for understanding how Daisetz felt about his child can be discovered in how Daisetz talked about his cat. While Daisetz loved all animals, he was especially fond of cats. In his later years, he would often cuddle his cat and speak to it in English as though it were a member of the family. I think that Daisetz projected Alan onto his cats, especially kittens.

On the subject of Zen and cats, there is a well-known koan—"Nanquan Kills a Cat"—which is found in *The Gateless Gate* (Case 14) and *The Blue Cliff Record* (Case 63). The story relates how the Tang-dynasty priest Nanquan Puyuan (ca. 749–ca. 835) happened upon some monks who were arguing over a cat. Nanquan picked up the cat and said to the monks: "Say something. If you don't say something, I will kill this cat!" When none of the monks could answer him, Nanquan killed the cat. After his senior disciple

Zhaozhou Congshen (778–897) returned that evening, Nanquan told him what had happened. When Zhaozhou heard this, he put his straw sandals on his head and left the room. Nanquan said that had Zhaozhou been there, he could have saved the cat.

Among the koans involving Nanquan, Daisetz often quoted "Ordinary Mind Is the Way" from *The Gateless Gate* (Case 19), in which in response to the question "What is the Way?" Nanquan replies, "Ordinary mind is the Way." However, Daisetz practically never mentioned "Nanquan Kills a Cat," which is just as well known as "Ordinary Mind Is the Way."[39] The only place Daisetz discusses this koan at any great length is the English-language *An Introduction to Zen Buddhism*, where he comments as follows:

> What does all this mean? Why was a poor innocent creature sacrificed? What has Jōshū's (Zhaozhou's) placing his sandals over his head to do with the quarreling? Did Nansen (Nanquan) mean to be irreligious and inhuman by killing a living being? Was Jōshū really a fool to play such a strange trick? And then the "absolute denial" and "absolute affirmation"—are these really two? There is something fearfully earnest in both these actors, Jōshū and Nansen. Unless this is apprehended, Zen is, indeed, a mere farce.[40]

"Nanquan Kills a Cat" is probably illustrating the state of being beyond affirmation and negation. Even realizing this, I think that Daisetz disliked this koan, where a cat is killed without mercy.

Daisetz saw the compassion of the Buddha in the way a mother cat takes care of her kittens. In a lecture at the Engakuji temple in 1960, Daisetz spoke about how one of his pet cats gave birth to a litter of kittens.[41] He related how one minute the mother would be nursing the kittens, only to go out the next minute and then, after she had eaten something, immediately come back to her kittens. She would go out for some exercise, come back again, and check on her children, even going so far as to lick up their waste. Unable to care for them, Daisetz gave the kittens away to neighborhood families, but he spoke about how sorry he felt for the mother cat, searching for her kittens, who had suddenly disappeared. Daisetz went so far as to say the following: when a cat carries her young, she grasps them in her mouth

---

39. Daisetz's comments on this koan are found in *SDZ* 27, 69; 31, 7; and 32, 377.
40. Daisetz Teitaro Suzuki, *An Introduction to Zen Buddhism*, 41; *SDZ* 14, 255.
41. *SDZ* 29, 32–33. Other cat stories are found in *SDZ* 6, 353; 28, 126; and 29, 398.

by the nape of the neck and carries the kittens one at a time. The kitten depends completely on the mother. However, monkeys do not do this: since the mother monkey carries the baby monkey on her back, the baby has to hang on using his arms, legs, and tail. Daisetz said that the way a mother cat carries her kittens resembles the "other power" of the Jōdo Shinshū sect, while the way the baby monkeys are carried recalls the "self-power" of the Zen sect.[42]

These divergent means of salvation symbolize the "Great Compassion" of the Shin sect and the "Great Wisdom" of the Zen sect, respectively. Let us remember that Daisetz was not just a Zen man; he was a scholar of Buddhism who was interested in both Zen and Shin Buddhism. Fiercely attacking his "undutiful son" was Daisetz's "salvation of the monkey," Zen side talking; never giving up on Alan was Daisetz's "salvation of the cat," Shin side talking. Daisetz possessed both aspects: Zen and Shin, "Great Wisdom" and "Great Compassion." If we lose this perspective, Daisetz's feelings toward his son appear to be ambiguous, and looking at his actions superficially might lead one to mistakenly assume that his attitude toward Alan was simply inconsistent.

In his later years, Daisetz often used the metaphor of the mother cat in explaining Buddhist teachings. Ishida Masami (ca. 1980–1979), who later became the president of and consultant to the Idemitsu Kosan Company, witnessed Daisetz bent over his desk and weeping at a lecture he gave at the Idemitsu-ryō lodging in Karuizawa in the summer of 1963 as he spoke of the mother cat and her kittens.[43] The spirit of the mother cat, filled with concern for her children, must have indeed tugged at Daisetz's heartstrings.

In Daisetz's conception of the Shin sect, a person could not have recourse to the "other power" just by waiting quietly; he believed that this power would not be attainable "unless one exerted every effort to reach that shore, no matter how foolish, incompetent, or powerless one might be."[44] Even when Alan, who must have been aware of how severe his drinking problem was, brought himself to ruin through his inability to stop drinking, Daisetz did not extend the "salvation of the cat" to him. Perhaps, however, in edging close to Alan and murmuring, "Ohh, ohh," Daisetz was offering his final act of "Great Compassion" to his son.

---

42. Suzuki Daisetsu, *Shinshū nyūmon*, trans. Satō Taira (Tokyo: Shunjūsha, 2011), 61–62. Originally published in 1983. The original English text is unpublished.

43. Ishida Masami, "Omoidasu mama," in Hisamatsu et al., *Suzuki Daisetsu*, 343. Originally published in *Suzuki Daisetsu zenshū geppō* (June 1970).

44. Suzuki, *Shinshū nyūmon*, 63.

I am confident that Daisetz's "Great Compassion" reached Alan. The last words spoken to a person left behind are decisive in forming feelings for the dead. Leaving the son with the unforgettable impression that his father had forgiven him despite what he had done, father and son parted ways forever.

Father and Son

After the incident, Alan and Mikako's relationship collapsed and they formally divorced in March 1965. It appears that Alan maintained his relationship with the Yashika Camera Company, but no one knows how he made his living. Hayashida Kumino wrote that Alan visited the Matsugaoka Bunko to offer incense around two to three months after Daisetz died.

> Even though Alan had just turned fifty, his steps were unsteady, and he looked much older than his years. He was a heavy drinker, after all, and it was probably because he had been living an intemperate and none too healthy life for some time. After appearing in the garden, he slowly walked up the stone steps, and, after what seemed to be a long time, he finally reached the veranda adjoining the room where the Buddhist altar was located and sat down on the cushion I offered him.
>
> Then, while looking at the Kita-Kamakura mountains, tinged with the approach of autumn, as though seeing them for the first time, he muttered wistfully: "I was a bad son, and I caused my parents all sorts of trouble. But I think I did one good thing: I didn't ruin your life."[45]

I would like to believe that this self-confession regarding how badly he treated his parents represents Alan's true feelings unclouded by alcohol. Even so, the old womanizing Alan, with his affected and flattering compliments to the ladies, had not changed at all. Kumino wrote that Alan told her: "Even though I was the one who was supposed to look after my father, you lived with him and looked after him. I'm sure that my father was happy. Thank you."[46] Kumino does not remember what she said in response.

In the spring of 1970, about four years after Daisetz's death, Ike Mariko

---

45. Hayashida, *Ōoji Suzuki Daisetsu kara no tagami*, 66.
46. Hayashida, *Ōoji Suzuki Daisetsu kara no tagami*, 66.

received a phone call from Suzuki Rei notifying her that Alan had been hospitalized with cancer of the pharynx and entreated her to visit him. Mariko
and Maya, who was a high school student at the time, went to see Alan
at a hospital in Hiroo, Shibuya-ku, Tokyo. Maya had already heard from
Mihoko that Daisetz was not her birth father, but she does not remember
who informed her that Alan was her father. According to Maya, Alan told
her and her mother, while dropping a joke in here and there, that his cancer
had been discovered accidentally and that he and Mikako had been divorced
for quite some time. He also spoke happily to Maya about the early years of
his marriage to Mariko. It was the first time that Alan and Maya had spoken
together when both were aware that they were father and daughter. Telling
Alan to take care of himself, Mariko left the hospital first, leaving the two of
them together. It was the last time Alan and Mariko saw each other.

From that point on, Alan was in and out of the hospital. When Alan
was hospitalized, Maya would often make sandwiches for him and look in
on him. She has a strong recollection that in one of the hospitals to which
he was admitted, her father had been placed in a very dingy space in the
corner of a room, his bed separated from the rest of the room by only a cur-
tain. Maya says that she kept her meetings with her father a secret but that
Mariko was aware of them.

One day, according to Maya, two middle-aged women she did not know
came to visit Alan, who was being treated at home. One of the women,
noticing that Maya was wearing a yellow T-shirt with "MAYA" written on
it, said: "Oh, so you're Maya, right? My, you've grown up. I remember you
when you were small." It was Shikiba Mikako. Maya remembers the conversation between Alan and Mikako being basically small talk.

Alan passed away in a small hospital in Setagaya-ku, Tokyo. Even when
he was in critical condition, Mariko did not come, and the only family
member who was with him at the end was Maya, the daughter whom he did
not raise. On June 27, 1971, after a battle with cancer lasting a little more
than a year, Alan died with his daughter looking after him. Maya's presence
was probably Alan's only comfort during those last, lonely years.

The funeral was held at Shin'nō-in on Mt. Kōya, the sub-temple with
which Beatrice had been connected. It was a very quiet affair and, in addition
to Maya, was only attended by Suzuki Rei, Suzuki Ichio, and Alan's friends
from Yashika Camera. Alan's posthumous Buddhist name was "Daishō-in
Shasei Kyūshin Koji" (Great Excellence, he who pursues truth through true
images), a reference to his love of photography.[47] It was arranged that sutras

---

47. The Chinese character *shō* from "Daishō" is the same character as Alan's Japanese given

would be said in perpetuity for Alan at Shin'nō-in, but none of his ashes were interred at either Tōkeiji or Nodayama in Kanazawa. There is no grave marker for Masaru Suzuki anywhere.

I would like to end this book by giving a brief description of what happened after Alan died to the women with whom he had been deeply connected. Ike Mariko continued singing until the age of eighty-three. However, immediately after performing "Sentimental Journey" at a party on May 28, 2000, she collapsed from subarachnoid bleeding and died on May 30, bringing her life devoted to singing to a close. It is not known what happened to Shikiba Mikako. In addition to her duties as a housewife, as a hobby Hayashida Kumino practiced the Japanese folk craft of *kumihimo*, in which cords are braided together to form colorful patterns. She published *Letters from My Granduncle D. T. Suzuki* in 1995 and died from illness in July 2011. Alan's daughter by Nobu was blessed with grandchildren and is living happily in the United States. Ike Maya, after studying music at a university, was active for a while in the entertainment world. She later studied pottery in the United States and ran an art gallery for a time. She had two sons and one daughter. Today she operates an English conversation school in Tokyo and is also busy with overseeing a nursery school for children called Gokan no Mori (Forest of Five Senses), which she regards as her life's work.

Maya has named her company the Daisetsu-sha (Daisetz House).

---

name, Masaru; the character *sha* of "Shasei" and the character *shin* of "Kyūshin" together form the word *shashin* (photograph).

Appendix

Family Tree

(facing page)

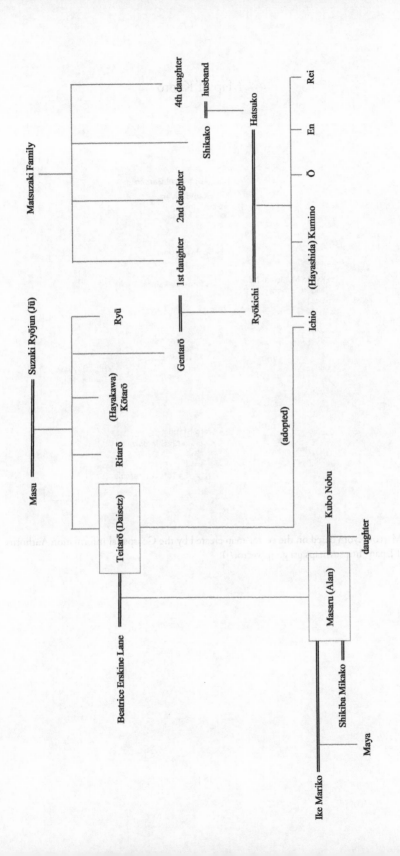

Map of Kyoto

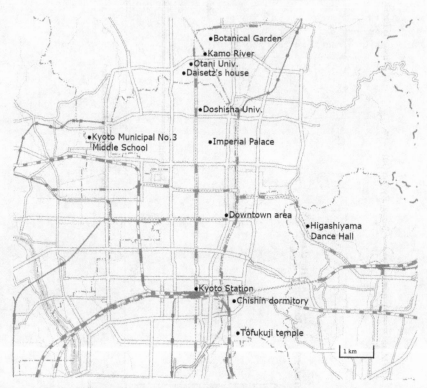

(Map of Kyoto based on the vector map created by the Geospatial Information Authority of Japan [https://maps.gsi.go.jp/vector/])

Chronology

	D.T. Suzuki		Masaru "Alan" Suzuki
	Age		Age
Oct. 18, 1870	0	Born in Honda-machi, Kanazawa city.	
Nov. 16, 1876	6	Ryōjun (father) died.	
Apr. 21, 1878	7	Birth of Beatrice Lane.	
Apr. 1882	11	Admitted to the Ishikawa Prefectural Technical School.	
Oct. 1887.	16	Admitted to the Number Four Higher Middle School.	
July 1, 1888	17	Dropped out of the Number Four Higher Middle School. Practiced Zen at Kokutaiji temple?	
July 8, 1888	17	Became an assistant at the Elementary School in Iida-machi, county of Suzu, Ishikawa prefecture.	
Apr. 8, 1890	19	Masu (mother) died.	
Jan. 12, 1891	20	Left for Kobe city, where brother Kōtarō lived.	
May 1891	20	Went to Tokyo and lived in Kyūchōkan dormitory.	
June 1, 1891	20	Admitted to the Tokyo Professional School.	
July 27, 1891	20	Became a disciple of Imakita Kōzen at Engakuji temple.	
Oct. 1891	20	Dropped out of the Tokyo Professional School.	
Jan. 16, 1892	21	Imakita Kōzen died.	
Apr. 11, 1892	21	Became a disciple of Shaku Sōen.	
Sep. 1892	21	Became a special student of the Faculty of Philosophy, College of Letters of Tokyo Imperial University.	
July 1893	22	Translated Shaku Sōen's speech for the first World's Parliament of Religions.	
Dec. 1894	24	Around this time, received the Buddhist name "Daisetsu" from Shaku Sōen.	

	D.T. Suzuki		Masaru "Alan" Suzuki
	Age		Age
May 1895	24	Dropped out of Tokyo Imperial University.	
Dec. 5, 1896	26	Achieved enlightenment at Engakuji temple.	
Feb. 7, 1897	26	Departed for the United States.	
July 14, 1905	34	Until the next April, served as the translator of Shaku Sōen, who was visiting the United States.	
Apr. 8, 1906	35	Met Beatrice in New York.	
Mar. 26, 1909	38	After a one-year stay in the UK, returned to Japan.	
Aug. 31, 1909	38	Appointed as an English instructor at Gakushuin University.	
Oct. 15, 1909	38	Appointed as an instructor at the College of Letters, Tokyo Imperial University.	
Feb. 14, 1911	40	Beatrice arrived in Japan.	
Apr. 1911	40	Lived in Oimatsu-cho, Koishikawa-ku, Tokyo.	
Dec. 12, 1911	41	Married Beatrice. Lived in Takadaoimatsu-cho, Koishikawa-ku.	
July 1915	44		Birth of Alan?
July 7, 1916	45		0 Birth date recorded in the family register.
July 21, 1916	45	Registration of Masaru's birth.	0
Nov. 1, 1919	49	Shaku Sōen died.	3
Mar. 22, 1921	50	Resigned from Gakushuin Univeristy. Appointed as professor at Shinshū Otani University.	4
May 19, 1921	50	Lived in the dormitory of Otani University.	4
Sep. 1921	50	Lived in Rikkyoku-an at Tōfukuji temple.	5
Jan. 1926	55	Around this time, lived in Chishin dormitory of Otani sect located in Imakumano, Kyoto city.	9

	Age	D.T. Suzuki	Age	Masaru "Alan" Suzuki
Mar. 23, 1926	55	Moved to a new house in Koyamaōno-cho, Kamigyō-ku, Kyoto city.	9	
Apr. 1929	58		12	Enrolled in Kyoto Municipal Number Three Middle School.
July 7, 1931	60		15	Went to Iwakura Masaji's hometown in Toyama prefecture and spent the summer there.
Sep. 1931	60		15	Transferred to Mt. Kōya Middle School.
Nov. 1932	62		16	Suspended from Mt. Kōya Middle School.
Sep. 1933	62		17	Violent incident at Mt. Kōya Middle School.
Apr. 1934	63		17	Entered Doshisha University.
Aug. 1936	65		20	Participated in the Japan-America Students Conference at Waseda University.
Aug. 1937	66		21	Participated in the Japan-America Students Conference at Stanford University. Met Kubo Nobu.
Summer 1937	66		21	Around this time or in the next summer, met Ike Mariko at Higashiyama Dancehall.
Mar. 15, 1938	67	Beatrice hospitalized.	21	
May 1938	67		21	Affair with Ōtani Kinuko.
Mar. 1939	68		22	Graduated from Doshisha University.
May 28, 1939	68	Revealed to Alan that he was adopted.	22	
July 16, 1939	68	Beatrice died.	23	
Nov. 3, 1939	69		23	Wedding ceremony with Kubu Nobu.
Apr. 11, 1940	69		23	Registered his marriage with Nobu.
July 4, 1940	69	Adopted Suzuki Ichio.	23	
Jan. 1942	69		25	Employed by Dōmei News Agency after leaving Japan Times.
Mar. 1942	71		25	Nobu gave birth to a daughter.

	D.T. Suzuki			Masaru "Alan" Suzuki
	Age		Age	
Oct. 1942	72		26	Dispatched to Shanghai as a reporter of Dōmei News Agency.
Dec. 1942	72	Around this time, completion of construction of Matsugaoka Bunko.	26	
Dec. 1945	75		29	Returned from Shanghai and lived in Shirokane-sankō-cho, Shiba-ku, Tokyo. Reunion with Ike Mariko.
Dec. 1946	76		30	Introduced Ike Mariko in *Spotlight* magazine.
1947	76		30	Translated the lyrics of "Tokyo Romance."
Sep. 10, 1947	76		31	Wrote the lyrics for "Tokyo Boogie-woogie." Recorded the song on this day.
Nov. 1, 1947	77		31	Published an English conversation lesson in *Keikō* magazine.
Jan. 1948	77		31	Record of "Tokyo Boogie-woogie" released.
July 2, 1948	77	Sekiguchi Kono died.	31	
July 25, 1948	77		32	Published the translated book *Shukujo to shinshi*.
Oct. 1948	77	Moved out of house in Kyoto.	32	
Nov. 21, 1948	78		32	Marriage ceremony with Ike Mariko at Engakuji temple.
Dec. 1, 1948	78		32	Published the translated book *Amerikashiki kaseihō*.
Jan. 18, 1949	78		32	Amicable divorce with Nobu.
Feb. 9, 1949	78		32	Article introducing Alan and Mariko appeared in *Asahi gurafu* magazine.
June 16, 1949	78	Traveled to Hawaii.	32	
Nov. 3, 1949	79	Awarded the Order of Culture.	33	
Dec. 1, 1949	79		33	Published a Japanese translation of *Baseball for Everyone*.
Feb. 1, 1950	79	Moved to San Francisco. Lectured at Claremont College and others.	33	
June 1950	79		33	Translated the lyrics of "Buttons and Bows." Record released.

	Age	D.T. Suzuki	Age	Masaru "Alan" Suzuki
Sep. 21, 1950	79	Moved to New York. Lectured at Columbia University and others.	34	
June 9, 1951	80	Temporarily returned to Japan.	34	
June 1951	80		34	Mariko gave birth to a girl.
Sep. 13, 1951	80	Moved to the United States again. Lectured at Claremont College and others.	35	
Nov. 20, 1951	81		35	Registered his marriage with Mariko and the birth of their daughter.
Dec. 1951	81		35	Disappeared from home and started living with Shikiba Mikako.
Feb. 1, 1952	81	Appointed as a lecturer of Columbia University and moved to New York.	35	
June 30, 1952	81	Temporarily returned to Japan.	35	
Sep. 14, 1952	81	Moved to the United States again.	36	
Nov. 8, 1952	82		36	Amicable divorce with Mariko.
Feb. 27, 1953	82		36	Registered his marriage with Mikako.
Jan. 10, 1954	83	Moved to Okamura family's apartment in New York.	37	
Sep. 10, 1954	83	Temporarily returned to Japan with Okamura Mihoko.	38	
Jan. 17, 1955	84	Moved to the United States again.	38	
1956	85		39	Around this time, lived in Tomisaka 2, Bunkyō-ku, Tokyo. Engaged in the translation of films.
Jan. 15, 1957	86	Introductory article published in *Vogue* magazine.	40	
Feb. 4, 1957	86	Introductory article published in *Time* magazine.	40	
Aug. 31, 1957	86	Introductory article published in *New Yorker* magazine.	41	
Jan. 1958	87	Introductory article published in *Mademoiselle* magazine.	41	
Oct. 1958	87	Beat writers visited Daisetz.	42	

	D.T. Suzuki		Masaru "Alan" Suzuki
	Age		Age
Nov. 22, 1958	88	Returned to Japan with Okamura Mihoko. Lived in Matsugaoka Bunko.	42
June 4, 1961	90		44 Arrested for suspected violence to a woman. Incident reported in newspapers the next morning.
June 19, 1961	90		44 Publication of *Shūkan shinchō* magazine, which reported the incident.
Mar. 18, 1965	94		48 Amicable divorce with Mikako.
July 12, 1966	95	Died at St. Luke's International Hospital in Tokyo.	50
June 27, 1971			54 Died at a hospital in Setagaya-ku, Tokyo.

Note: Compiled from Kirita Kiyohide, *Suzuki Daisetsu kenkyū kiso shiryō* (Kamakura: Matsugaoka Bunko, 2005) and other sources.

Bibliography

Adams, Phoebe. "The Atlantic Bookshelf: Reader's Choice." *Atlantic Monthly* 200, no. 4 (October 1957): 178–80.

Alcott, Louisa May. *Little Women*. Boston: Roberts Brothers, 1868.

Andō Reiji. *Daisetz*. Tokyo: Kōdansha, 2018.

Ariyama Teruo and Nishiyama Takesuke, eds. *Dōmei Tsūshinsha kankei shiryō*. Vol. 10. Tokyo: Kashiwa Shobō, 1999.

Aronowitz, Alfred G. "The Beat Generation." *New York Post* (March 19, 1959).

Asahina Sōgen. "Daisetsu sensei iku." In *Kaisō Suzuki Daisetsu*, edited by Nishitani Keiji, 182–86. Tokyo: Shunjūsha, 1975. Originally published in *Engaku* (September 1, 1966).

Asahina Sōgen. "Katei ni okeru Daisetsu sensei." In *Suzuki Daisetsu: Hito to shisō*, edited by Hisamatsu Shin'ichi et al., 117–22. Tokyo: Iwanami Shoten, 1971. Originally published in *Suzuki Daisetsu zenshū geppō* (April 1969).

Beruwuddo, Vikutā [Suzuki, Masaru]. "Eigo kaiwa kōza dai 2 kō: Beigo no rekishi." *Keikō* 22 (1947): 7–8.

Bradshaw, Roberta V. "Clubs and Club People." *Washington Post* (April 8, 1906).

Breen, John et al., eds. *Beyond Zen: D.T. Suzuki and the Modern Transformation of Buddhism*. Honolulu: University of Hawai'i Press, 2022.

Bronstein, Daniel J. "Search for Inner Truth." *Saturday Review* (November 16, 1957): 22–23.

Bungei Shunjū. *Bungei Shunjū 70 nenshi honpen*. Tokyo: Bungei Shunjū, 1991.

Cage, John. *Silence*. Hanover: Wesleyan University Press, 1973. Originally published in 1961.

Carus, Paul. *The Gospel of Buddha according to Old Records*. Chicago: Open Court Publishing, 1894.

Charters, Ann. "Foreword." In *Dictionary of Literary Biography*, vol. 16: *The Beats: Literary Bohemians in Postwar America. Part 1: A–L*, edited by Ann Charters, ix–xiv. Detroit: Gale Research, 1983.

Charters, Ann. "Introduction: Variations on a Generation." In *The Portable Beat Reader*, edited by Ann Charters, xv–xxxvi. New York: Penguin Classics, 1992.

Ciardi, John. "Epitaph for the Dead Beats." *Saturday Review* (February 6, 1960): 11–13.

Cleary, Thomas, and J. C. Cleary, trans. *The Blue Cliff Record*. Vol. 2. Boulder: Shambhala, 1977.

Deimajio, Jō [Joe DiMaggio]. *Hyakumannin no yakyū*. Translated by Bikutā Beruwuddo [Victor Bellwood (Masaru Suzuki)]. Tokyo: Hōmu Jānarusha, 1949. Originally published as *Baseball for Everyone: A Treasury of Baseball Lore and Instruction for Fans and Players*, by Joe DiMaggio (New York: Whittlesey House, 1948).

Dempsey, David. "In Pursuit of 'Kicks.'" *New York Times* (September 8, 1957).

Eberhart, Richard. "West Coast Rhythms." *New York Times* (September 2, 1956).

Emerson, Ralph Waldo. *Nature*. Boston: James Munroe and Company, 1836.

Emerson, Ralph Waldo. *Representative Men*. Boston: Phillips, Sampson and Company, 1850.

Endō Tomoyuki, ed. "Aren Ginzubāgu nenpu." In *Gendaishi techō tokushūban: Sōtokushū Aren Ginzubāgu*, 304–19. Tokyo: Shichōsha, 1997.

Enomoto Yasuko. *Shanhai: Takokuseki toshi no hyakunen*. Tokyo: Chūkō Shinsho, 2009.

Executive Committee of the Fourth America-Japan Student Conference, ed. *Report of the Fourth America-Japan Student Conference August, 1937*. Executive Committee of the Fourth America-Japan Student Conference, 1938.

"Famed Buddha Scholar Finds Sanctuary Here." *Los Angeles Times* (March 11, 1950).

Fields, Rick. *How the Swans Came to the Lake: A Narrative History of Buddhism in America*. 3rd edition. Boston: Shambhala, 1992. The first edition was published in 1981.

Furuta Shōkin. "Daisetsu sensei to yūen no hitobito (1)." *Suzuki Daisetsu zenshū zōho shinban geppō* 18 (March 2001): 8–15.

Furuta Shōkin. "Ohimareru kotodomo." In *Suzuki Daisetsu: Hito to shisō*, edited by Hisamatsu Shin'ichi et al., 300–302. Tokyo: Iwanami Shoten, 1971. Originally published in *Suzuki Daisetsu zenshū geppō* (July 1971).

Ginsberg, Allen. "Howl for Carl Solomon." In *The Portable Beat Reader*, edited by Ann Charters, 62–70. New York: Penguin Classics, 1992.

Ginzubāgu, Aren [Allen Ginsberg]. "Watashi ni totte Tōyō to wa." Translated by Katagiri Yuzuru. In *Gendaishi techō tokushūban: Sōtokushū Aren Ginzubāgu*, 178–87. Tokyo: Shichōsha, 1997.

Ginzubāgu, Aren [Allen Ginsberg]. "Intabyū [interview]: Ginzubāgu to bukkyō." Translated by Shigematsu Sōiku. In *Gendaishi techō tokushūban: Sōtokushū Aren Ginzubāgu*, 254–63. Tokyo: Shinchōsha, 1997.

Gold, Herbert. "The Beat Mystique." *Playboy* 5: 2 (February 1958): 20, 84–87.

Gold, Herbert. "Hip, Cool, Beat — and Frantic." *The Nation* 185: 16 (November 16, 1957): 349–355.

Harada Ryōsuke and Saeki Ryūjō, eds. *Gakuen kaiko roku*. Kōya: Kōyasan Kōtōgakkō, 1956.

Harley, Jack. "Jack Rips Magazine." *Chicago Daily News* (October 25, 1958).

Hattori Ryōichi. *Boku no ongaku jinsei*. Tokyo: Chūō Bungeisha, 1982.

Hayashida Kumino. *Ooji Suzuki Daisetsu kara no tegami*. Kyoto: Hōzōkan, 1995.

Heard, Gerald. "On Learning from Buddha." *New York Times* (June 4, 1950).

Herrigel, Eugen. *Zen in der Kunst des Bogenschiessens*. Munich: Otto Wilhelm Barth-Verlag, 1948.

Hinohara Shigeaki. *Shi o dō ikitaka*. Tokyo: Chūkō Shinsho, 1983.

"Hito: Suzuki Daisetsu no omoide o shuppan shita moto hisho Okamura Mihoko-san." *Asahi Shimbun* (June 27, 1997).

Hōburaito, Ānesuto [Earnest Hoberecht]. *Shukujo to shinshi: Demokuratikku etiketto*. Translated by Vikutā Beluwuddo [Victor Bellwood (Masaru Suzuki)]. Tokyo: Rajio Shinbunsha, 1948.

Hōburaito, Ānesuto [Earnest Hoberecht]. *Tokyo romansu*. Translated by Ōkubo Yasuo. Tokyo: Kobarutosha, 1946. The English edition is *Tokyo Romance* (New York: Didier, [1947]).

Hokkoku Shinbunsha Henshūkyoku, ed. *Zen: Suzuki Daisetsu botsugo 40 nen*. Kanazawa: Hokkoku Shinbunsha, 2006.

Holmes, Clellon. "This Is the Beat Generation." *New York Times* (November 16, 1952).

Iinuma Nobuko. *Noguchi Hideyo to Merī Dājisu: Meiji Taishō ijintachi no kokusai kekkon*. Tokyo: Suiyōsha, 2007.

Ike Maya. "Daisetsu papa to watashi." In *Tsuisō Suzuki Daisetsu: Botsugo 40 nen kinen kikōshū*, edited by Kaneko Tsutomu, 6–7. Kamakura: Matsugaoka Bunko, 2006.

"In a Nutshell." *Washington Post* (June 19, 1949).

Ishida Masami. "Omoidasu mama." In *Suzuki Daisetsu: Hito to shisō*, edited by Hisamatsu Shin'ichi et al., 342–46. Tokyo: Iwanami Shoten, 1971. Originally published in *Suzuki Daisetsu zenshū geppō* (June 1970).

Iwakura Masaji. "Ōtani Daigaku jidai no Suzuki Daisetsu." In *Suzuki Daisetsu no hito to gaku-mon*, edited by Furuta Shōkin, 87–100. Tokyo: Shunjūsha, 1961.

Iwakura Masaji. *Shin'nin Suzuki Daisetsu*. Kyoto: Hōzōkan, 1986.

Jaffe, Richard M. "D.T. Suzuki and Two Cranes: American Philanthropy and Suzuki's Global Agenda." *Kōeki Zaidanhōjin Matsugaoka Bunko kenkyū nenpō* 32 (2018): 29–58.

Jitsuda Jidao. *Teisō jūrin to sono saiban*. Tokyo: Nishōdō Shoten, 1930.

"Jottings." *Spotlight* 1: 1 (1946): 1.

Jugaku Bunshō. "Kateijin to shite no Daisetsu koji." In *Suzuki Daisetsu: Hito to shisō*, edited by Hisamatsu Shin'ichi et al., 206–10. Tokyo: Iwanami Shoten, 1971. Originally published in *Suzuki Daisetsu zenshū geppō* (July 1969).

Kamoto Itsuko. *Kokusai kekkon no tanjō: "Bunmei koku Nippon" eno michi*. Tokyo: Shin'yōsha, 2001.

Kerouac, Jack. *The Dharma Bums*. New York: Viking Press, 1958.

Kerouac, Jack. *On the Road*. New York: Viking Press, 1957.

Kerouac, Jack. *Selected Letters, 1957–1969*. Edited by Ann Charters. New York: Viking, 1999.

Kerouac, Jack. [no title.] *Berkeley Bussei* (1960): [unpaginated].

Kirita Kiyohide. "Chūki Suzuki Daisetsu eibun nikki ni tsuite." *Zaidanhōjin Matsugaoka Bunko kenkyū nenpō* 19 (2005): 157–58.

Kirita Kiyohide, ed. "D.T. Suzuki's English Diaries." *Zaidanhōjin Matsugaoka Bunko kenkyū nenpō* 19–29 (2005–2015).

Kirita Kiyohide. "Kōki." *Zaidanhōjin Matsugaoka Bunko kenkyū nenpō* 29 (2015): 59–60.

Kirita Kiyohide. "Matsugaoka Bunko to Suzuki Daisetsu kenkyū." *Zaidanhōjin Matsugaoka Bunko kenkyū nenpō* 18 (2004): 83–93.

Kirita Kiyohide. *Suzuki Daisetsu kenkyū kiso shiryō*. Kamakura: Matsugaoka Bunko, 2005.

Kirita Kiyohide. "Zenshū no kanketsu ni atatte: Kongo no Daisetsu kenkyū no tameni." *Suzuki Daisetsu zenshū zōho shinban geppō* 40 (December 2003): 9–12.

Kondō Akihisa. "Jōshū shakkyō—Suzuki hakase to seishin bunseki." In *Kaisō Suzuki Daisetsu*, edited by Nishitani Keiji, 278–89. Tokyo: Shunjūsha, 1975. Originally published in *Eastern Buddhist* (August 1967).

Kubo Hisaji. *Kin kaikin bōkokuron*. Tokyo: Kubo Hōsei Keizai Kenkyūjo, 1929.

Kusunoki Kyō. "Okono-san no tsuioku." In *Suzuki Daisetsu: Hito to shisō*, edited by Hisamatsu Shin'ichi et al., 389–92. Tokyo: Iwanami Shoten, 1971. Originally published in *Suzuki Daisetsu zenshū geppō* (June 1970).

Kyokutō Gakugei Tsūshin Shuppansha, ed. *Amerikashiki kaseihō*. Tokyo: Kyokutō Gakugei Tsūshin Shuppansha, 1948.

Masutani Fumio, "Suzuki Daisetsu ron." In *Suzuki Daisetsu botsugo 40 nen*, edited by Matsugaoka Bunko, 122–37. Tokyo: Kawade Shobō Shinsha, 2006. Originally published in *Zaike bukkyō* 1490 (1966).

"Meiokusama bakari de kataru enman kokoroe uchiake kai." *Shufu to seikatsu* (March 1, 1948): 36–40.

Millstein, Gilbert. "Books of the Times." *New York Times* (September 5, 1957).

Miyamura Takamichi, ed. *Ruporutāju [reportage]: The Fourth America-Japan Student Conference 1937*. Tokyo: Miyamura Takamichi, 1938.

Mizukami Tsutomu. *Watakushiban Tōkyō zue*. Tokyo: Asahi Bunko, 1999. Originally published in *Asahi Shinbun*, Tokyo and Tama district edition (June 5, 1994, to September 10, 1995).

Nagahara, Hiromu. *Tokyo Boogie-Woogie: Japan's Pop Era and Its Discontents*. Cambridge, MA: Harvard University Press, 2017.

Nancy Wilson Ross Papers 1913–1986. Held by Harry Ransom Center, University of Texas at Austin.

Nishimura Eshin. *Suzuki Daisetsu no genfūkei*. Tokyo: Daizō Shuppan, 1993.

Nobe Yōko. *Yōshi engumi no shakaigaku: "Nippon-jin" ni totte "ketsuen" to wa nanika.* Tokyo: Shin'yōsha, 2018.

Ōhashi Tadanari. "San-chū kōshinkyoku." In *Kyō san-chū Yamashiro-kō sōritsu 60 shūnen kinengō,* edited by Hirao Kiyoshi, 176–80. Kyoto: Sōryō Dōsōkai, 1971.

Okamura Mihoko. "Daisetsu-sensei ni oai shite." In *Suzuki Daisetsu to wa dareka,* edited by Ueda Shizuteru and Okamura Mihoko, 26–36. Tokyo: Iwanami Gendai Bunko, 2002. Originally published in *Chichi* (September 2001).

Okamura Mihoko. "Hongan ga nobotta." In *Suzuki Daisetsu towa dareka,* edited by Ueda Shizuteru and Okamura Mihoko, 187–94. Tokyo: Iwanami Gendai Bunko, 2002. Originally published in *Zen bunka* 181 (July 2001).

Okamura Mihoko. "Myōyō." In *Kaisō Suzuki Daisetsu,* edited by Nishitani Keiji, 106–22. Tokyo: Shunjūsha, 1975. Originally published in *Daihōrin* (September 1, 1966) and *Tosho* (January 1, 1971).

Okamura Mihoko. "'Shi'nin' Daisetsu." In *Suzuki Daisetsu: Hito to shisō,* edited by Hisamatsu Shin'ichi et al., 368–72. Tokyo: Iwanami Shoten, 1971. Originally published in *Suzuki Daisetsu zenshū geppō* (August 1970).

Ōtake Hideo, Takeda Akira, and Hasegawa Zenkei, eds. *Gisei sareta oyako: Yōshi.* Tokyo: Sanseidō, 1988.

Ōtani Kōsho. "'Tenkan' no taiken." In *Kaisō Suzuki Daisetsu,* edited by Nishitani Keiji, 134–40. Tokyo: Shunjūsha, 1975. Originally published in *Daihōrin* (September 1, 1946).

"People Are Talking about." *Vogue* (January 15, 1957).

Prothero, Stephen. "Introduction." In *Big Sky Mind: Buddhism and the Beat Generation,* edited by Carole Tonkinson, 1–20. New York: Riverhead Books, 1995.

Pryce-Jones, Alan. "A Road with No Turning." *The Listener* 60: 1527 (July 3, 1958): 15–16.

"Religion: Zen." *Time* (February 4, 1957): 65–66.

Ross, Nancy Wilson. "What Is Zen?" *Mademoiselle* (January 1958): 64–65, 116–17.

Ross, Nancy Wilson. *The World of Zen: An East-West Anthology.* New York: Random House, 1960.

Sargeant, Winthrop. "Profiles: Great Simplicity." *New Yorker* (August 31, 1957): 34–53.

Satō Taira. "Taikō." In *Kaisō Suzuki Daisetsu,* edited by Nishitani Keiji, 145–51. Tokyo: Shunjūsha, 1975. Originally published in *Daihōrin* (September 1, 1966).

Sekiguchi Waichi, ed. *Kaisen zen'ya no disukasshon: Nichibei gakusei kōryū 50 nen no kiroku.* Tokyo: Nichibei Gakusei Kaigi 50 Shūnen Kinenjigyō Jikkō Iinkai, 1984.

Shimizu Hideo, ed. *Ike Mariko shō.* Tokyo: Ike Mariko Ongaku Jimusho, 2000.

Shimoji Rōrensu [Lowrence] Yoshitaka. *"Konketsu" to "Nihonjin": Hāfu, daburu, mikkusu no shakaishi.* Tokyo: Seidosha, 2018.

Shinreikyō Shinja Ichidō. *Shinreikyō nyūmon.* Tokyo: Īsuto Puresu, 2000.

Shiroyama Saburō. *Yūjō chikara ari.* Tokyo: Kōdansha Bunko, 1993. Originally published in 1988.

"Shōwa saidai no fushō no musuko: Bunka kunshō jushōsha no chōnan ga guredasu made." *Shūkan shinchō* 6: 25 (June 26, 1961): 30–36.

Sims, Barbara R. *Traces That Remain: A Pictorial History of the Early Days of the Baha'i Faith among the Japanese.* Tokyo: Baha'i Publishing Trust Japan, 1989.

Snyder, Gary. "Notes on the Beat Generation." In *Beat Down to Your Soul: What Was the Beat Generation?,* edited by Ann Charters, 517–21. New York: Penguin Books, 2001. Originally published in *Chūō kōron* (January 1960) in Japanese.

Sueki Fumihiko. *Nihon Bukkyō no kanōsei: Gendai shisō to shite no bōken.* Tokyo: Shinchō Bunko, 2011. Originally published by Shinchōsha in 2006.

Suzuki, Alan M. [Masaru Suzuki]. "Editorial Page." *Spotlight* 1: 5–6 (1946): 14.

Suzuki, A. M. [Masaru Suzuki]. "The Spotlight Album of Beauty: Mariko Ike, Moonlight ans Roses." *Spotlight* 1, no. 7 (1946): 18–19, 30–31.

Suzuki, Beatrice [Lane]. "Buddhism and Practical Life." In *Bukkyō to jissai seikatsu*. Translated by Yokogawa Kenshō. Nagoya: Shindō Kaikan, 1933.

Suzuki Biatorisu [Beatrice Lane Suzuki]. *Shōren bukkyō shōkan*. Kyoto: Suzuki Teitarō, 1940.

Suzuki Biatorisu Rēn [Beatrice Lane Suzuki]. "Saiai naru Tei-sama." Translated by Yokoyama Uein [Wayne] Shigeto. In *Suzuki Daisetsu botsugo 40 nen*, edited by Matsugaoka Bunko, 78–83. Tokyo: Kawade Shobō Shinsha, 2006.

Suzuki Daisetsu [Daisetz Teitarō Suzuki]. *Ichi shinjitsu no sekai*. Tokyo: Kondō Shoten, 1941.

Suzuki Daisetsu [Daisetz Teitarō Suzuki]. *Shinshū nyūmon*. Translated by Satō Taira. Tokyo: Shunjūsha, 2011. Originally published in 1983.

Suzuki Daisetsu [Daisetz Teitarō Suzuki]. "Shiseiji o chūshin ni shite." In *Zen: Zuihitsu*. Tokyo: Daiyūkaku, 1927. Originally published in *Chūgai nippō* (September 1924).

Suzuki Daisetsu [Daisetz Teitarō Suzuki]. *Suedenborugu* [Swedenborg]. Tokyo: Hinoeuma Shuppansha, 1913.

Suzuki Daisetsu [Daisetz Teitarō Suzuki]. *Suzuki Daisetsu zenshū*. Tokyo: Iwanami Shoten, 1968–1971.

Suzuki Daisetsu [Daisetz Teitarō Suzuki]. *Suzuki Daisetsu zenshū zōho shinban*. 40 vols. Tokyo: Iwanami Shoten, 1999–2003.

Suzuki Daisetsu [Daisetz Teitarō Suzuki], "Yopparai to shinjū to shūkyō." In *Zen: Zuihitsu*. Tokyo: Daiyūkaku, 1927

Suzuki Daisetsu [Daisetz Teitarō Suzuki]. *Zen Buddhism and Its Influence on Japanese Culture*. Kyoto: Eastern Buddhist Society, 1938.

Suzuki Daisetsu and Hisamatsu Shin'ichi. "Taidan: Amerika no zen o kataru." *Zen bunka* 14 (1959): 16–29.

Suzuki Daisetsu [Daisetz Teitarō Suzuki] and Tsuji Sōmei. "Bīto zenerēshon sonota no koto." In *Suzuki Daisetsu zadanshū 5: Zen no sekai*, edited by Furuta Shōkin, 49–73. Tokyo: Yomiuri Shimbunsha. Originally published in *Kiitsu* (March 1960).

Suzuki Daisetsu Kyōjyu Kiju Shukugakai, ed. *Bukkyō no taii*. Kyoto: Hōzōkan, 1947.

Suzuki, Daisetz [Teitarō]. "Introduction." In *Zen in the Art of Archery*, by Eugen Herrigal, translated by R.F.C. Hull, vii–x. New York: Vintage Spiritual Classics, 1989. Originally published in 1953.

Suzuki, Daisetz [Teitarō]. *Japanese Spirituality*. Translated by Norman Waddell. Tokyo: Japan Society for the Promotion of Science, 1972.

Suzuki Daisetz [Teitarō]. "Zen in the Modern World." *Japan Quarterly* 5: 4 (October–December 1958): 452–61.

Suzuki, Daisetz Teitaro. *Essays in Zen Buddhism, First Series*. London: Luzac and Company, 1927.

Suzuki, Dr. Daisetz Teitaro. Historical Biographical Files. Columbia University Libraries Archival Collections.

Suzuki, Daisetz Teitaro. *An Introduction to Zen Buddhism*. Foreword by Carl Jung. New York: Grove Press, 1964. Originally published in 1934.

Suzuki, Daisetz Teitaro. *Outlines of Mahâyâna Buddhism*. London: Luzac and Company, 1907.

Suzuki Ichio. "Shōden-an no Daisetsu." In *Suzuki Daisetsu: Hito to shisō*, edited by Hisamatsu Shin'ichi et al., 418–21. Tokyo: Iwanami Shoten, 1971. Originally published in *Suzuki Daisetsu zenshū geppō* (November 1969).

Suzuki Masaru. "Sutanfōdo [Stanford] kaigi 9: The Role of the Arts." In *Ruporutāju: The Fourth America-Japan Student Conference 1937*, edited by Miyamura Takamichi, 72–73. Tokyo: Miyamura Masamichi, 1938.

Suzuki, Masaru. "Zen Buddhism and Its Effects on the Culture of Japan." In *The Third America-Japan Student-Conference 1936*, edited by Nozue Kenzō. Tokyo: Nichibei Eigo Gakusei Kyōkai, 1937.

Takanashi Yoshio. "Emason [Emerson] to Suzuki Daisetsu: 'Tōyōtekina mikata' o chūshin to suru hikakuteki kōsatsu." *Nagano-ken Tanki Daigaku kiyō* 70 (2015): 81–91.

Takayanagi Kenzō, ed. *Gakusei nichibei kaidan*. Tokyo: Nihon Hyōronsha, 1939.

Takeda Akira. "Yōshi no gainen to mokuteki: Yōshi kenkyū no sōkatsu o megutte." In *Gisei sareta oyako: Yōshi*, edited by Ōtake Hideo, Takeda Akira, and Hasegawa Zenkei, 301–21. Tokyo: Sanseidō, 1988.

T. M. [Miyamura]. "Pen sukecchi daihyōshū." In *Ruporutāju: The Fourth America-Japan Student Conference 1937*, edited by Miyamura Takamichi, 101–5. Tokyo: Miyamura Takamichi, 1938.

Thoreau, Henry David. *Walden; or, Life in the Woods*. Boston: Ticknor and Fields, 1854.

Torii Hideharu. *Kokusaku tsūshinsha "Dōmei" no kōbō: Tsūshin kisha to sensō*. Tokyo: Kadensha, 2014.

Tsūshin Shashi Kankōkai, ed. *Tsūshin Shashi*. Tokyo: Tsūshin Shashi Kankōkai, 1958.

Ueda Ken'ichi. *Shanhai bugiugi 1945: Hattori Ryōichi no bōken*. Tokyo: Ongaku no Tomo Sha, 2003.

Ueda Shizuteru. "Suzuki Biatorisu fujin." In *Suzuki Daisetsu to wa dareka*, edited by Ueda Shizuteru and Okamura Mihoko, 224–47. Tokyo: Iwanami Gendai Bunko, 2002. Originally published in *Zen bunka* 175 (2000).

Victoria, Brian. "The Emperor's New Clothes: The Buddhist Military Chaplaincy in Imperial Japan and Contemporary America." *Journal of the Oxford Centre for Buddhist Studies* 11 (2016): 155–200.

Watts, Alan. *The Spirit of Zen: A Way of Life, Work and Art in the Far East*. New York: Dutton, 1936.

"The Yabyum Kid." *Time* 72: 14 (October 6, 1958).

Yamada, Shoji. *Shots in the Dark: Japan, Zen, and the West*. Translated by Earl Hartman. Chicago: University of Chicago Press, 2009. Originally published as *Zen to iu na no Nihon-maru*. Tokyo: Kōbundō, 2005.

Yamamoto Ryōkichi. *Daisetsu ate Yamamoto Ryōkichi shokan: Suzuki Daisetsu mikōkai shokan [bessatsu]*. Kyoto: Zen Bunka Kenkyūjo, 1989.

Yokoyama Uein [Wayne] Shigeto. "Eibun shokan no mado kara mita Suzuki Daisetsu: 'The immediate present is a despot'." *Suzuki Daisetsu zenshū zōho shinban* 35 geppō (August 2002): 1–4.

Yokoyama Uein [Wayne] Shigeto. "Kaisetsu: Biatorisu [Beatrice] fujin no tegami ni han'ei sareru ningen Suzuki Daisetsu no shōzō." In *Suzuki Daisetsu botsugo 40 nen*, edited by Matsugaoka Bunko, 75–77. Tokyo: Kawade Shobō Shinsha, 2006.

Yoshimura Akira. *Mutsu bakuchin*. Tokyo: Shinchō Bunko, 1979. Originally published in 1970.

"Zen: Beat & Square." *Time* 72: 3 (July 21, 1958).

Index